Communications in Computer and Information Science 2798

Rationale

The CCIS series is devoted to the publication of proceedings of computer science conferences. Its aim is to efficiently disseminate original research results in informatics in printed and electronic form. While the focus is on publication of peer-reviewed full papers presenting mature work, inclusion of reviewed short papers reporting on work in progress is welcome, too. Besides globally relevant meetings with internationally representative program committees guaranteeing a strict peer-reviewing and paper selection process, conferences run by societies or of high regional or national relevance are also considered for publication.

Topics

The topical scope of CCIS spans the entire spectrum of informatics ranging from foundational topics in the theory of computing to information and communications science and technology and a broad variety of interdisciplinary application fields.

Information for Volume Editors and Authors

Publication in CCIS is free of charge. No royalties are paid, however, we offer registered conference participants temporary free access to the online version of the conference proceedings on SpringerLink (http://link.springer.com) by means of an http referrer from the conference website and/or a number of complimentary printed copies, as specified in the official acceptance email of the event.

CCIS proceedings can be published in time for distribution at conferences or as post-proceedings, and delivered in the form of printed books and/or electronically as USBs and/or e-content licenses for accessing proceedings at SpringerLink. Furthermore, CCIS proceedings are included in the CCIS electronic book series hosted in the SpringerLink digital library at http://link.springer.com/bookseries/7899. Conferences publishing in CCIS are allowed to use Online Conference Service (OCS) for managing the whole proceedings lifecycle (from submission and reviewing to preparing for publication) free of charge.

Publication process

The language of publication is exclusively English. Authors publishing in CCIS have to sign the Springer CCIS copyright transfer form, however, they are free to use their material published in CCIS for substantially changed, more elaborate subsequent publications elsewhere. For the preparation of the camera-ready papers/files, authors have to strictly adhere to the Springer CCIS Authors' Instructions and are strongly encouraged to use the CCIS LaTeX style files or templates.

Abstracting/Indexing

CCIS is abstracted/indexed in DBLP, Google Scholar, EI-Compendex, Mathematical Reviews, SCImago, Scopus. CCIS volumes are also submitted for the inclusion in ISI Proceedings.

How to start

To start the evaluation of your proposal for inclusion in the CCIS series, please send an e-mail to ccis@springer.com.

Walid A. Mahmoud · Kosai Raoof ·
Safaa O. Al-Mamory · Ali Al-sherbaz ·
Fahad Mohammed Abdulhussein Al-zubaidi ·
Mohammad Reza Feizi Derakhshi ·
Haqi Khalid Ismail
Editors

Advanced Communications and Digital Networks

First International Conference, ACDN 2025
Baghdad, Iraq, December 2–3, 2025
Proceedings

Springer

Editors
Walid A. Mahmoud
Uruk University
Baghdad, Iraq

Safaa O. Al-Mamory
University of Babylon
Hillah, Iraq

Fahad Mohammed Abdulhussein Al-zubaidi
Uruk University
Baghdad, Iraq

Haqi Khalid Ismail
University of Technology
Baghdad, Iraq

Kosai Raoof
Laboratoire d'Acoustique de l'Université du Maine
Le Mans, France

Ali Al-sherbaz
University of Cambridge
Cambridge, UK

Mohammad Reza Feizi Derakhshi
University of Tabriz
Tabriz, Iran

ISSN 1865-0929 ISSN 1865-0937 (electronic)
Communications in Computer and Information Science
ISBN 978-3-032-15447-7 ISBN 978-3-032-15448-4 (eBook)
https://doi.org/10.1007/978-3-032-15448-4

This Springer imprint is published by the registered company Springer Nature Switzerland AG
The registered company address is: Gewerbestrasse 11, 6330 Cham, Switzerland

Preface

We are very pleased to introduce the proceedings of the First International Conference on Advanced Communications and Digital Networks (ACDN 2025), which was hosted and organized by Uruk University, Iraq, on December 2–3, 2025. It was an international conference focusing on specific topics in Communications and Digital Networks. The conference brought together graduate students, lecturers, researchers, and industry leaders to share novel findings and practical experiences in the aforementioned fields.

The call for papers resulted in a total of 50 submissions from which only 32 manuscripts passed the prescreening stage. Then, the PC Chairs decided to accept only 9 papers based on a highly selective review process. Finally, only 28% of the reviewed papers were accepted for oral presentation during the conference. The main fields for accepted papers were wireless digital communications, optical fiber communications, and advanced signal processing. The double-blinded peer reviewing process was based on up to 10 reviewers per paper. All review reports were discussed independently by the PC Chairs before the final decision was taken. We hope that we have put the first milestone to exchange experiences in the field of advanced digital communication systems and are looking forward to preparing the next conference in the near future.

The ACDN 2025 PC Chairs deeply thank the involved reviewers because they spent valuable time and energy to read, evaluate, and make suggestions to enhance the quality of the submitted papers and finally make the right decision. Furthermore, we would like to convey our gratitude to the keynote speakers for their excellent presentations. Words of thanks are extended to all authors who submitted their papers and for letting us evaluate their work. Thanks to the Springer team for making these proceedings possible. We hope that all participants enjoyed a successful conference, made a lot of new contacts, engaged in fruitful discussions, and had a pleasant stay in Baghdad.

December 2025

Walid A. Mahmoud
Kosai Raoof
Safaa O. Al-Mamory
Ali Al-Sherbaz
Fahad Mohammed Abdulhussein Al-zubaidi
Mohammad Reza Feizi Derakhshi
Haqi Khalid Ismail

Organization

General Chair

Qais Saeed Al-Sabbagh	Uruk University, Iraq

Program Committee Chairs

Walid A. Mahmoud	Uruk University, Iraq
Kosai Raoof	ENSIM Le Mans Université, France
Safaa O. Al-Mamory	University of Babylon, Iraq
Ali Al-Sherbaz	University of Cambridge, UK
Fahad Mohammed Abdulhussein Al-Zubaidi	Uruk University, Iraq
Mohammad Reza Feizi Derakhshi	University of Tabriz, Iran
Haqi Khalid Ismail	University of Technology, Iraq

Program Committee Members

Aarti Bansal	Thapar Institute of Engineering and Technology, India
Abdullah H. Ali	University of Diyala, Iraq
Ahmed Al-Talabi	AlShaab University, Iraq
Ahmad Jalili	Gonbad Kavous University, Iran
Ahmed Musa Dinar	University of Technology, Iraq
Ali Z. K. Matloob	University of Babylon, Iraq
Amal Ibrahim Mahmood	Middle Technical University, Iraq
Amit Mishra	Thapar Institute of Engineering and Technology, India
Ammar Ali Zakzouk	Al-Esraa University, Iraq
Aqeel Abdulazeez Mohammed	University of Baghdad, Iraq
Bayan M. Sabbar	Al-Mustaqbal University, Iraq
Bharat Garg	Thapar Institute of Engineering and Technology, India
Dalia Raad	Mustansiriyah University, Iraq
Donya Abbas Khalid	Al-Nahrain University, Iraq
Elnaz Zafarani Moattar	Islamic Azad University, Tabriz Branch, Iran

Emad Salman	University of Diyala, Iraq
Essam N. Abdulla	University of Technology, Iraq
Fahad Al-Zubaidi	Uruk University, Iraq
Faris Ali Jasim Shaban	Imam Jaafar Al-Sadiq University, Iraq
Firas Abedi	Al-Furat Al-Awsat Technical University, Iraq
Firas Al-Hasani	Al Iraqia University, Iraq
Francesco Zirilli	Università di Roma La Sapienza, Italy
Gaganpreet Kaur	Thapar Institute of Engineering and Technology, India
Geetika Dua	Thapar Institute of Engineering and Technology, India
Ghassan Muslim Hassan	Ashur University, Iraq
Habib Ahmad	Georgia Institute of Technology, USA
Hadeel N. Abdullah	University of Technology, Iraq
Haider Alzaki	University of Diyala, Iraq
Haqi Khalid	University of Technology, Iraq
Harpreet Vohra	Thapar Institute of Engineering and Technology, India
Hasan Abdulameer	University of Babylon, Iraq
Hussein Alaa Al-Kaabi	Vocational Education, Iraq
Ibrahim Khidir Eltahir	University of Gezira, Sudan
Ibrahim Ismael Hamad	Salahaddin University, Iraq
Ilham Hameed Qaddoori	University of Diyala, Iraq
Jalal J. Hamad Ameen	University of Salahaddin, Iraq
Jawad K. Ali	University of Technology, Iraq
Kadhim B. Swadi	Al-Esraa University, Iraq
Kasturi Vasudevan	IIT Kanpur, India
Khalifa Abboud	Uruk University, Iraq
Kholee Phimu	NIT Mizoram, India
Khomdram Jolson Singh	Manipur University, India
Kosai Raoof	Université du Maine, France
Layla Mahdi Salih	Kirkuk University, Iraq
Lwaa Faisal Abdulameer	University of Baghdad, Iraq
Mahdi Siasifar	Imam Khomeini International University, Iran
Mahesh S. Chaudhari	Thapar Institute of Engineering and Technology, India
Majid Ul Ghafar	Hazara University, Sudan
Manu Bansal	Thapar Institute of Engineering and Technology, India
Maryam Khalifa Abboud	Middle Technical University, Iraq
Maryam Mahdi Alhusseini	Middle Technical University, Iraq
Mazen M. Abdullatif	Al-Esraa University College, Iraq

Md. Tofael Ahmed	Comilla University, Bangladesh
Md. Sharif Hossen	Comilla University, Bangladesh
Mohammad-Reza Feizi Derakhshi	University of Tabriz, Iran
Mohammed Aboud Kadhim	Middle Technical University, Iraq
Mohammed Saeed Mohammed	Middle Technical University, Iraq
Mohsen Aljazaery	University of Babylon, Iraq
Muhammad Fahad Munir	International Islamic University, Pakistan
Muhammed A. Ibrahim	University of Salahaddin, Iraq
Murtadha Ali Nsaif Shukur	Al-Furat Al-Awsat Technical University, Iraq
Mushreq Al-Tamimi	Mustansiriyah University, Iraq
Pradeep R.	College of Engineering Trivandrum, India
Praneetha Kotla	ERP Smartlabs, India
Ravi Kumar	Thapar Institute of Engineering and Technology, India
Rawaa Kadhim	Middle Technical University, Iraq
Raya M. Alsharfa	Middle Technical University, Iraq
Reem Jamal Abbass	Middle Technical University, Iraq
Robin Singla	Thapar Institute of Engineering and Technology, India
Saad Ahmed Ayoob	University of Mosul, Iraq
Saad Wasmi Luhaib	University of Mosul, Iraq
Sarah Mohammed Najim	University of Technology, Iraq
Sarah Najm	Ministry of Higher Education and Scientific Research, Iraq
Sarah Saadoon Jasim	Middle Technical University, Iraq
Sarah W. Abdulmajeed	Al-Iraqia University, Iraq
Sarmad K. Ibrahim	Mustansiriyah University, Iraq
Saurabh Sharma	Thapar Institute of Engineering and Technology, India
Shiva Krishna Deepak	Benchling, India
Siva Krishna Jampani	Asurion LLC, India
Sura Fawzi Ismail	University of Information Technology and Communications, Iraq
Sura Khalil Ibrahim	University of Baghdad, Iraq
Surbhi Sharma	Thapar Institute of Engineering and Technology, India
Thamer M. Jamel	University of Technology, Iraq
Yasameen F. Azeez	Al-Farabi University, Iraq
Yaseen H. Ismael	University of Mosul, Iraq
Yazen Mahmood	Cihan University, Iraq
Zahraa Niema Kamal	University of Babylon, Iraq
Zahraa Khduair Taha	Al Iraqia University, Iraq

Contents

Optical Fiber

Capacity and Security Enhancing of 4 Gigabit Passive Optical Networks Based on Hill Algorithm

Essam N. Abdulla[1](✉), Salah A. Adnan[2], Rusul Musadaq[3], Reem A. Hussien[1], and Akram Sh Ahmed[1]

[1] Optoelectronics Engineering Department, Laser and Optoelectronics College, University of Technology, Baghdad, Iraq
{Essam.N.Abdulla,reem.a.hussien, akram.s.ahmed}@uotechnology.edu.iq
[2] Laser and Optoelectronics Engineering Department, Al-Ma'moon University, Baghdad, Iraq
salahaldeen.a.taha@almamonuc.edu.iq
[3] Wireless Communication Engineering Branch, Communications Department, University of Technology, Baghdad, Iraq
11459@uotechnology.edu.iq

Abstract. Based on FTTH systems and according to secure 4-GPON technology, a network system with an optimum distance of 75 km could support up to 128 customers with 10/5Gbps at a least quality acceptable factor of 6 and level of BER 10−9, with an optimal reach of 20 km.

Keywords: FTTH · Hill · GPON · Security · MATLAB-Opti-System simulation program · PON

1 Introduction

It is crucial to construct a strong optical network that can offer quality customer service with a high security rate. This is more imperative especially in light of the increasing need for capacity from many end users [1]. Passive optical network (PON) techniques are extensively utilized [2]. The vulnerability of the fiber communication link to attacks is one of the most important problems. It is possible to intercept sensitive data if someone manages to find access to the data. Improvements must be made to the optical access network's physical layer to maintain the privacy of clients. Several networking solutions have been offered by telecom organizations, such as the ITU-T. These days, GPON is widely used in Asia for optical networks. Bidirectional communication speeds of 2.5/1.25 Gbps are provided by GPON, the first PON specification. The G.984.6 [3] is the ITU-T common organization that specifies GPON. Operators typically employ GPON to create FTTH and support high-applications bandwidth such as Play triple and computing cloud. With a single broadband connection, triple-play enables the provision of a phone and two intensive-bandwidth services (such as high-access internet speed,

W. A. Mahmoud et al. (Eds.): ACDN 2025, CCIS 2798, pp. 3–15, 2026.
https://doi.org/10.1007/978-3-032-15448-4_1

television, and low-services capacity) [4]. PONs usually consist of optical network units (ONUs), optical line termination (OLT) units, and distribution optical network (ODN), or optical network terminals, which are often called ONTs [5]. Internet communication, medical imaging, multimedia systems, military communication, telemedicine, etc. all use image encryption and decryption. As a result, protecting and ensuring the secrecy of data have become absolutely essential [6]. It is difficult to support the large amounts of data needed by both transportation and security at the same time. Cryptography is among the most promising methods to ensure security of communications. Numerous methods for protecting data have been proposed. Optical safe communication utilizing a novel 5d chaos distribution separation introduced the new DDD-MD technology (Dynamic Diffeo-Difference Multi-Dimensional). A new cryptosystem built on the chaotic stream segmentation (CSS) technique uses it as a key [7], as well as features secure optical communication using the hill method cipher [8] [9], optical based protected chaos [10], and a security system using the technique of the Rivest Cipher 4 [11]. The dynamic wavelength and bandwidth allocation (DWBA) algorithm has been investigated as a TWDM-PON hotspot. Some DWBA studies concentrate on load balancing and energy conservation; however, they overlook time latency, which makes them inapplicable to 5G fronthaul networks [12]. Numerous encryption methods have been created to raise OAN's physical security layer. Zhang et al. used 2- chaos scrambling dimensional methods to develop OFDM-PON that is physically safe [13]. In order to provide structural stability for fast-range communication, Kumari et al. established a wheel-network according to resilient PON and used mode OCDMA and division multiplexing (MDM) networks [14]. To improve OFDM-PON security, Cheng et al. implemented fractional transformation Fourier. Recently a high-security speed WDM method has been developed that uses the blowfish ciphering to enhance safety image and rate information conveyance through remote regions [15]. The analysis of designs for unique algorithms research investigations based on the performance analysis is shown in Table 1. A high-security speed GPON method has been developed that uses the Blowfish ciphering to enhance photo rate of information and safety transmission for PON. According to G.984.6 ITU-T specifications, a network design with an optimum reach of 65 km can support up to 64 consumers utilizing technology of secure GPON at a minimal quality acceptable factor of 6, an optimum level of BER around 10−9, and an optimal distance between optical successive terminals network of 20 km. GPON has reached a minimum permitted reception sensitivity about −35.8 dBm for U/S and −34.3 dBm for D/S, allowing it to transmit data at 2.5 Gbps D/S and 1.25 Gbps U/S [16]. To enhance information throughput, receiving sensitivity, link communication distance, and performance of security for PON, a unique secure 4-GPON was proposed that uses For both U/S and D/S paths Time Division Multiple (TDM) using the encryption of Hill. Compared to blowfish ciphers, hill ciphers are safer and more suitable for optical communications, and they are utilized in several real-world scenarios, like storage cloud, secure communication requirements, and image encryption for *steganography* [17]. To the best of our knowledge, no study has ever employed the Hill method to enhance security PON on GPON asymmetric for a distance link of 75 km and a ratio of splitting of 128 based on the standard ITU-T criteria G.984.6. Moreover, the asymmetrical 10/5 Gbps security optical 4-GPON proceed shows the degree to which this organization upholds transmission reliable while enhancing system efficiency, which has a minimum permitted reception sensitivity of –37.2 dBm for uplink and -36.7dBm for downlink. Security tests have also been carried out to display how well the algorithm of Hill withstands different cryptanalytic techniques. These assessments comprise analysis of time, analysis of histogram, entropy data, private key space, and correlation evaluations.

The rest of the paper is organized as follows: A summary is provided in Sect. 1. Section 2 presents the simulated scenario, Sect. 3 presents the outcomes, and Sect. 4 examines the conclusion.

Table 1. Studies and their contributions

Reference	Contribution
[7]	(1) Putting forward a novel 5D continuous chaotic system for key generation. (2) A numerical analysis evaluating the suggested chaotic system's effectiveness in terms of its dynamic characteristics. (3) Using the circuit design concept as a guide, a circuit schematic of the suggested chaotic system was drawn
[8]	Hill coding used initially in a secure FSO (WDM-SFSO) system communication operating at a large capacity of 80 Gb/s
[9]	Using the Hill cipher technique, suggested a picture encryption scheme that used wavelength-division-multiplexing (WDM) to transfer large bitrates up to 80 Gbits. The encrypted image was sent 178 km away via optical fiber
[10]	To secure an optical fiber system, created a chaotic waveform and incorporated an information signal inside it using a chaos masking approach. Three distinct DCF configurations were studied and compared
[11]	The performance of an FSO system deteriorates when optical chaos is introduced because it creates a noise signal with bigger and more erratic amplitudes on the signal
[12]	Proposed a new DWBA algorithm for TWDM-PON that was based on the reinforcement learning (RL) algorithm Q-learning. In order to meet the low latency requirement, this DWBA method can efficiently limit latency
[13]	Expanded the key space and improved the chaotic nature of logistic mapping. Additionally, by combining time slots and frequency subcarriers, 2-D scrambling increased the system's resilience to eavesdroppers
[14]	Suggested using multi-weight zero cross-correlation (MWZCC) cipher in a hybrid bidirectional MDM-OCDMA-PON design of 10/2.5 Gbit/s. In the suggested system, the MDM approach incorporated donut modes 0 and 1
[18]	Proposed a way to encrypt and compress images at the same time. The two main methods introduced are permutation-diffusion type picture encryption and compressed sensing (CS) employing structurally random matrix (SRM)
[19]	Presented a brand-new color image encryption technique that used spatiotemporal chaos, one-time keys, and DNA sequence operations

(*continued*)

Table 1. *(continued)*

Reference	Contribution
[20]	Addressed the growing need for secure real-time image communication. Several chaos-based image cryptosystems were studied. Permutation and diffusion were two separate processes with fixed control parameters in the permutation-diffusion architecture that formed the basis of the majority of them

2 Simulation Setup

The algorithm Hill cipher proposed by Lester S. Hill, is among the most significant algorithms based on symmetric linear algebra. It offers a number of advantages for data encryption. Nevertheless, it is not always possible to pass the matrix encryption key backwards. To decrypt text or images, the matrix encryption array key needs to be reversed. The reversible non-matrix composition technique is encoded using a reversible primary matrix [21]. As illustrated in Fig. 1, the matrix inverse of the recovered original photo was multiplied by the block of the image encrypted in order to decode this transmitted data. The OLT, ODN, and ONU are components of the D/S system and the corresponding U/S system make up the two components of the network architecture.

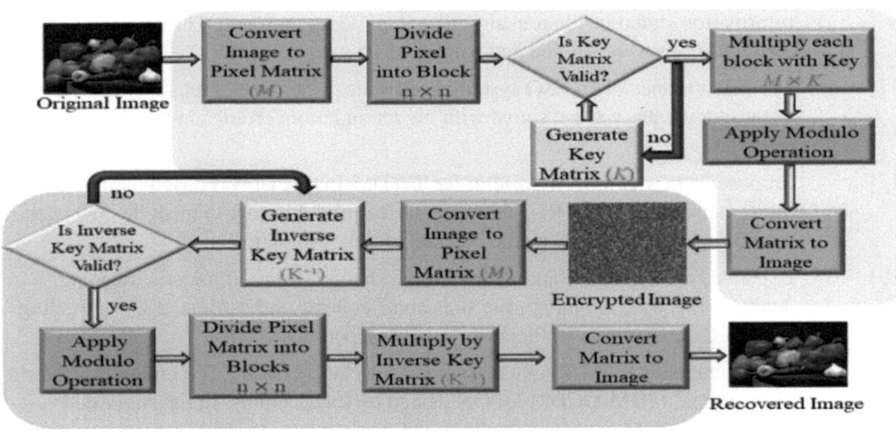

Fig. 1. Block diagram for Hill encryption/decryption [21].

2.1 Down-Link

The pulse generator NRZ receives the pixels, which transforms them into a signal that is electrical. The binary picture is already encoded and run via a pseudo random binary sequence (PRBS) of (4 * 2.5) Gbps. A continuous laser pulse and a Mach-Zehnder modulator (MZM) with a 30dB ratio of extinction are utilized to change a signal that is electrical into an optical signal. The collected signal is blended straight onto a bidirectional SMF. With insertion losses of 1 dB and return losses of 65 dB, an optical circulator is then used to separate the signal U/S. Signals are divided among ONUs using the fiber distance via a passive splitter bidirectional at the remote node (RN). The ODN employs two power stages splitter to achieve a 128 split ratio: a 1:4 bidirectional splitter with loss insertion of 4 dB, followed by a 1:32 splitter/combiner passive. A divisor's number of outputs and the losses it causes have the inverse mathematical connection formula that follows [22]:

$$PL = 10 \times \text{Log}(\frac{1}{\mathbf{N}}) \quad (1)$$

The loss insertion caused by the passive splitter is denoted by PL, where N is the configuration of the splitter. The average power is set at 5 dBm in order to supply a GPON system on D/S wavelengths. In the S band, the D/S wavelength is between λ1 and λ4 (1490–1491.2 nm), with a channel spacing of 50GHz. The optical signal is received at the receiver of D/S by an avalanche photodiode (APD), which converts it into an electrical impulse before returning it to its original pixel structure. The responsivity of APD's is 0.9 A/W at unity gain, and 9 A/W of MR corresponds to a multiplication factor (M) of about 10 [23]. There are insertion losses in every ONU of 3 dB, because it has an optical filter to select the D/S channel wavelength direction when using various wavelengths, as shown in Fig. 2.

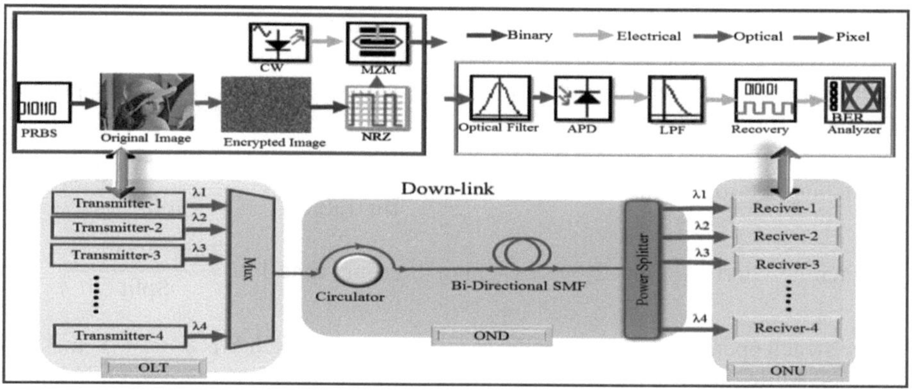

Fig. 2. The down-link protecting 4-GPON system configuration includes OLT, ODN, and ONU.

2.2 Up-Link

The OLT at the downlink is comparable to the ONU transmitter. A 4-GPON network is ensured by setting the U/S communication directionality wavelength power mean launched to 0.5 dBm. With a channel spacing of 50GHz, the O band's U/S wavelength is between λ5 and λ8 (1310 and 1311.2 nm). After using a passive 32:1 splitter/combiner at the optical network unit, a certain wavelength is transmitted to the appropriate optical line network receiver. After choosing the most repetition simulated using a buffer picker at the upstream receiver, the data is recovered using an APD and a band-pass filter. As seen in Fig. 3, it is additionally filtered utilizing a low-Bessel pass filter before being analyzed utilizing an analyzer of BER.

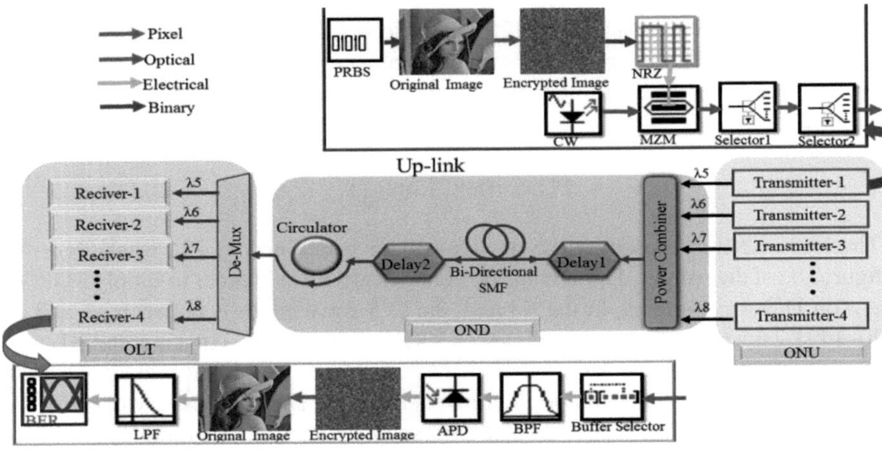

Fig. 3. The U/S OLT, ODN, and ONU of the 4-GPON network system.

When there are numerous channels sharing the identical wavelength, time division multiple access (TDMA) needs to be taken into consideration in the U/S channel. Two dynamic Y-switches are utilized to make sure that data is only sent within the time designated intervals. The method at hand aids in avoiding interruptions between multiple consumers. For an optical network unit with Y-dynamic switches 1 and 2, the equations are given by formulas (2) and (3) [24, 25]:

$$\text{Switching Starting time } 1 = \text{Time Slot} \times \left(\frac{1}{\text{Bit rate}}\right) \times \left(\frac{\text{Sequence length}}{\text{Split}}\right) \quad (2)$$

$$\text{Switching Starting time } 2 = \text{Switching Starting time } 1 + \frac{\text{Time window}}{\text{Split}} \quad (3)$$

The switch opening time (T2) for the second dynamic switch Y is 8×10^{-10} to 3.976 $\times 10^{-7}$ s, while the switch beginning time (T1) for the first dynamic switch Y is 0 to 3.968×10^{-7} s. There are 32 U/S users that share the same wavelength, denoted as N. 256 bits making up the sequence length (SeqL), 1.25 Gbps is the bit rate (Br), 25.6 $\times 10^{-9}$ s is the time window (t), and 0 to 31 is the timeslot (τ). In this instance, the OLT side detected the ONUs' U/S communication directionality 5 Gbps (4 * 1.25 Gbps) traffic. Only one of the 32 time slots is available for sending the signal. To broadcast a 1.25 Gbps signal in an upstream direction at a specific wavelength, two switch Y selections are used by every of the 32 ONUs. By splitting the 1.25 Gbps capacity inserted into the optical signal among 32 clients, the 5 Gbps network can give a specific speed of 39.06 Mbps to 128 users.

3 Results and Discussion

The productivity of the 4-GPON approach was assessed utilizing receiver sensitivity measures and BER. The GPON criteria, which require −27 dBm for D/S communication directionality and −28 dBm for U/S communication directionality at the OLT, must be met by the receiver sensitivity, according to ITU-T 984.6 [3]. The major purpose of this research was to deliver safe capacity over a 75-km link communication distance link at a pace of 10 Gbps D/S communication directionality and 5 Gbps U/S communication directionality data transmission, utilizing Hill ciphering to assure reception clear. The quality factor (Q factor) and logarithm of bit error rate (BER) values are plotted against the receiver's sensitivity over a range of link distances at 1490 nm and 1310 nm for U/S communication directionality and D/S communication directionality, respectively (Fig. 4). The capacity shows that the performance of the system declines with increasing network communication distance, causing the BER to surpass 10–9 and the Q factor to drop less than the threshold 6. The measured BER was 10–10 at −36.7 dBm for D/S communication directionality and 10–10 at −37.2 dBm for U/S communication directionality at a distance of 75 km. The corresponding Q factors were 6.3 for the downstream direction and 6.5 for the upstream direction. This demonstrates that the ITU-T 984.6 minimal sensitivity standards are fulfilled. Table 2 lists the acquired network parameters from simulations and calculations with the expected 4-GPON values. The characteristics that are noted, which exhibit minor but acceptable enhancements, are aligned with ITU-T standards G.984.6 for a 4-GPON asymmetric network access.

Table 2. ITU-T G.984.6 parameters are compared with the findings of asymmetric secure 4-GPON.

Channels direction	Communication link		Sensitivity		BER		Q-factor	
Capacity	[3]	Acquired	[3]	Acquired	[3]	Acquired	[3]	Acquired
10 Gbps D/S	20 km	75 km	−27 dBm	−36.7 dBm	10^{-3}	10^{-10}	5	6.3
5Gbps U/S	20 km	75 km	−28 dBm	−37.2 dBm	10^{-3}	10^{-10}	5	6.5
Splitting ratio			Known 64 at 20 km			Acquired 128 at 75 km		

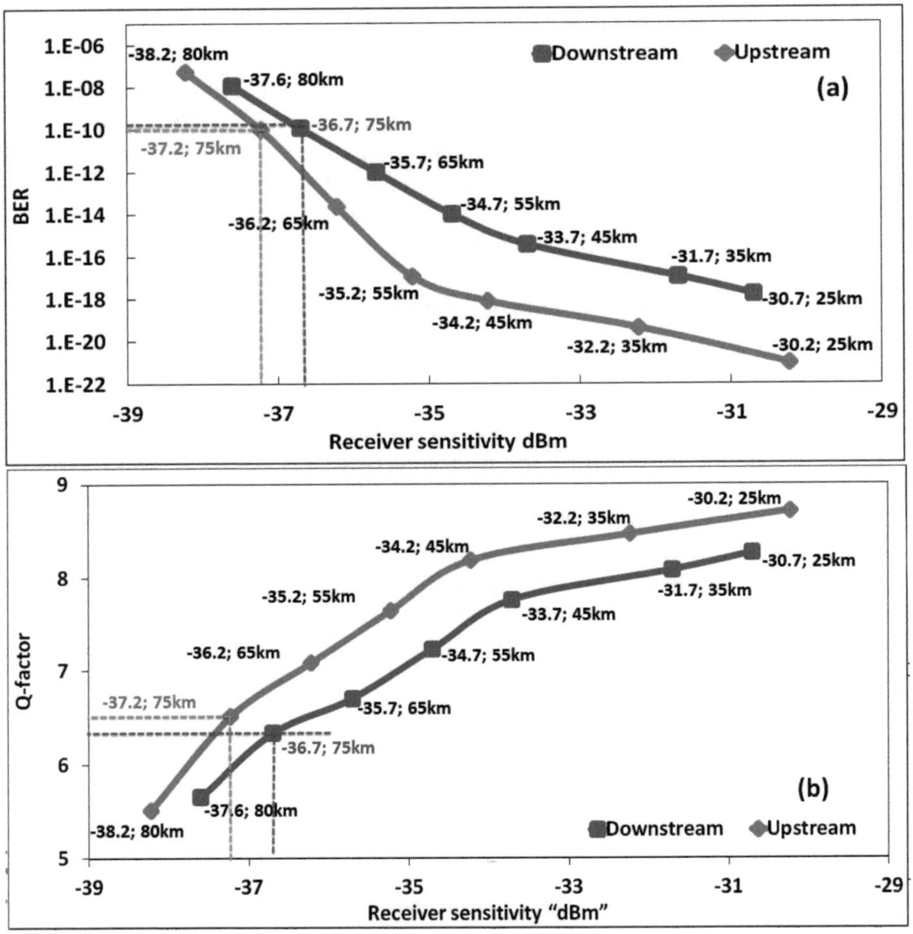

Fig. 4. At different link distances, (a) the BER and (b) the Q-factor versus receiver sensitivity for the D/S and U/S directions.

The decryption procedure utilizes the criteria that follow: (1) the initial values x0, y0, and z0 are also included in the key, paired with the parameters r2, μ, and r1. (2) r2 = 0.61247892775319, r1 = 0.14785214785423, μ = 3.98745632101279, z0 = 0.61247892775319, y0 = 0.92791237172793 and x0 = 0.75147854321781 are the parameters that are employed (3). If the precision is 10–14, the key space may be at least 1084 ≈ 2279 > 2128. Since the space key should be at least 2128 from a cryptographic perspective, it is large enough to survive brute-force attacks [21] to assure a high degree of security. So, the system design meets the specifications for a PON security network. Ciphers of Hill have been utilized in various real-world applications, including storage of cloud, biometrics identity, copy software safeguarding, encryption of image for surveillance, and safe communication requirements. The key spaces of the proposed system and those of existing systems that have been reported in academic publications are listed in Table 3.

Table 3. A comparison between the references and the recommended key space.

Cipher	[26]	[18]	[19]	[20]	[27]	Proposed Cipher
Key space	2^{186}	2^{149}	2^{203}	2^{199}	$3.4 \times 10^{80} \approx 2^{267}$	$10^{84} \approx 2^{279}$

Histograms are widely utilized to analyze images. To have a better understanding of the image pixel distribution, the quantity of pixels at every level of intensity needs to be examined. By displaying the amount, the discrepancies between the image of plain and the equivalent image ciphering must be displayed in order to prevent statistical attacks. The Lena photo's 256x256 histograms were recognized, along with the matching encrypted pictures. For the Lena image, the original photos A1 and the related histogram A2 are demonstrated in Fig. 5; however, the encrypted image A3 and histograms A4 are similarly significantly and distributed differently from the plain photos. The recovered image is displayed in A5. The ciphering picture is noise and completely different from the image of plain, therefore no attributes of the image plain can be discerned from it. As a result, the recommended encryption method is quite safe. The findings showed the effectiveness of the proposed approach in thwarting statistical attacks.

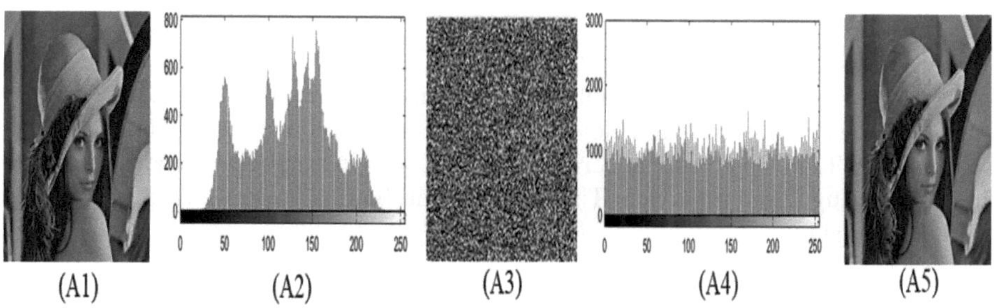

Fig. 5. The simulation result: original image (A1), the corresponding histogram (A2), image of encryption (A3), the corresponding histogram (A4), and the recovered photo (A5).

The Lena test images' pixel distribution in the D', V', and Directions are shown in Fig. 6. For well-defined imaging, nearby pixels in the horizontal (H'), vertical (V'), and diagonal (D') planes usually have strong correlations with one another. An encrypted image should have correlations equivalent to zero, which suggests that it is different sufficiently from the plain image. It seems that every pixel in the encrypted image is evenly spaced throughout the system of coordinates.

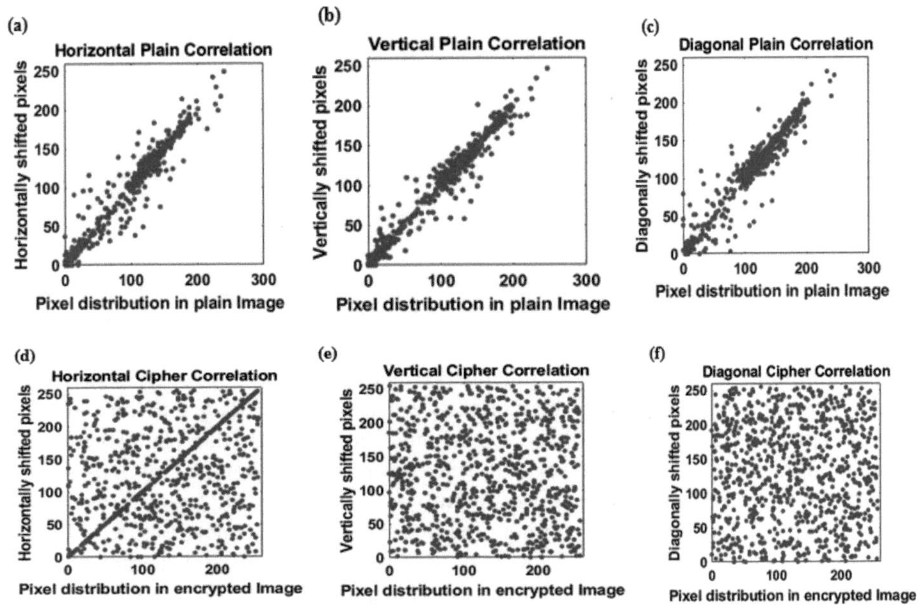

Fig. 6. The correlation analysis for the original Lena image: a–c and corresponding Lena image's encrypted pixels d–f.

A comparison of the security of the proposed cipher for Lena image compared to other works [16] is shown as in Table 4. The accuracy, encryption speed, and security of the Hill code compared to the blowfish code are indicated in Table 3. The coefficient association in Table 3 is closer to zero compared to previous studies, demonstrating the safety of the suggested approach. This implies that there is greater unpredictability in the ciphered data.

Table 4. The security analyses of hill cipher compared to blowfish cipher.

Security analysis	Parameter security analysis	Proposed cipher	[16]
Perceptual security analysis	peak signal-to-noise ratio (PSNR)	9.45	9.33
	mean square error (MSE)	7681.78	7653.58
	mean absolute error (MAE)	74.51	72.53
	Structural Similarity Index (SSIM)	1	1
	Visual Information Fidelity (VIF)	0.99987	0.99836
Correlation analysis	Horizontal	0.0720	0.0720

(*continued*)

Table 4. *(continued)*

Security analysis	Parameter security analysis	Proposed cipher	[16]
	Vertical	−0.0054	−0.0110
	Diagonal	0.0025	−0.0323
Differential attack analysis	NPCR (Number of Pixels Change Rate)	99.59	99.420
	UACI (Unified Average Changing Intensity)	28.79	27.02
Entropy analysis	Entropy of ciphered image	7.9972	7.9811
Time encryption analysis		2.01	2.22

The outcomes were contrasted with those of other projects. The results demonstrated how much larger the data rate, splitting ratio, and link communication distance were higher compared to other approaches (Table 5).

Table 5. Illustration of prior research with the suggested plan

Ref.	Secure techniques	Bitrate	Transmission distance (km)	Splitting ratio
[4]	No security	2.5D/S/1.25U/S Gbps	60	128
[28]	No security	2.5D/S/1.25U/S Gbps	17	32
[29]	No security	2.5D/S/1.25U/S Gbps	40	Not defined
[30]	No security	2.5D/S/1.25U/S Gbps	20	128
[16]	Blowfish ciphering	2.5D/S/1.25U/S Gbps	65	64
Proposed work	Hill ciphering	10D/S/5U/S Gbps	75	128

4 Conclusion

A novel security solution for 4-GPONs was proposed that enhanced network security against fiber failure or breakage, as specified by the ITU-T G.984.6 standard, alleviated the impacts of breaks in the connection between OLT and optical network unit, and provided a dependable technique for quick communication. GPON is utilized by telecom providers to cut costs. The fact that this technology supports data is one of its benefits over the same backbone network as FTTH. Triple play is made easy by the latency, high bandwidth, outstanding Quality of Service (QoS) support, and high reliability of four-GPON low technology. Opti-System and MATLAB tools were integrated to produce a 4-GPON security system based on the Hill cipher. For 75 km at a data rate of 10/5Gbps, a minimum of −37.2 dBm direction of U/S and −36.7 dBm direction of D/S are needed to provide a suitable BER and Q-factor. The analysis of the suggested network reveals a significant space key, with little correlation between coefficients, a comparable distribution of histograms and improved resistance to common assaults including brute-force, statistical, and anti-differential attacks. Grayscale graphics were successfully utilized for secure communication. Above all, the strong encryption properties of the employed method provided a high level of protection for sensitive data. Secure physical layer communications may benefit from the application of this security-enhanced 4-GPON technique in the future. As part of future work, more advanced cryptographic techniques such as AES or ECC can be explored to enhance the security of GPON systems, especially in scenarios involving long-reach transmission and high split ratios.

References

1. Tang, R., et al.: High security OFDM-PON based on an iterative cascading chaotic model and 4-D joint encryption. Opt. Commun. **495** (2021)
2. Bindhaiq, S., Zulkifli, N., Supa'at, A.M., Idrus, S.M., Salleh, M.S.: 128 Gb/s TWDM PON system using dispersion-supported transmission method. Opt. Fiber Technol. **38**, 87–97 (2017)
3. ITU-T G.984.6. Gigabit-capable passive optical networks (GPON): Reach extension. ITU-T G-Series Recomm. (2008)
4. Abdellaoui, Z., Dieudonne, Y., Aleya, A.: Design, implementation and evaluation of a Fiber To The Home (FTTH) access network based on a Giga Passive Optical Network GPON. Array **10**, 100058 (2021)
5. Abdulla, E.N., Hussien, R.A., Rashid, F.F., Abdulkafi, A.A., Abass, A.K., Saleh, M.A.: Design and performance analysis of symmetrical 160 Gbps TWDM-PON utilizing bidirectional configuration. J. Opt. (2023)
6. Thakur, P., Rana, A.: A symmetrical key cryptography analysis using blowfish algorithm. Int. J. Eng. Res. **5**, 235–238 (2016)
7. Al-Saidi, N.M., Ali, M.H., Al-Azzawi, W.K.H., Abass, A.K.: Secure optical communication using a new 5D chaotic stream segmentation. Int. J. Sustain. Dev. Plan. **17**, 1553–1560 (2022)
8. Mushatet, A.F., Fadil, E.A., Abdulla, E.N.: High bit rate secure FSO system utilizing Hill coding. J. Opt. Commun. **0147**, 1–14 (2025)
9. Mohammed, S.H., Abass, A.K., Ali, M.H., Rashid, F.F.: Design and simulation of secure fiber optic communication system utilizing hill cipher algorithm. J. Opt. **53**, 1499–1507 (2023)
10. Fadil, E.A., et al.: Design and performance analysis of optical communication system utilizing optical chaos. J. Opt. **53**, 2435–2440 (2024)
11. Mohammed, S.H., Ali, M.H., Abass, A.K., Al-Azzawi, W.K.: Design and implementation of cipher algorithm based secure optical communication system. Opt. Quant. Electron. **55**, 86 (2023)
12. Liang, S., Zhao, F., Jiang, W.: A learning algorithm for TWDM-PON' DWBA with 5G fronthaul networks. Opt. Fiber Technol. **53**, 102039 (2019)
13. Zhang, L., Xin, X., Liu, B., Yin, X.: Physical secure enhancement in optical OFDMA-PON based on two-dimentional scrambling. Eur. Conf. Opt. Commun. ECOC **20**, 32–37 (2012)

14. Kumari, M., Arya, V., Al-Khafaji, H.M.R.: Wheel-based MDM-PON system incorporating OCDMA for secure network resiliency. Photonics **10** (2023)
15. Hussien, R.A., Radhi, S.S., Rashid, F.F., Abdulla, E.N., Abass, A.K.: Design and performance analysis of secure optical communication system by implementing blowfish cipher algorithm. Results Opt. **16**, 100708 (2024)
16. Musadaq, R., Abdulwahid, S.N., Abd Alwahed, N.N., Abdulla, E.N.: Security analysis of an image encryption algorithm based on Blowfish in GPON. J. Opt. Commun. 32–34 (2025)
17. Chen, L., Guo, G., Peng, Z.: A hill cipher-based remote data possession checking in cloud storage. Secur. Commun. Networks **7**, 511–518 (2014)
18. Chen, J., Zhang, Y., Qi, L., Fu, C., Xu, L.: Exploiting chaos-based compressed sensing and cryptographic algorithm for image encryption and compression. Opt. Laser Technol. **99**, 238–248 (2018)
19. Wu, X., Wang, K., Wang, X., Kan, H., Kurths, J.: Color image DNA encryption using NCA map-based CML and one-time keys. Signal Process. **148**, 272–287 (2018)
20. Xin Chen, J., liang Zhu, Z., Fu, C., Yu, H., bo Zhang, L.: A fast chaos-based image encryption scheme with a dynamic state variables selection mechanism. Commun. Nonlinear Sci. Numer. Simul. **20**, 846–860 (2015)
21. Radhi, S.S., Hussien, R.A., Abdulla, E.N., Abass, A.K., Rashid, F.F.: Design a secure TWDM-PON via the Hill cipher algorithm. Opt. Contin. **4**, 1051–1064 (2025)
22. Mousa, E., Abdulla, E.N., Adnan, S.A.: Enhancing network security based on 10G-EPON with the use of the Hill cipher algorithm. J. Opt. Commun. 1–13 (2025)
23. Abdulla, E.N., Abass, A.K., Abdulkafi, A.A.: Asymmetric 160/80 Gb/s TWDM PON with supported transmission method utilizing FBG and DML. J. Opt. Commun. **45**, s611–s618 (2022)
24. Abdulla, E.N., Abass, A.K., Abdulkafi, A.A.: Asymmetric 160/80 Gbps TWDM PON utilizing dispersion compensation technique. J. Opt. 1683–1693 (2022)
25. Abdulla, E.N., Safa Salam Radhi, F.F.R., Hussien, M.M.S.R.A., Abass, A.K., Fadil, A.E.A.: Security improvement for TWDM-PON utilizing blowfish cryptography. Appl. Opt. **63** (2024)
26. Wang, X., Zhu, X., Wu, X., Zhang, Y.: Image encryption algorithm based on multiple mixed hash functions and cyclic shift. Opt. Lasers Eng. **107**, 370–379 (2018)
27. Guesmi, R., Farah, M.A.B., Kachouri, A., Samet, M.: A novel chaos-based image encryption using DNA sequence operation and Secure Hash Algorithm SHA-2. Nonlinear Dyn. **83**, 1123–1136 (2016)
28. Awalia, W., Pantjawati, A.B.: Performance simulation of fiber to the home (FTTH) devices based on optisystem. IOP Conf. Ser. Mater. Sci. Eng. **384** (2018)
29. Kherici, C., Kandouci, M.: Performance study of a coexistence system in a PON network taking into account the stimulated scattering of Raman. In: 10th International Conference on Innovation, Modern Applied Science & Environmental Studies (ICIES'2022), vol. 351, pp. 4–8 (2022)
30. Kaur, R., Singh, S.: Polarization multiplexing and hybrid modulation based bandwidth efficient NG-PON2 coexisting with GPON and XG-PON. J. Opt. Technol. **88**, 196 (2021)

Design a Robust FTTB-GPON-Based Directly Modulated VCSEL Sources Using an Identity Row Shifting Matrix Coding Scheme

Sura Khalil Ibrahim[1,2](✉), Ghusoon M. Ali[2], and Ali Khalid Jassim[2]

[1] Electronic and Communication Engineering Department, College of Engineering, University of Baghdad, Baghdad, Iraq
sura.k@coeng.uobaghdad.edu.iq

[2] Electrical Engineering Department, College of Engineering, Mustansiriyah University, Baghdad, Iraq
{eng.ghusoom_ali,alijassim}@uomustansiriyah.edu.iq

Abstract. The giga-passive optical network (GPON) systems use spectral amplitude coding-optical code division multiple access (SAC-OCDMA) to enhance user security. However, this technique has shortcomings. Expanding user capacity requires extra components or channels, which increases system complexity. These networks also use broadband spectrum sources to maintain acceptable performance. This paper addresses these challenges. It presents a robust fiber-to-the-building gigabit passive optical network (FTTB-GPON). The network uses the Identity Row-Shifting Matrix (IRSM) SAC-OCDMA code scheme and four narrow-band, directly modulated vertical-cavity surface-emitting laser (VCSEL) sources, which are distributed across four channels to serve 16 buildings. The network is evaluated under this configuration. It is tested with (1490.05/1310.05) nm downlink/uplink (DL/UL), 0.6 nm channel spacing, and 0.15 nm bandwidth over a 20 km fiber optic backbone at 2.5 Gbps. The results showed that this scenario achieved an acceptable bit error rate (BER) and Q-factor. The network demonstrated a BER of −13.6 dB and a Q-factor of approximately 7.53.

Keywords: FTTB-GPON · IRSM code · VCSEL · SAC-OCDMA · ZCC

1 Introduction

Several techniques have been used for SAC-OCDMA, like IRSM codes, which are used to address the problems in SAC-OCDMA systems, like the associated phase-induced intensity noise (PIIN) and multiple access interference (MAI) [1, 2]. Numerous academics have introduced various encoding strategies to reduce MAI. Spectral amplitude coding (SAC) is preferred above all other OCDMA types because it can remove MAI with the use of the code sequences with fixed in-phase cross-correlation. SAC-OCDMA, which is an incoherent OCDMA system type, has the main benefit of utilizing all-optical processing for performing networking functions like routing and addressing. For this reason, SAC is a preferred choice for the upcoming optical access system generation [3, 4].

W. A. Mahmoud et al. (Eds.): ACDN 2025, CCIS 2798, pp. 16–29, 2026.
https://doi.org/10.1007/978-3-032-15448-4_2

The incoherent source noise level increases with the number of users [5]. When the rate of transmission reaches 1250 Mbps, Ayotte has demonstrated that error correction codes (ECC) may be utilized in order to enhance performance of SAC-OCDMA systems to compensate for the noise [6, 7]. Numerous code schemes, including Reed-Solomon (RS) codes [8], turbo codes (TC) [9], and low spectral density parity check (LDPC) codes [10], have been proposed. Vasic et al. have demonstrated that LDPC codes perform better than TC in terms of quality transmission and design complexity [11]. Additionally, another scheme has been introduced to enhance system performance. It employs a bi-directional 10/2.5 Gbps hybrid mode-division multiplexing (MDM) and OCDMA-PON system that incorporates multi-weight zero cross-correlation (MWZCC) coding [12]. Furthermore, OCDMA has been presented for free-space optical and optical sensor networks. This approach offers a quality-of-service difference at the physical layer [13, 14]. Different types of optical signal superposition (incoherent or coherent) or various encoding methods (amplitude/phase, time/wavelength) can be used to classify OCDMA [15, 16].

An FTTB-GPON system is proposed using four narrowband directly modulated VCSEL sources integrated with a WDM (MUX/DEMUX/MUX) encoder based on the IRSM-SAC-OCDMA code scheme distributed on four channels in the downlink to improve security. The proposed design uses (1490.05/1310.05) nm (DL/UL) with a 0.6 nm spacing and a 0.15 nm bandwidth. This design feeds 16 buildings in four blocks. The 4-FBG decoders are used in receiver spread according to the code scheme.

This paper is designed as follows: Sect. 2, presents the literature review of GPON-SAC-OCDMA. Section 3 explains the design of the proposed FTTB-GPON system. Section 4 shows the coding scheme of IRSM SAC-OCDMA, while Sect. 5 illustrates the IRSM SAC-OSDMA encoder design. Section 6 presents results and their discussion. Section 7 concludes the paper. Section 8 outlines the proposed future work.

2 Literature Review

SAC-OCDMA plays an important role in GPON security. By introducing spectral/spatial codes for an OCDMA-based PON, Memon et al. demonstrated a system where the two-dimensional (2-D) multi-diagonal code assigns each user a unique spectral and spatial pattern. As a result, secure, interference-free transmission was ensured for 6-users, each at 15 Gbps over 25 km of single-mode fiber (SMF). Their architecture operated with four downstream wavelengths (1546–1548.1 nm) and 4 upstream wave-lengths (1310–1312.1 nm). System performance was evaluated based on BER and Q-factor across various data rates [17]. Imtiaz *etal.* proposed a two-dimensional (2D) double-weight zero cross-correlation system, compatible with spectral-spatial as well as spectral-temporal 2D-OCDMA architectures. Supporting 2 Gbps for the same parameters, this design achieved a BER of 10^−9 [18]. Similarly, Kehkashan A. Memon *et al.* developed a high-speed giga-passive optical network (GPON) that features one-dimensional (1D) spectral amplitude coding and free-space optical (FSO) channels. The network eliminates multiple access interference (MAI) for 5-locations at 10 Gbps per user. Their results were notable: the BER reached 10^−18 in haze, 10^−11 at 1200 m in clear air, and 10^−14 at 1200 m or 550 m in rain [19]. In another relevant study, Ahmed N. et al. presented a hybrid OCDMA/wavelength division multiplexing (WDM) system for GPON, utilizing a modified double-weight (MDW) code and differential phase shift keying (DPSK) with several detection methods. In this approach, one light-emitting diode (LED) was split into three channels, each modulated at 1 and 2.5 Gbps with a Mach-Zehnder modulator (MZM). These three OCDMA channels, along with one WDM channel, were transmitted simultaneously. A (4 $\times$ 4) demultiplexer/multiplexer was employed to separate and combine signals. At the receiver, the multiplexer recombined signals into their respective channels. Detection was direct for the WDM channel, while each OCDMA channel passed first through an AND detector and then a complementary detector [16].

In summary, the reviewed studies illustrated that researchers have utilized broadband sources (BBs) to reduce multiple access interference (MAI) and increase user capacity in optical networks. However, this approach requires additional network components such as filters (devices that separate or combine different wavelengths) and amplifiers. Furthermore, several OCDMA techniques can be adapted for short-reach optical links leveraging BBs. While OCDMA systems contribute to data confidentiality, they also introduce phase-induced intensity noise (PIIN), which complicates code implementation and necessitates sophisticated detection methods. To address this, the identity row shift matrix (IRSM) code, applied within spectral amplitude coding (SAC)-OCDMA, achieved zero cross-correlation and effectively eliminates PIIN.

This paper presents an FTTB-GPON system that employs four narrowband, directly modulated VCSEL sources, seamlessly integrated with a WDM (MUX/DEMUX/MUX) encoder and based on the IRSM-SAC-OCDMA code scheme. Data is distributed across four downlink channels, which enhances security. The design operates at 1490.05 nm for downlink and 1310.05 nm for uplink, utilizing a 0.6 nm spacing and a 0.15 nm bandwidth. The system serves 16 buildings grouped into four blocks. At the receiver, 4-FBG decoders are employed according to the code scheme to recover the original data for each user.

3 Design of the Proposed FTTB-GPON System

The proposed FTTB-GPON downlink and uplink system includes the transmitter, cables, and receiver. At the downlink, the transmitter, at the optical line terminal (OLT), modulates the signal information directly with an optical carrier provided by optical sources. The type of optical source is a directly modulated VCSEL, which operates jointly like a modulator and an optical source distributed on four channels. The modulated signals are then encoded using a WDM (MUX/DEMUX/MUX) encoder based on the IRSM-SAC OCDMA technique. The combined encoded signal will be transmitted over a bidirectional backbone fiber-optic cable, representing the system's second part, as optical distribution network (ODN). At the receiver, the decoder consists of a single FBG filter that detects each channel directly and decodes the received signals. These are distributed by splitters to the 16 buildings (each 4-buildings in one block) at optical network units (ONUs) over two stages of fiber optic feeders. At the uplink, an optical transmitter is used, which is set up to use an externally modulated laser without using the IRSM code technique. At the uplink receiver, the PIN detector is utilized for direct detection. The proposed design is implemented using Opti-system software v.15 as shown in Fig. 1.

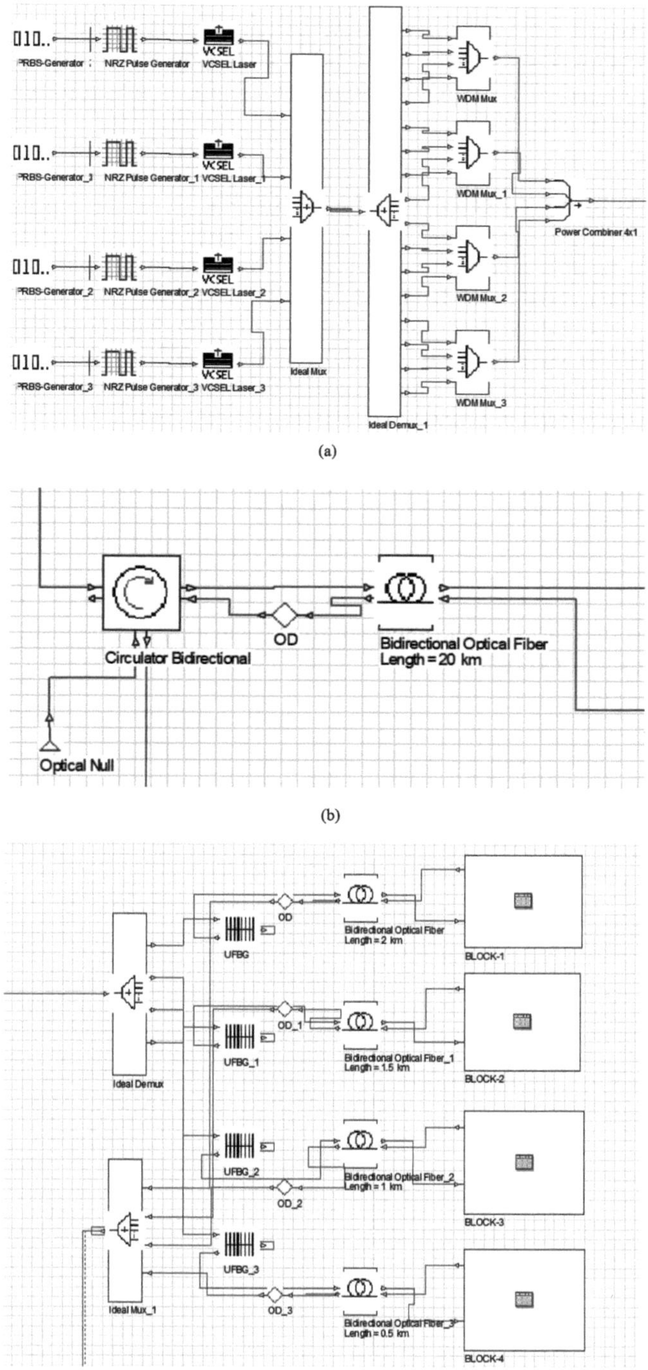

Fig. 1. FTTB-GPON using IRSM-SAC-OCDMA (1490.05/1310.05) (DL/UL) at 2.5 Gbps over 20 km (a) transmitter;(b) fiber cable; (c) receiver.

Real-time WDM (DEMUX/MUX/DEMUX) encoders and FBG decoders increase both cost and complexity. In contrast, the IRSM code reduces processing overhead. As a result, the proposed FTTB-GPON architecture achieves a strong balance in terms of scalability, security, and hardware simplicity.

4 Coding Scheme of IRSM SAC-OCDMA

IRSM code is a suitable scheme for an SAC-OCDMA system. The main characteristics of the IRSM code consist of the length of code (A), weight of code (M), and number of channels (N), with high auto-correlation and a cross-correlation equal to zero (ZCC). The IRSM code scheme comprises the following steps [1, 2]:

The first step consists of an identity matrix, i, of order $m = 4$. Here, an identity matrix of (4 × 4) is used in Eq. (1) as follows:

$$i_4^0 = \begin{bmatrix} 1\,0 & 0\,0 \\ 0\,1 & 0\,0 \\ 0\,0 & 1\,0 \\ 0\,0 & 0\,1 \end{bmatrix}_{4\times4} \tag{1}$$

The second step involves shifting each row of the matrix downward $(m-1)$ times, as shown in Eqs. (2), (3), and (4).

$$i_4^1 = \begin{bmatrix} 0\,1 & 0\,0 \\ 0\,0 & 1\,0 \\ 0\,0 & 0\,1 \\ 1\,0 & 0\,0 \end{bmatrix}_{4\times4} \tag{2}$$

$$i_4^2 = \begin{bmatrix} 0\,0 & 1\,0 \\ 0\,0 & 0\,1 \\ 1\,0 & 0\,0 \\ 0\,1 & 0\,0 \end{bmatrix}_{4\times4} \tag{3}$$

$$i_4^3 = \begin{bmatrix} 0\,0 & 0\,1 \\ 1\,0 & 0\,0 \\ 0\,1 & 0\,0 \\ 0\,0 & 1\,0 \end{bmatrix}_{4\times4} \tag{4}$$

Then, in the third step, it will arrange each of i_4^0, i_4^1, i_4^2, and i_4^3 in row matrices of (1 × 16) to construct the IRSM matrix of (4 × 16) as below in Eq. (5):

$$i_{IRSM} = \begin{bmatrix} 1000010000100001 \\ 0100001000011000 \\ 0010000110000100 \\ 0001100001000010 \end{bmatrix}_{4\times 16} \tag{5}$$

Consequently, the code length is calculated by multiplying the weight (M) by the number of channels (N), as shown in Eq. (6).

$$A_{IRSM} = M \times N \tag{6}$$

Following the IRSM code matrix, the code word of each channel can be in Eq. (7):

$$\begin{aligned} &\text{First channel} \rightarrow \lambda 1,\ \lambda 6,\ \lambda 11,\ \lambda 16 \\ &\text{Second channel} \rightarrow \lambda 2,\ \lambda 7,\ \lambda 12,\ \lambda 13 \\ &\text{Third channel} \rightarrow \lambda 3,\ \lambda 8,\ \lambda 9,\ \lambda 14 \\ &\text{Fourth channel} \rightarrow \lambda 4,\ \lambda 5,\ \lambda 10,\ \lambda 15 \end{aligned} \tag{7}$$

Where λ_x is the wavelength for each code, $x = 1, 2, 3 \ldots A$. ($A = 16$).

The ZCC function for the IRSM code can be calculated by summing the products obtained by multiplying each pair of code sequences, C_i and C_j, as in Eq. (8):

$$\lambda_C = \sum_{k=1}^{A} C_{ik} \times C_{jk} \tag{8}$$

Where $i \neq j$. $C_{ik}.C_{jk} = 0$ for all k, $\lambda c = 0$.

For example, ZCC for two codes in the IRSM code (channel 1 and 2) for $k = 1, 2\ldots$ $A = 16$:

$\lambda c = 1 \times 0 + 0 \times 1 + 0 \times 0 + 0 \times 0 + 0 \times 0 + 1 \times 0 + 0 \times 1 + 0 \times 0 + 0 \times 0 + 0 \times 0 + 1 \times 0 + 0 \times 1 + 0 \times 1 + 0 \times 0 + 0 \times 0 +$
$1 \times 0 = 0$.

5 IRSM-SAC-OCDMA Encoder Design

An FTTB-GPON system is examined in one setting at 2.5 Gbps. The set uses wavelengths of 1490.05/1310.05 nm as downlink/uplink (DL/UL) spacing of 0.6nm and BW = 0.15 nm. 4-VCSEL sources are connected with WDM (MUX/DEMUX/MUX) at the downlink to achieve the secured modulated signals. The WDM MUX collects the modulated VCSEL signals and distributes them over the WDM DEMUX to encode them with four WDM MUXs related to the IRSM code scheme, as shown in Table 1.

Table 1. IRSM code wave-lengths at BW = 0.15 nm for (1490.05 nm/1310.05 nm) (DL/UL)

Wave-length	λ 1 (nm)	λ 2 (nm)	λ 3 (nm)	λ 4 (nm)	λ 5 (nm)	λ 6 (nm)	λ 7 (nm)	λ 8 (nm)
Channel	1489.8	1489.95	1490.1	1490.25	1490.4	1490.55	1490.7	1490.85
1st	1	0	0	0	0	1	0	0
2nd	0	1	0	0	0	0	1	0
3rd	0	0	1	0	0	0	0	1
4th	0	0	0	1	1	0	0	0
Wave-length	λ 9 (nm)	λ 10 (nm)	λ 11 (nm)	λ 12 (nm)	λ 13 (nm)	λ 14 (nm)	λ 15 (nm)	λ 16 (nm)
Channel	1491	1491.15	1491.3	1491.45	1481.6	1481.75	1491.9	1492.05
1st	0	0	1	0	0	0	0	1
2nd	0	0	0	1	1	0	0	0
3rd	1	0	0	0	0	1	0	0
4th	0	1	0	0	0	0	1	0

6 Results and Discussion

The results highlighted the simulated features of the design, BER, and Q-factor. The Q-Factor and BER can be numerically estimated based on the Eqs. (9), and (10) [20, 21]:

$$Q = \frac{|\mu 1 - \mu 0|}{\sigma 1 + \sigma 0} \tag{9}$$

$$BER = 0.5 \times erfc\left(\frac{Q}{\sqrt{2}}\right) \tag{10}$$

Where $\mu 0, \mu 1, \sigma 0$, and $\sigma 1$ are average values and standard deviations of sampled values.

The simulation covered ASE, shot, and thermal noises. Optical impairments like chromatic dispersion (17 ps/nm.km) and nonlinear effects (SPM, XPM, and FWM) are covered by limiting input power below 10 dBm. To examine the effects, the FTTB-GPON using IRSM code maintained BER $\leq 10^{-9}$, and Q-factor over 6.

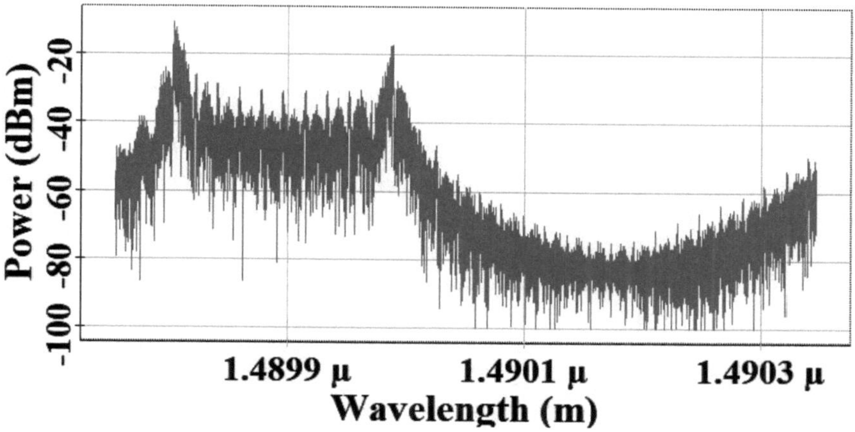

(a)

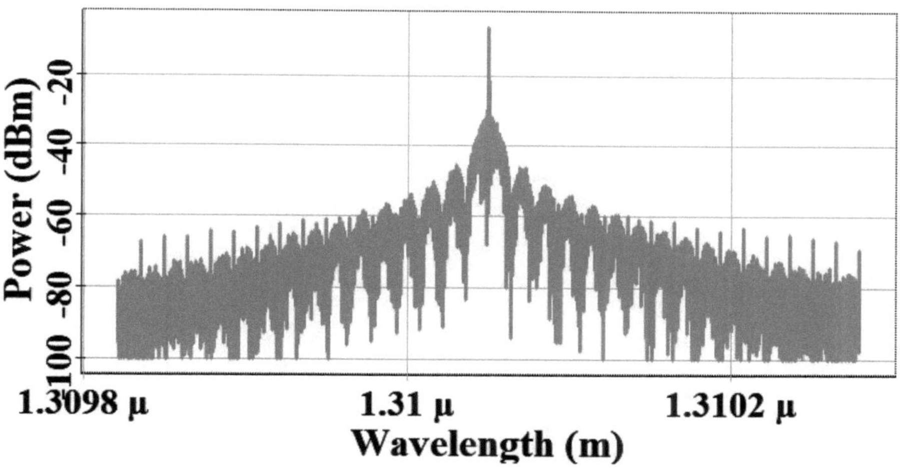

(b)

Fig. 2. Transmitted signals of downlink and uplink for proposed FTTB-GPON using (a) VCSEL (DL-1490.05 nm), (b) EML (UL-1310.05 nm) at 2.5 Gbps over 20 km.

When the VCSEL-GPON system is implemented without OCDMA codes, the modulated signals exhibited narrow-band properties. Which explains why the system does not function accurately when utilizing DM- VCSEL in GPON method [22]. The proposed FTTB-GPON design implemented the IRSM code scheme with 4-VCSEL of transmitted power of 4.76 dBm for sixteen buildings at 2.5 Gbps over a 20 km backbone fiber optic. It is implemented at wavelengths of (1490.05/1310.05) nm (DL/UL) with a spacing of 0.6 nm between optical sources and a bandwidth of 0.15 nm using a WDM (MUX/DEMUX/MUX) encoder. In the ITU-G.984 standard of the GPON system, the

VCSEL sources have narrowband features when operating at 1490 nm. Therefore, 4-VCSELs are used to cover the IRSM coding scheme in the proposed design, as shown in Fig. 2. Block-4 shows the best performance due to the short distance compared to the others.

Figure 3 shows the optical received power vs. Q-factor and BER at 20 km. The suggested design increases the Q-factor by increasing the optical power to −17 dBm, achieving a quality factor above 15, as can be seen in Fig. 3a.

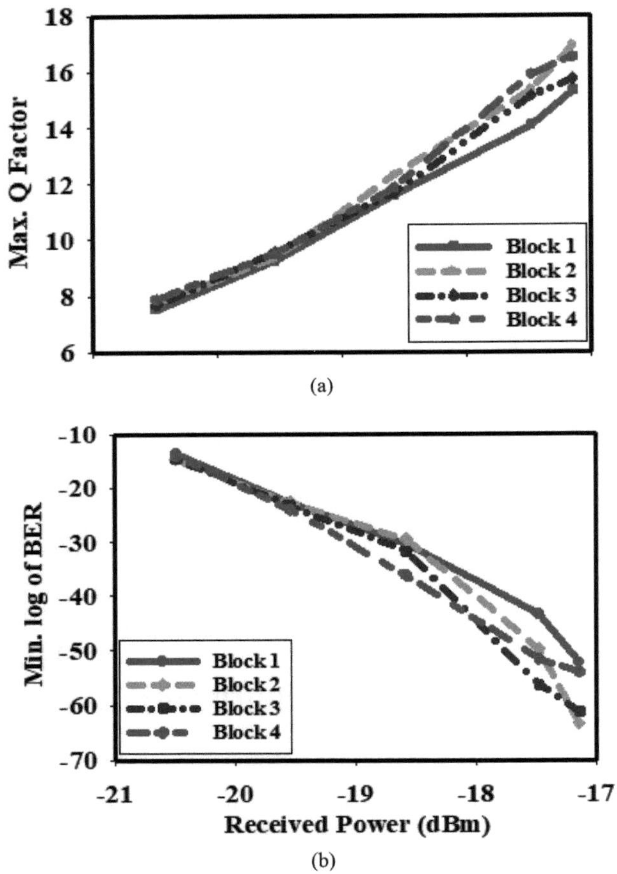

Fig. 3. Total received optical power of FTTB-GPON-IRSM system (1490.05/1310.05) nm versus (a) Q-factor; (b) BER over 20 km at 2.5 Gbps.

Figure 3b indicates the BER in dB decrements gradually below −10 dB with optical power increasing towards −17 dBm for 4-blocks of design. The Q-factor indicates results above the value of 6, and the BER result is below −10 dB. The proposed design operates with an acceptable optical power of more than -28 dBm, meeting the ITU-G. 984 standard.

Figure 4 shows the length versus Q-factor at 3–20 km. The Q-factor decreases with increasing fiber optics length. At 20 km, the quality factor is about 7.53, while the BER is about −13.6 dB. The FTTB-GPON-OCDMA demonstrates good characteristic results. The number of buildings increased to 25. The percentage improvement achieved by the proposed model compared to RD and MDW models is 38.89% and 92.31%, respectively. It is realized that the maximum number of buildings is 25 for the proposed design with IRSM code, RD code of 18, and MDW of 13 for $M = 4$.

Figure 5 indicates the eye diagrams of 4-blocks of the secure proposed design using the IRSM technique. The results show a good open-eye diagram, low min. log BER, and acceptable-quality factors at a distance of 20 km backbone of the fiber channel. The results are examined with the use of Optisystem v. 15.0. The simulation systems of the 4-receivers' BER values are also provided in Table 2.

The BER values of the systems vary by −13 to −16 dB at 2.5 Gbps. This variation happens because the structure of two-adjacent "1"s in IRSM code can help reduce interference.

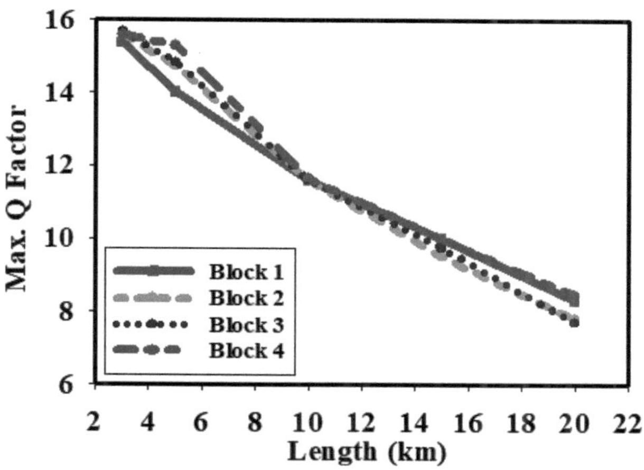

Fig. 4. Optical fiber length versus Q-factor for (1490.05/1310.05) nm at 2.5 Gbps over 3–20 km.

Table2. BER values and Q-factors of the 16- buildings for the 4-blocks at 20 km.

Receiver	1st receiver 2 km + 50 m		2nd receiver 1.5 km + 50 m		3rd receiver 1 km + 50 m		4th receiver 550m	
Blocks	BER	Q	BER	Q	BER	Q	BER	Q
1st Block	−13.6	7.53	−13.16	7.40	−13.66	7.55	−13.88	7.62
2nd Block	−14.04	7.66	−13.40	7.47	−13.06	7.37	−13.10	7.38
3rd Block	−14.83	7.89	−13.94	7.63	−15.32	8.03	−14.88	7.91
4th Block	−15.92	8.20	−15.37	8.05	−15.07	7.96	−14.71	7.86

Table 3. Comparison between the related works and the state of art.

Ref.	Network	Technique	Light sources	Data rate (Gbps)	Distance (km)	BER
[17]	GPON	2D-MD	CW-Laser	15	25	$4.41 * 10^{-12}$
[18]	PON	2D-DWZCC	LED	2	25	$1.77 * 10^{-10}$
[19]	GPON	1D-MD	CW-Laser	10	20	$1.12 * 10^{-11}$
[16]	GPON	MDW	LED	1/2.5	15/8	$3.45 * 10^{-9}$/ $9.12*10^{-9}$
This work	FTTB-GPON	IRSM	VCSEL	2.5	20	$3.27 * 10^{-14}$

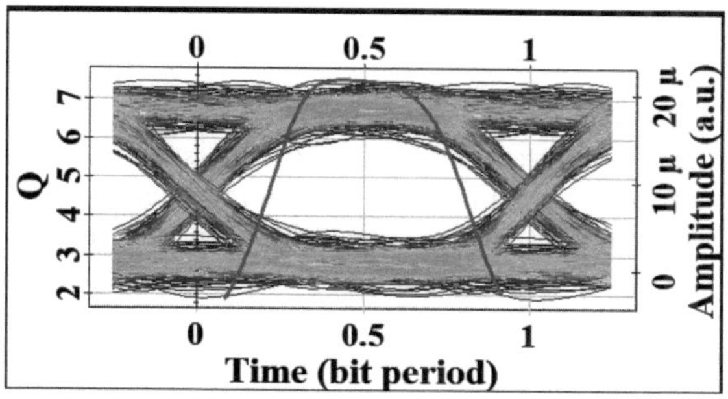

Block -1

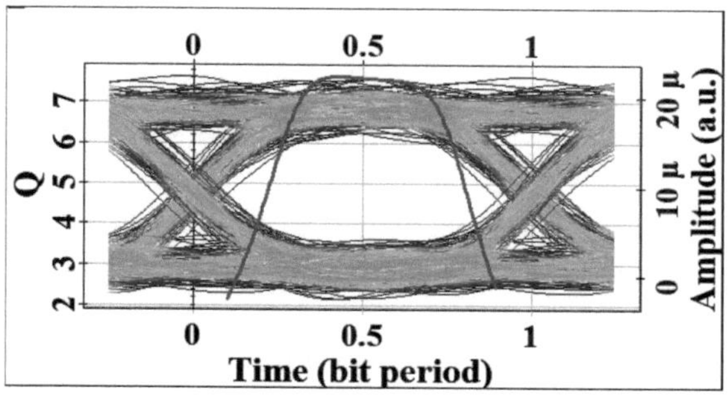

Block -2

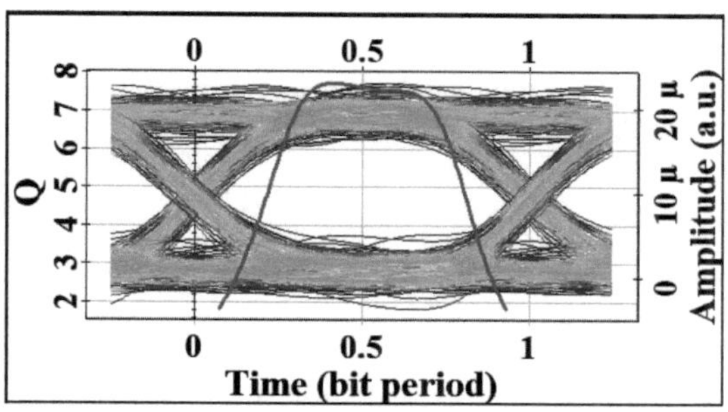

Block -3

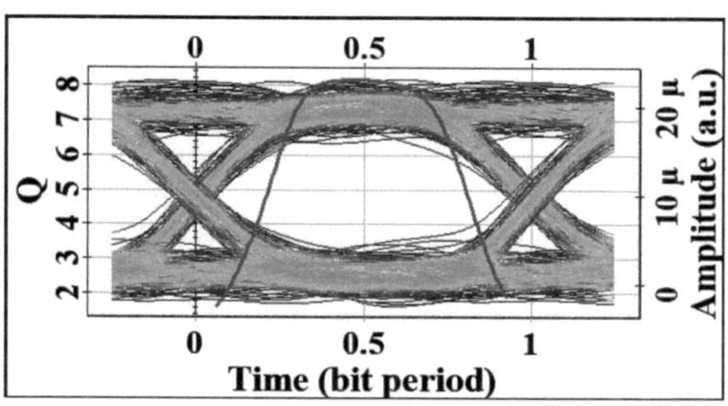

Block-4

Fig. 5. Eye diagrams for the 4-blocks, including 16 buildings of the secure-proposed FTTB-GPON-OCDMA design (1490.05/1310.05) nm at 2.5 Gbps over 20 km of backbone distance.

7 Conclusion

A robust FTTB-GPON system is designed and investigated using the IRSM-SAC-OCDMA code scheme with direct modulated VCSEL sources. The network deploys (1490.05/1310.05) nm downlink/uplink (DL/UL) with a spacing of 0.6 nm and a bandwidth of 0.15 nm over a fiber optic backbone of 20 km. The results indicated that an acceptable BER and Q-factor are achieved. The proposed design gives a value of 7.53 for Q-factor, while the BER is about −13.6 dB. The Q-factor indicated results above a value of 6, and the BER result below −10 dB. Table 3 indicates the performance improvement compared with previous studies. The percentage improvement achieved by the proposed model compared to RD and MDW models is 38.89% and 92.31%, respectively. The proposed design operated with an acceptable optical power of more than -28 dBm, meeting the ITU-T G.984 standard. Therefore, the IRSM is a good candidate for the FTTB-GPON technique with narrowband VCSEL sources.

8 Future Work

The proposed work may be extended to FTTH/FTTX systems and WDM PON hybrids to support next-generation network access. Future research could also evaluate system performance at higher data rates and explore hybrid-coding methods, such as IRSM with FEC, or compatibility with NG-PON2 standards.

References

1. Alayedi, M., Cherifi, A., Ferhat Hamida, A., Bouazza, B.S., Rashidi, C.B.M.: Performance enhancement of SAC-OCDMA system using an identity row shifting matrix code. In: Ullah, A., Anwar, A., Rocha, Á., Gill , S. (eds.) BT - Proceedings of International Conference on Information Technology and Applications, pp. 547–559. Springer Nature Singapore, Singapore (2022)
2. Alayedi, M., Cherifi, A., Hamida, A.F., Matem, R., El-Mottaleb, S.A.A.: Performance improvement of SAC-OCDMA network utilizing an identity column shifting matrix (ICSM) code. In: Abd El-Latif, A.A., Maleh, Y., Mazurczyk, W., ELAffendi, M., I. Alkanhal, M. (eds.) Advances in Cybersecurity, Cybercrimes, and Smart Emerging Technologies. CCSET 2022. Engineering Cyber-Physical Systems and Critical Infrastructures, vol. 4. Springer, Cham (2023). https://doi.org/10.1007/978-3-031-21101-0_21
3. Hasoon, F.N., Al-Mansoori, M.H., Shaari, S.: Different detection schemes using enhanced double weight code for OCDMA systems. In: IAENG Transactions on Engineering Technologies, pp. 287–299. Springer, Dordrecht (2013):
4. Abd El-Mottaleb, S.A., Singh, M., Alshathri, S., El-Shafai, W., Aly, M.H.: Enhancing security and capacity in FSO transmission for next-generation networks using OFDM/OCDMA-based ICSM codes. Front. Phys. **11**, 1–12 (2023). https://doi.org/10.3389/fphy.2023.1231025
5. Ayotte, S., Rusch, L.A.: Increasing the capacity of SAC-OCDMA: forward error correction or coherent sources. IEEE J. Sel. Top Quantum Electr. **13**, 1422–1428 (2007)
6. Lokesha, H.R.: Performance analysis of different detection techniques for SAC-OCDMA system. Int. J. All Res. Educ. Sci. Methods **12**(5), 4875–4888 (2024)
7. Koetter, R., Vardy, A.: Algebraic soft-decision decoding of Reed- Solomon codes. IEEE Trans. Inf. Theory **49**, 2809–2825 (2003)

8. Glavieux, A.: Channel coding in communication networks: from theory to turbocodes. Wiley, United Kingdom (2013)
9. Franceschini, M., Ferrari, G., Raheli, R.: LDPC coded modulations. Springer, London New York (2009)
10. Vasic, B., Djordjevic, I.B., Kostuk, R.K.: Low-density parity check codes and iterative decoding for long-haul optical communicationsystems. J. Lightwave Technol. **21**, 438 (2003)
11. Boukricha, S., Ghoumid, K., Ar-Reyouchi, E.M., Elmar, Y., Yahiaoui, R., Elmazria, O.: Evaluation of SAC-OCDMA system performance in terms of BER and Q-factor using FBGs and M-sequence code. In: Q2SWinet 2020 - Proceedings of the 16th ACM Symposium on Quality of Service and Security for Wireless and Mobile Networks (Q2SWinet), pp. 1–5 (2020). https://doi.org/10.1145/3416013.3426444
12. Kumari, M., Arya, V., Al-Khafaji, H.M.R.: Wheel-based MDM-PON system incorporating OCDMA for secure network resiliency. Photonics **10**(3) (2023). https://doi.org/10.3390/photonics10030329
13. Fadhil, H.A., Aljunid, S.A., Ahmed, B.: Performance of OCDMA systems using random diagonal code for different decoders architecture schemes. Int Arab. J. Inf. Technol. **7**, 1–5 (2010)
14. Seyedzadeh, S., Mahdiraji, G.A., Sahbudin, R.K., Abas, A.F., Anas, S.B.: Experimental demonstration of variable weight SAC-OCDMA system for QoS differentiation. Optl. Fiber. Technol. **20**, 495–500 (2014)
15. Yin, H., Richardson, D.J.: Optical code division multiple access communication networks. Chap. **1**, 36–37 (2008)
16. Ahmed, N., Rashid, M.A.: Effects of modulation techniques RZ, NRZ, and CSRZ on the operation of hybrid OCDMA/WDM system for gigabit passive optical networks. Int. J. Microw. Opt. Technol. **12**(4) (2017)
17. Memon, K.A., Atieh, A., Umrani, A.W., Unar, M.A., Shah, W.: Design and performance analysis of GPON-employed two-dimensional multidiagonal OCDMA code. Opt. Eng. **59**(07), 1 (2020). https://doi.org/10.1117/1.oe.59.7.076105
18. Imtiaz, W.A., Yousef, H., Zeghid, M., Sharma, T., Mirza, J.: Techno-economic analysis of two dimensional optical code division multiple access systems. Opt. Quantum Electron. **53**(1) (2021). https://doi.org/10.1007/s11082-020-02630-z
19. Memon, K.A., Umrani, A.W., Unar, M.A., Shah, W., Umrani, F.A.: Design and analysis of high-speed bottleneck-free one-dimensional OCDMA based gigabit symmetric PON. Wirel. Pers. Commun. **126**(4), 3147–3165 (2022). https://doi.org/10.1007/s11277-022-09857-x
20. Jaiswal, A.K.: To study the effect of BER and Q-factor in Intersatellite optical wireless communication system. IOSR J. Electron. Commun. Eng. **3**(4), 19–21 (2012). https://doi.org/10.9790/2834-0341921
21. Sarr, M., et al.: Design and implementation of a hybrid FTTH-FSO network for the deployment and maintenance of GPON-based FTTH Network in inaccessible areas or construction civil engineering sites. Int. J. Phys. **11**(4), 180–186 (2023). https://doi.org/10.12691/ijp-11-4-3
22. Ibrahim, S.K., Ali, G.M., Jasim, A.K.: Evaluation of effectiveness of FTTX-GPON technology-based narrowband direct modulation using shared WDM-SAC-OCDMA system. Results Opt. **21**, 100841 (2025). https://doi.org/10.1016/j.rio.2025.100841

Signal Processing

Implementation and Test of Capon DOA Estimation Algorithm on FPGA Platform Using MATLAB

Abed Alnaser Ramadan[1](✉), Shahad A. Mnati[1], R. Kh. Al-Janabi[2], Mohammed Q. Mohammed[1,3], and Istabraq M. Al-Joboury[4]

[1] Cyber Security Engineering Department, Al-Esraa University, Baghdad, Iraq
{abdulnaser,dr.mohammed}@esraa.edu.iq,
shahed.ali1202a@kecbu.uobaghdad.edu.iq

[2] Medical Instrumentation Engineering Department, Al-Esraa University, Baghdad, Iraq
Ranakk@esraa.bis.edu.iq

[3] University of Information Technology and Communications, Baghdad, Iraq

[4] Cert-IQ Team Member, Baghdad, Iraq
info@cert.gov.iq

Abstract. The estimation of Direction-of-Arrival (DOA) of radio signals in a smart antenna system (SAS) is crucial in various applications, including air and space navigation, radar, sonar, and other systems. In this paper, a proposed method is presented for implementing and testing the Capon DOA estimation algorithm on an FPGA platform. In this method, the software features of MATLAB are leveraged and the algorithm code is modified to accommodate the hardware features of the FPGA platform. The method is an integration of MATLAB software and FPGA platform. The proposed method addresses the problem of hardware complexity connected with the FPGA platform, and all the results of DOA measurements are shown on the FPGA platform. The performance of the Capon algorithm is tested on the FPGA platform taking into account the effects of the number of signal samples and SNR on DOA estimation accuracy.

Keywords: Smart Antenna System (SAS) · Direction of Arrival (DOA) · Capon algorithm and FPGA

1 Introduction

Smart Antenna System (SAS) is defined as a set of array antenna elements with a digital signal processing unit. It can effectively change its radiation pattern, directing the main radiation loop towards the user (the desired signal), and forming a zero gain (null) towards the unwanted signals [1, 2].

The direction of arrival (DOA) estimation is the process of determining the angle of the incoming signal. This is accomplished by processing the relative phases of the incident signal as observed by each of the antenna elements [3]. The DOA estimate is used to form beamforming, which is the process of creating the radiation pattern

W. A. Mahmoud et al. (Eds.): ACDN 2025, CCIS 2798, pp. 33–43, 2026.
https://doi.org/10.1007/978-3-032-15448-4_3

coming off the antenna array in specific directions. Therefore, the performance of a smart antenna system (SAS) is highly dependent on the performance of these algorithms and the complexity of signal processing [3].

Historically, signal processing hardware has limited the practical implementation of sophisticated DOA and beamforming algorithms [4]. The computation time and physical size of the hardware needed to estimate DOA often limit their practical deployment in modern mobile communications systems. Recently, progress and development in digital integrated circuit manufacturing has led to renewed interests in deploying smart antenna systems in mobile communications devices [4].

Most equipment and practical applications in communications and radars require real-time DOA estimation, and thus, hardware implementation and experimental testing are important and necessary. The computational complexity required to implement the DOA estimation algorithm is an important factor in the hardware implementation of the algorithm, which directly affects both the execution time and resource requirements. The efficiency and cost of the computational complexity of these algorithms depend on the matrix operations used and the size of the matrices [5].

Implementing DOA estimation with high performance on platforms such as FPGA, DSP, GPU and CPU is very important. FPGAs are characterized by their parallel processing, ease of implementation, high speed, strong flexibility, and multiple resources. They have become a mainstay in the implementation of DOA algorithms [6, 7].

The possibility of implementing all signal processing operations on a single chip facilitates the practical implementation of smart antennas in mobile communication devices [3].

Several papers have addressed implementation of DOA algorithms using FPGAs. In [3] implementation of Bartlett DOA algorithms using FPGAs with 8-element circular array antennas was discussed. In [8] FPGA hardware implementation of subspace-based DOA estimation algorithms employing LU matrix decomposition was presented. Authors in [9] focused on implementation of MUSIC algorithm on FPGA platform in real time. Authors in [5] studied a performance comparison for matrix decomposition methods of subspace-based DOA estimation algorithms and implementation on the FPGA platform. In [10] QR decomposition of received data matrix and implementation of subspace-based DOA estimation algorithm on FPGA platform were discussed. Moreover, authors in [11] provided a practical test of the LMS beamforming algorithm on a Xilinx FPGA chip.

In this paper, a method for the Capon DOA algorithm implementation on Altera Cyclone II FPGA platform was proposed. FPGA implementation of single source DOA estimation processing of a 4-antenna uniform linear array (ULA) was carried out with one-degree resolution. This method exploits the software features of MATLAB and the hardware features of FPGA chips. It is integration of MATLAB software and FPGA hardware and enables the estimation of DOA in real-time. It takes into account the effects of the number of samples and SNR on DOA estimation accuracy. The proposed method has solved the problem of hardware complexity connected with the FPGA, and all the results of DOA measurements are shown on the FPGA platform.

2 The Capon DOA Algorithm

One of the most popular algorithms with spectral estimation and good resolution is Capon's Minimum Variance Method, also called Minimum Variance Distortionless Response (MVDR), which was proposed by Capon [12].

This approach seeks to address the issues associated with low resolution in the Delay-and-Sum technique [13]. Capon's algorithm focuses on deliberately forming the radiation pattern in the desired direction using some degrees of freedom while using the remaining degrees of freedom to form zeros, or Nulls, in the directions where interference signals are considered unwanted [13, 14].

This technique minimizes the effects of nuisance interference signals by lowering output power while keeping gain in the preferred direction constant. This gain is typically set to unity [13–15].

In other words, this algorithm realizes the following equation [13–16]:

$$\min E\left[|y(k)|^2\right] = \min \mathbf{w}^H \mathbf{R}_{uu} \mathbf{w}$$
$$\text{subject to} \mathbf{w}^H \mathbf{a}(\phi_0) = 1 \quad (1)$$

Where $\mathbf{w}$ is the weight vector and is expressed by $\mathbf{w} = [w_1 w_2 \cdots w_M]^T$, and M is the element or sensor number of the array antenna. The matrix $\mathbf{R}_{uu}$ is the covariance matrix of the output data of the array antenna elements. $\mathbf{a}(\phi_0)$ is the steering vector with dimension $(M \times 1)$ associated with the direction of incidence at angle ϕ_0 and is expressed as [15, 16]:

$$\mathbf{a}(\phi_0) = [1 e^{-J\frac{2\pi d}{\lambda}\sin\phi_0} \ldots e^{-J\frac{2\pi d}{\lambda}(\mathrm{M}-1)\sin\phi_0}]^T \quad (2)$$

Where d is the distance between two consecutive array elements and is equal to $d = \lambda/2$.

That is, the variance (power) of the antenna output is reduced in all directions, and at the same time the signal coming from the desired direction is passed without distortion (unity gain and zero phase shift) [15–17].

By solving the problem shown in Eq. (1), we obtain the following weight vector [13, 15–18]:

$$\mathbf{w} = \frac{\mathbf{R}_{uu}^{-1}\mathbf{a}(\phi)}{\mathbf{a}^H(\phi)\mathbf{R}_{uu}^{-1}\mathbf{a}(\phi)} \quad (3)$$

Then the spatial spectrum of Capon's algorithm is given by [13–16, 18, 19]:

$$P_{capon}(\phi) = \frac{1}{\mathbf{a}^H(\phi)\mathbf{R}_{uu}^{-1}\mathbf{a}(\phi)} \quad (4)$$

By calculating and plotting the Capon spectrum over the total range of ϕ, the DOA can be estimated by determining the locations of the peaks in this spectrum [18, 19]. The Capon method provides better resolution than the Delay-and-Sum method; however, it depends on the aperture (number of elements) of the antenna and the signal-to-noise ratio SNR. It also requires calculating the inverse of the array antenna correlation matrix $\mathbf{R}_{uu}^{-1}$ [15, 16, 18, 19].

3 Implementation of Capon DOA Estimation Algorithm on FPGA

One of the smart antenna system algorithms, represented by the Capon algorithm for estimating the directions of arrival of signals received by the array antenna, was tested. The implementing the Capon algorithm on an FPGA chip can be explained as follows:

3.1 Creating the Code for the Capon Algorithm in MATLAB

The code for the Capon algorithm for estimating the direction of arrival of signals is formed in the MATLAB programming environment using two parts: the main program, represented by the Function; and the program inputs, represented by the Test Bench.

The program is coded in the MATLAB programming environment, and then converted to the VHDL language. Therefore, some unsupported functions, which are available in the MATLAB environment, are replaced with their detailed code. For example, the function of the matrix inverse inv($\mathbf{R}_{uu}$) was replaced with a code in the MATLAB environment that performs the same function. The unsupported exponential function, which returns a variable value, was also replaced by the sum $\mathrm{e}^{\mathrm{x}} = \sum_{k=0}^{\infty} \frac{x^k}{k!}$ and it is implemented using code in the MATLAB environment.

3.2 Converting the MATLAB Code to VHDL

The MATLAB code is converted into the VHDL language using the HDL Coder application available in the MATLAB environment. After calling both the Function and the Test Bench, the following steps are performed:

- Define Input Types, which are automatically of the Double type. It is possible to change it to the appropriate data type.
- Converting floating point to fixed point. The unsupported Exponential Function is replaced with the Look-Up Table. This table includes the Interpolation Method, which is selected as Linear, and the number of points expressing this function is set at 1000 points.
- Select Code Generation Target. The Altera QUARTUS II board is selected from Cyclone II Chip Family, and the device type of EP2C35F672C6.
- HDL Code Generation.

3.3 Matching the VHDL Code with the Inputs and Outputs of the FPGA Platform

After developing the Capon algorithm code in VHDL with the help of the HDL Coder application available in the MATLAB environment, it was modified to fit the inputs and outputs (display) of the FPGA platform.

The basic modification process in this code, in the VHDL language, lies in converting both the input and output data for the direction of arrival value, whether the actual value of the direction of arrival (algorithm input), or the estimated value of the direction of arrival (algorithm output), into data that is compatible with display on 7-segments.

The Altera Cyclone II EP2C35F672C6 FPGA platform has eight 7-segments. In this test, the first Seven Segment Digit 0 and the fourth Seven Segment Digit 3 were used, and the modified part of the code was assigned to them.

3.4 Simulation of the Capon Algorithm Code on FPGA Platform

The simulation was carried out using the ModelSim program due to its relative ease of performing the simulation. The Capon algorithm code written in VHDL was called and tested, and the simulation was executed. Figure 1 shows the ModelSim simulation program interface and the simulation results.

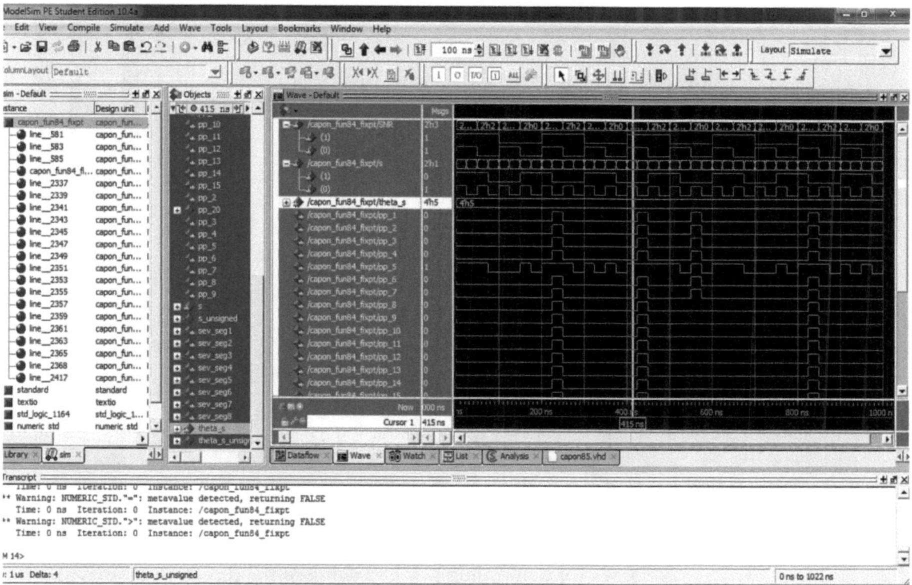

Fig. 1. ModelSim simulation program interface and simulation results.

4 Implementation of Capon DOA Estimation Algorithm on FPGA

After downloading the Capon DOA estimation algorithm code onto the Cyclone II EP2C35F672C6 FPGA platform, the algorithm and its capabilities in estimating DOA were tested. Figure 2 shows the inputs and outputs of the Cyclone II EP2C35F672C6 FPGA platform including switches, LEDs, and 7-segments.

4.1 Representing the Electronic Situation

The electronic situation included the selection of the spatial scanning range within the sector $[1^\circ \div 15^\circ]$. Assuming a signal coming from a direction within this specific spatial sector.

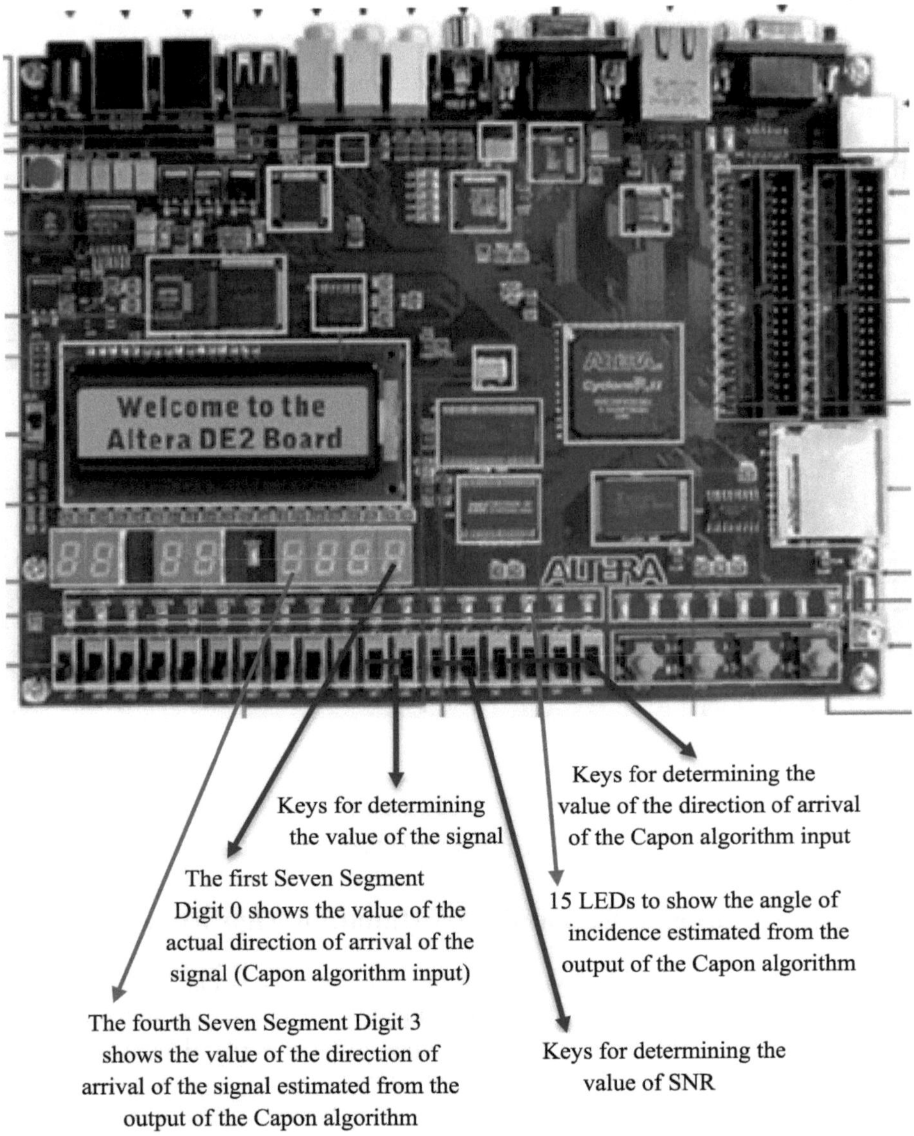

Fig. 2. The FPGA Cyclone II platform's inputs and outputs include switches, LEDs and 7-segments.

The SNR values, the number of signal samples, and the DOA of the signal were also represented. The value of SNR can be controlled through two keys that make up four values, and each value of these keys [0 ÷ 3] corresponds to a specific value for the SNR. The signal sample values will also be represented by two input keys. These two keys constitute four values, and each value of these keys [0 ÷ 3] corresponds to a specific value for the number of samples.

Regarding the DOA of this signal, the value of the angle of arrival was determined through the position of four on-off switches covering values within the range [1° ÷ 15°].

The value corresponding to the actual direction of arrival of the signal (algorithm input) was also shown by the first Seven Segment Digit 0, on the platform.

As for showing the results of the Capon algorithm, there are two ways to do so. The first way is to indicate the direction by lighting the relevant LED out of 15 LEDs placed on the platform in a sequential manner. The second way is to show the DOA of the signal estimated from the output of the Capon algorithm on the fourth Seven Segment Digit 3.

4.2 Implementation of the Test

We conduct a test of Capon algorithm on FPGA platform for single source angle estimation and using 4-element antenna ULA with one-degree resolution. The Capon DOA estimation algorithm was tested for an incoming signal within the angular sector [1° ÷ 15°]. The output of the algorithm and its ability to estimate the direction of arrival were tested assuming the signal is coming from an angle of 9°, and at different SNR ratios and the number of samples (N). Table 1 shows the ability of the Capon algorithm to estimate the DOA within the angular sector [1° ÷ 15°].

The results of the practical test indicated the ability of this algorithm to estimate the direction of the signal coming from an angle of 9°, with N = 128, and at all values of SNR = 0, 5, 10 and 20 dB. This algorithm can also estimate the direction of arrival when N = 64 and SNR = 20 dB.

The results also indicate that for N = 32, 64, and SNR = 0, 5, 10 dB, a wide angular range was obtained in the output of the algorithm including [8° ÷ 10°]. This means that the accuracy of angular resolution worsen and fluctuates around 9°.

As for the output of this algorithm at SNR = 0, 5, 10, and 20 dB, and the number of samples N = 16, the output of all LEDs was equal to 1, meaning that it is absolutely impossible to distinguish the direction of arrival of the signal.

Figure 3 shows a picture of the Cyclone II EP2C35F672C6 FPGA platform during practical testing of the Capon algorithm (case 1). The figure represents the case of a signal arriving from an angle of 9°, at SNR = 10 dB, and number of samples N = 128. Clearly the LED number 9 is ON, which represents the direction of the arrival. In addition, number 9 displayed on each of the two 7-segments expresses the direction of the arrival, as an input to the algorithm (the first Seven Segment Digit 0), and the output of the Capon algorithm (the fourth Seven Segment Digit 3).

Figure 4 shows a picture of the Cyclone II EP2C35F672C6 FPGA platform during practical testing of the Capon algorithm (case 2). The figure represents the case of a signal arriving from angle 9°, for SNR = 5 dB, and N = 64. Clearly, the LEDs No. 8, 9, and 10 are ON, which represent a wide angular range [8° ÷ 10°]. In addition, number 9 displayed on the first Seven Segment Digit 0 expresses the direction of the arrival as input to the algorithm; while no number is displayed on the fourth Seven Segment Digit 3 as an indication of inaccuracy in estimating the direction of the arrival. This means that the accuracy of the angular resolution of the Capon algorithm deteriorates and fluctuates around the angle 9°.

Table 1. The ability of the Capon algorithm to estimate DOA within the sector [1° ÷ 15°].

SNR (dB)	Samples (N)	Algorithm Output														
		LED number [1° ÷ 15°]														
		1°	2°	3°	4°	5°	6°	7°	8°	9°	10°	11°	12°	13°	14°	15°
0	16	1	1	1	1	1	1	1	1	1	1	1	1	1	1	1
	32	0	0	0	0	0	0	0	1	1	1	0	0	0	0	0
	64	0	0	0	0	0	0	0	1	1	1	0	0	0	0	0
	128	0	0	0	0	0	0	0	0	1	0	0	0	0	0	0
5	16	1	1	1	1	1	1	1	1	1	1	1	1	1	1	1
	32	0	0	0	0	0	0	0	1	1	0	0	0	0	0	0
	64	0	0	0	0	0	0	0	1	1	1	0	0	0	0	0
	128	0	0	0	0	0	0	0	0	1	0	0	0	0	0	0
10	16	1	1	1	1	1	1	1	1	1	1	1	1	1	1	1
	32	0	0	0	0	0	0	0	1	1	1	0	0	0	0	0
	64	0	0	0	0	0	0	0	1	1	1	0	0	0	0	0
	128	0	0	0	0	0	0	0	0	1	0	0	0	0	0	0
20	16	1	1	1	1	1	1	1	1	1	1	1	1	1	1	1
	32	0	0	0	0	0	0	0	1	1	1	0	0	0	0	0
	64	0	0	0	0	0	0	0	0	1	0	0	0	0	0	0
	128	0	0	0	0	0	0	0	0	1	0	0	0	0	0	0

Fig. 3. Picture of the FPGA platform during practical testing of the Capon algorithm (case 1).

Fig. 4. Picture of the FPGA platform during practical testing of the Capon algorithm (case 2).

5 Conclusions

A practical test was carried out on one of the smart antenna system algorithms, the Capon DOA estimation algorithm. The test was performed using Cyclone II EP2C35F672C6 FPGA platform for single source angle estimation and using 4-elements antenna uniform linear array (ULA) with one-degree resolution.

The testing process was carried out for an incoming signal within the angular sector $[1^\circ \div 15^\circ]$ and at different values of the signal-to-noise ratio (SNR) and the number of samples. It was designed to observe the output of the algorithm and its ability to estimate the direction of arrival within this sector.

The results of the practical test indicated the ability of this algorithm to estimate the direction of arrival of a single signal at SNR $\geq$ 0 dB and N = 128; and at SNR = 20 dB and the number of N = 64.

The purpose of this test was to design a small, portable smart antenna system available to a large number of users by taking advantage of the development of digital chip technologies and their advantages.

References

1. Dhope, T.S., Simunic, D., Zentner, R.: Comparison of DOA estimation algorithms in SDMA system. AUTOMATIKA. **54**(2), 199–210 (2013)
2. Rao T.N., Rao V.S.: Implementation of MUSIC algorithm for a smart antenna system for mobile communications. Int. J. Sci. Eng. Res. **2**(12), 6 pp. (2011)
3. LaMeres, B.J., Weber, R.J., Huang, Y., Abusultan, M., Harkness, S.: Design and test of FPGA-based direction-of-arrival algorithms for adaptive array antennas. IEEEAC paper. **7**, 1198–1205 (2011)
4. Abusultan, M., Harkness, S., LaMeres, B.J., Huang, Y.: FPGA implementation of a bartlett direction of arrival algorithm for a 5.8GHz circular antenna array. In: Conference Paper in IEEE Aerospace Conference Proceedings (2010)
5. Hussain, A., Tayem, N., Soliman, A.-H.: Matrix decomposition methods for efficient hardware implementation of DOA estimation algorithms: a performance comparison. In: 2019 4th International Conference and Workshops on Recent Advances and Innovations in Engineering (ICRAIE), IEEE (2019)
6. Chaudhari, M.G.: Smart antenna design for tracking multiple users using FPGA virtex-5, A thesis submitted in partial fulfillment of the requirements for the degree of Master of Technology in Electrical Engineering, Department of Electrical Engineering National Institute of Technology, Rourkela-769008, Odisha, INDIA May (2015)
7. Zhou, S., Li., Zhou: Field programmable gate array (FPGA) implementation of parallel jacobi for eigen-decomposition in direction of arrival (DOA) estimation algorithm. Remote Sens. **16**, 3892–3907 (2024)
8. Hussain, A.A., Tayem, N., Butt, M.O., Soliman, A.-H., Alhamed, A., Alshebeili, S.: FPGA Hardware Implementation of DOA Estimation Algorithm Employing LU Decomposition. vol. 6, pp. 17666–17680. IEEE (2018)
9. Sikka, P.: High-level synthesis assisted, low-latency, area- and power-optimized FPGA implementation of MUSIC algorithm for direction-of-arrival estimation. Sustain. Energy Technol. Assess. **57** (2023)
10. Alhamed, A., Tayem, N., Alshawi, T., Alshebeili, S., Alsuwailem, A., Hussain, A.: FPGA-based real-time implementation for direction-of-arrival estimation. J. Eng. **6**, 260–265 (2017)
11. Arathy Reghu kumar, K., Soman, P., Shanmuga Sundaram, G.A.: Beam forming algorithm implementation using FPGA. Int. J. Adv. Electric. Electron. Eng. **2**(3) (2013)
12. High-Resolution, C.J., Analysis, F.W.S.: Proc. IEEE **57**(8), 1408–1418 (1969)
13. Dhope (Shendkar), T.S., Simunic, D., Zentner, R.: Comparison of DOA estimation algorithms in SDMA system. AUTOMATIKA **54**, 199–209 (2013)
14. Devendra, M., Manjunathachari, K.: Literature survey on high resolution direction of arrival (DOA) algorithms. Int. Adv. Res. J. Sci. Eng. Technol. **2**(2) (2015)

15. Velasco, M.C.: Randomly spaced smart antennas, The University of New Mexico, THESIS Submitted in Partial Fulfillment of the Requirements for the Degree of Master of Science in Electrical Engineering (2013)
16. Elahian, B.: Estimating the time and angle of arrivals in mobile communications, The University of Québec, Canada, THESIS Submitted in Partial Fulfillment of the Requirements for the Degree of Master of Science in Electrical Engineering (2013)
17. Beham, A.R.: Performance analysis of DOA algorithms Int. J. Innov. Res. Comput. Commun. Eng. **4**(1) (2016)
18. Agrawal, P., Shandilya, M.: MATLAB simulation of subspace based high resolution direction of arrival estimation algorithm. Int. J. Comput. Appl. **130**(15) (2015)
19. Xiong, H.: BEng. Antenna Array Geometries and Algorithms for Direction of Arrival Estimation. Thesis submitted to the University of Nottingham for the degree of Master of Science (by Research) in Electromagnetics Design (2012)

Performance Analysis for Joint Channel Estimation and Equalization in OTFS Systems for High Mobility Channels

Sura H. Khadum[1], Thamer M. Jamel[1(✉)], and Hassan F. Khazaal[2]

[1] Department of Communication Engineering, University of Technology, Baghdad, Iraq
coe.23.02@grad.uotechnology.edu.iq,
thamer.m.jamel@uotechnology.edu.iq
[2] Department of Electrical Engineering, Wasit University, Wasit, Iraq
hfahad@uowasit.edu.iq

Abstract. Orthogonal Time-Frequency Space (OTFS) modulation is a viable alternative to Orthogonal Frequency Division Multiplexing (OFDM) in channels that experience both time and frequency variations, particularly in high-mobility scenarios. However, equalization and effective channel estimation (CE) are important to polarization diversity when using OTFS for maximizing its utility, especially over time-varying channels. The performance of OTFS and OFDM systems was determined using joint equalization and pilot-aided channel estimation, particularly in high-mobility scenarios, using Bit Error Rate (BER). For both systems, a system model was introduced that uses Delay Doppler (DD) domain pilot insertion and equalization based on predicted channel characteristics using a Minimum Mean Square Error (MMSE) technique. The performance was assessed using simulations that utilize popular high-mobility channel models (EVA, ETU, UAV, and TDL-C channels) with high Doppler frequencies. Regarding channels with fast temporal variations, the results indicated that OTFS outperformed OFDM. This benefit was particularly evident in terms of enhanced channel estimate accuracy and resilience to Doppler spread, as demonstrated by other studies. The findings underscored that OTFS could serve as a dependable waveshape for 5G, 6G, and forthcoming mobile transmission systems.

Keywords: OTFS · Channel Estimation · Equalization · High Mobility · Doppler spread · Bit Error Rate (BER) · Delay-Doppler Domain · MMSE

1 Introduction

The rapid development of wireless communication systems (5G and beyond) is driving up the demand for next-generation wireless networks to provide reliable and dependable high-data-rate connectivity. This increases the requirement for uniformity across diverse contexts, particularly in automobile-to-automobile communication at high speeds. OFDM, a conventional multicarrier modulation technique, is widely employed in LTE and 5G due to ease of implementation as well as optimal utilization of available

W. A. Mahmoud et al. (Eds.): ACDN 2025, CCIS 2798, pp. 44–66, 2026.
https://doi.org/10.1007/978-3-032-15448-4_4

bandwidth. However, the performance of OFDM severely drops in large Doppler spread channels, causing Inter-Carrier Interference (ICI) as well as error in channel estimates [1]. Orthogonal Time Frequency Space (OTFS) modulation has recently received a great deal of attention as a strong alternative to OFDM in situations where people are highly mobile [2].

Working based on the delay-Doppler (DD) rather than the time-frequency domain, the OTFS modulation provides a considerable advantage in doubly dispersive channels. It has been proposed as a formidable replacement for OFDM [3, 4]. OTFS modulation improves channel estimation and equalization by transforming the time-varying wireless channel into the delay-Doppler domain. In this domain, the channel presents a quasi-static and sparse representation, which enhances the robustness and efficiency of signal processing [5]. Owing to this, OTFS is best suited for use in 5G (TDL-C channel) as well as subsequent situations, like high-mobility user situations, UAV networks, as well as rapid vehicular communications [6]. However, as the wireless multipath channel is defined by convolution, OTFS systems can still be affected by inter-symbol interference (ISI) as well as inter-Doppler interference (IDI). Equalization is thus necessary on the receiver's end to deal with these impacts. The deconvolutional equalizer is important as it works to remove the convolutional impact from the transmission channel by finding the initially transmitted symbols from the received signal [7]. Deconvolutional equalizers in OTFS tend to use simple methodologies like zero-forcing (ZF) as well as minimum mean square Error (MMSE), taking advantage of the sparse as well as structured characteristics of the channel matrix within the DD domain to recover symbols effectively with precision [8]. The use of pilot-based systems and zero forcing (ZF) and Minimum Mean Square Error (MMSE), and other linear equalizers has been the subject of recent research on OTFS channel estimation and equalization methods [9, 10]. While researchers have thoroughly investigated these methods for OFDM, their performance within the OTFS framework remains an ongoing topic of study.

The present study focuses on the bit error rate (BER) effectiveness king an OTFS system that employs a realistic combined channel estimation (CE) and equalization approach, which proves effective for channels subjected to significant levels of mobility. The proposed channel estimation method relies on DD domain-embedded pilots. An MMSE equalizer was used to directly retrieve the broadcast data symbols from the estimated channel characteristics. Our primary achievements include:

1. Presenting an integrated OTFS system model with DD pilot-based CE and MMSE equalization, specifically considering high-mobility effects.
2. Conducting comprehensive simulations at different Doppler frequencies under typical high-mobility channel models (EVA, ETU, UAV, and TDL-C) to assess the end-to-end BER performance.
3. Evaluating the OTFS system within the same high-mobility environment as a conventional OFDM system.

This work does not optimize or compare different pilot placement design methods. Instead, it adopts a pre-fixed pilot-based iterative estimation scheme of paths. The rationale for this choice is two-pronged: first, it is a popular and practically employed technique in OTFS systems that offers credible channel estimation for high-mobility applications; secondly, the focus of this work lies in comparing the OTFS and OFDM performance against each other in BER over different channel models. Therefore, the main focus was placed on investigating the effects of modulation order and channel conditions, rather than investigating other pilot placement design options.

This research is significant in that it thoroughly and quantitatively analyzes performance across the multitude of existing channel models, such as EVA, ETU, UAV, and TDL-C. The study fulfills an important gap in the literature by evaluating OTFS performance for real propagation scenarios.

The rest of the paper is organized as follows: Section two covers a literature survey of estimation and equalization techniques on the OTFS system. Section three describes an OTFS-based concept. The joint channel estimation and equalization method are explained in Section four. Section five details the technique and the outcomes of the simulation setup for the performance analysis. Section six discusses the performance results, and section seven concludes the paper. Lastly, the projects for the future are presented in Section eight.

2 Literature Review

Channel estimation and equalization, two critical components in modern wireless communication systems, directly influence the accuracy and efficiency of data transmission. Recent advances have investigated the implementation of OTFS systems in mobility-rich environments with equalization and channel estimation. Some authors have used MMSE-based techniques in the time-frequency or delay-Doppler domains. In contrast, other authors have adopted simple equalization methods and simpler channel models. Unfortunately, many of these studies assume optimal or perfect channel state information (CSI), which limits their applicability to real-world situations. There is a limited understanding of how equalization performance interacts with actual channel estimate errors, particularly in models designed for extremely dynamic environments, such as ETU and UAVs. In contrast, this study proposes a hybrid methodology for channel estimation and equalization to analyze OTFS system performance. To provide a more practical solution, it integrates MMSE equalization with a realistic channel estimator in the delay-Doppler domain. Our approach demonstrated greater applicability to real-world scenarios by outperforming other approaches to the BER in high-mobility channels without relying on perfect CSI. To mitigate interference between symbols and carriers in dynamic channels, [11] utilized iterative detection, zero forcing (ZF), and maximum mean squared error (MMSE) equalization. Common methods for channel estimation, including Least Squares (LS), Minimum Mean Square Error (MMSE), and pilot-aided approaches are discussed in [12]. For OTFS systems, channel estimation has been the subject of several investigations. Raviteja et al. proposed an embedded pilot-based channel estimate method [13], which used isolated pilot symbols in the delay-Doppler grid. Their method outperformed the more conventional time-frequency domain estimate in doubly dispersive channels. Examining the operation of MMSE and ZF equalizers in OTFS with different channel conditions, [14] identified that OTFS with MMSE equalization, with scores at the packet level, frequently outperform OFDM in environments with large induced Doppler.

Under substantial channel variations, bit error rate (BER) performance rates in OTFS are superior relative to OFDM in still cases, when the situation is rapidly changing, both in Extended Typical Urban (ETU) environments and vehicle environments [15]. In high-speed wireless scenarios, where conventional OFDM struggles, studies have supported OTFS as a viable alternative. The processing complexity of equalizers, pilot overhead, and implementation in existing hardware are some of the practical problems that remain unsolved.

Researchers are actively studying hybrid methods that combine the best parts of OTFS and OFDM, as well as how to improve where pilots are placed and make things simpler by using sparsity [16]. One might imagine that a hybrid OTFS-OFDM system can achieve better performance than separate implementations by capitalizing on the complementary strengths of each scheme. OTFS has intrinsic merit under doubly dispersive, high-mobility channels since it makes maximum use of the delay-Doppler space by efficiently canceling Doppler spreads. On the other hand, OFDM benefits from low-complexity equalization and high spectral efficiencies for static or low-mobility links. A scheme that is a combination of both can dynamically adapt to variable channel conditions by assigning OTFS for high-mobility users or for mission-critical transmits and OFDM for stable, low-mobility links and high-data-rate communication. This overall design improves reliability, enhances BER performance, and ensures efficient use of spectrum for a wide array of applications. The design requires careful consideration for receiver complexities, estimation methods for the channel, and resource allocator methods. The hybrid OTFS-OFDM system is regarded as a promising candidate for future-generation wireless systems thanks to balanced robustness and efficiency that is difficult to achieve by individually employing a scheme.

Recently, deep learning-based channel estimation methods have been proposed for OTFS and OFDM systems. CNNs and autoencoders are used to capitalize on channel sparsity in the delay-Doppler domain. These approaches have shown better estimation performance in high-mobility and non-linear-channel situations than traditional pilot-based schemes [17]. The downside is that these deep learning methods are still not practical for real-world usage because they need large training datasets, are computationally intensive, and offer very little generalization ability for channels not included in the training dataset. In contrast, the proposed pilot-based MMSE approach does not require an offline training dataset and is computationally much less intensive, making it suitable for real-time processing [18]. Although this results in some loss of estimation accuracy, we believe that it is a small price to pay. It would be interesting to look into hybrid designs that mix pilot-based estimation with lightweight deep learning modules. It is possible to find a good balance between speed and accuracy [19].

3 OTFS System Model

The OTFS system under consideration contains M subcarriers, which act as delay taps, and N time slots, which act as Doppler taps. The system spans and $T_f = NT$, a frame time, and a bandwidth B that is equal to $M\Delta f$, where Δf is the subcarrier spacing and $T = 1/\Delta f$. Data symbols $X[k, l]$, extracted from a QAM constellation, are scattered across a DD domain grid; k denotes the Doppler index and l the delay index [20].

Figure 1 represents the OTFS modulation and demodulation system in the time-frequency, delay-Doppler, and time domains:

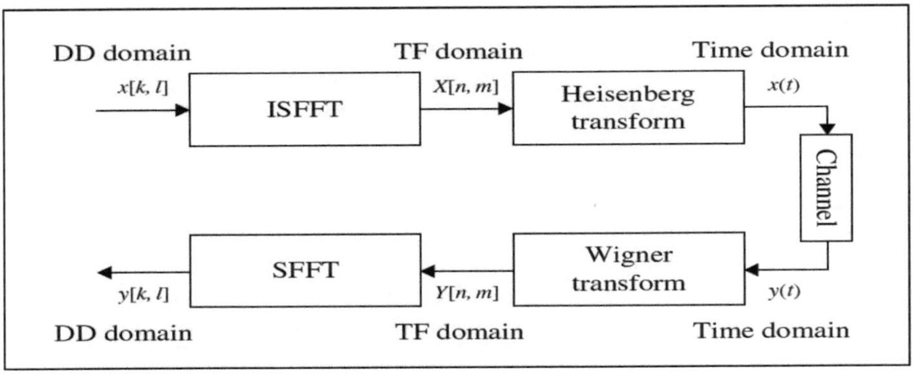

Fig. 1. OTFS System [20]

Using ISFFT, $x\ [k, l]$ from the DD domain, where $\mathrm{k} = 0, 1, \ldots, \mathrm{N} \rightarrow 1$, and $\mathrm{l} = 0, 1, \ldots, \mathrm{M} \rightarrow 1$, are converted to the TF domain. Equation (1) represents the conversion of transmitted symbols from the Delay-Doppler domain to the Time-Frequency domain before modulation.

$$\mathrm{X}[n, m] = \frac{1}{\sqrt{MN}} \sum\nolimits_{k=0}^{N-1} \sum\nolimits_{l=0}^{M-1} x[k, l]\ e^{(\mathrm{j}2\pi(\frac{nk}{N} - \frac{ml}{M}))} \tag{1}$$

Thereafter, through the use of the Heisenberg transform, the TF signal is converted into a signal $x(\mathrm{t})$ in the time domain as shown in Eq. (2):

$$x(t) = \sum\nolimits_{n=0}^{N-1} \sum\nolimits_{m=0}^{M-1} X\,[n, m]\ g t_{\mathrm{x}}(t - nT) e^{(j2\pi m\Delta f(t-nT))} \tag{2}$$

which gives the form of the transmit pulse as $\mathrm{g_{tx}(t)}$. Where τ and v are the delay and Doppler variables, respectively, and $h\ (\tau, \mathrm{v})$ is the channel response in the DD domain through which a transmitted signal travels. According to this model, the received signal $\mathrm{y}(t)$ is represented in time after passing through the multipath channel with Doppler and Delay added to it by AWGN noise, as shown in Eq. (3):

$$\mathrm{y}(t) = \iint h(\tau, v) x(t - \tau) e^{j2\pi v(t-\tau)} d\tau dv + w(t) \tag{3}$$

where $w\ (t)$ is the additive white Gaussian noise (AWGN).

The matched filter process represents the calculation of the ambiguity function ($\mathrm{A_{grx,\,y}}$) between the received signal and the reference pulse, as shown in Eq. (4):

$$A_{\mathrm{grx,}\,y}(t, f) = \int g *_{\mathrm{rx}} (t\prime - t) y(t) e^{-j^{2\pi f(t\prime - t)}} dt \tag{4}$$

A form of the received pulse is defined by $\mathrm{g_{rx}(t)}$.

Equation (5) shows that the received TF samples are obtained by evaluating the ambiguity function at discrete time and frequency grid points.

$$\mathrm{A_{grx,\,y}}(t, f) \text{ at } t = nT \text{ and } f = m\Delta f. \tag{5}$$

Equation (6) represents the reconversion of the signal that was received from the TF domain to the DD domain at the receiver.

$$Y[n,\ m]\ = A_{\text{grx},\,y}(t,\ f)|_{t=nT,f=m\Delta f} \tag{6}$$

The Wigner transform is defined using Eqs. (4) and (6). The matching DD domain samples, y [k, l], are then obtained by applying SFFT to the TF domain samples. Equation (7) represents the reconversion of the received signal from the TF domain to the DD domain at the receiver.

$$\text{y}\ [l, k] = \frac{1}{\sqrt{MN}}\sum\nolimits_{n=0}^{N-1}\sum\nolimits_{m=0}^{M-1} Y[n, m]e^{\left(-\text{j}2\pi\left(\frac{nk}{N}-\frac{ml}{M}\right)\right.} \tag{7}$$

Assume a channel with P pathways in the DD domain caused by P reflectors. Each reflector has a delay and a Doppler; therefore, the channel response h (τ, ν) in the delay-doppler domain is given by Eq. (8):

$$h(\tau, v) = \sum\nolimits_{i=1}^{p} hi\delta(\tau\ -\ \tau_i)\delta(\tau\ -\ \tau_i) \tag{8}$$

τi, νi, and h_i represent the ith path's delay, Doppler, and fade coefficients, respectively [20].

The TF domain's input-output relationship is provided by Eq. (9):

$$Y[n, m]\ = H[n, m]X[n, m]\ +V[n, m] \tag{9}$$

V [n, m] represents TF domain noise, and H [n, m] is expressed by Eq. (10):

$$H[n, m] = \int_{\tau}\int_{v} e^{j2\pi vnT}\ e^{(-\text{j}2\pi(v+m\Delta f)}\ dvd\tau \tag{10}$$

A 2D convolution can be used to approximate the connection between the input and output in the DD domain, as shown in Eq. (1):

$$\text{Y}\ [k, l] \approx \sum_{k\prime}\sum_{l\prime}\text{H}_{\text{eff}}\big[(k-k\prime)_N,\ (l-l\prime)_M\big]\cdot\text{X}\ [k\prime, l\prime]\ +\ \text{W}\ [k, l] \tag{11}$$

where H_{eff} [(k-k') refers to the effective discrete DD channel response that takes into account route gains, delays, and Dopplers, W [k, l] stands for the DD domain noise, and M and N represent the modulo-N and modulo-M, respectively. Inter-Doppler interference occurs when the Doppler (k, l) value is high because it causes a substantial spreading in the k-dimensional component of $\text{H}_{\text{eff.}}$ [21].

4 Integrated Equalization Technique and Channel Estimation

The OTFS modulation scheme handles the delay and frequency variations induced by the channel well. However, detection schemes should still have the ability to recover all information symbols contained in an OTFS frame, considering the channel state information (CSI) of the receiver when performing signal detection. Consequently, precise channel estimation at the receiver is vital, as it significantly influences detection performance. The dilemma of OTFS channel estimation is to estimate the time delays, Doppler shifts, and fading coefficients of all the identified paths (DD) with an estimate done in the DD domain. If P is the number of paths and (τ_i, ν_i, h_i) is the three-tuple representing the ith path's delay, Doppler, and fade coefficient, then channel estimation aims to find the estimated values of this three-tuple for each of the P paths, (τ_i, ν_i, h_i), where i ranges from 1 to P. The appropriate estimated channel matrix $\hat{\mathrm{H}}$ is constructed using these estimations, which are then utilized in the detection methods. To estimate the three-tuple (τ_i, ν_i, h_i) and achieve a channel matrix $\hat{\mathrm{H}}$ estimate, known pilot symbols in the DD domain are supplied as OTFS signal vectors x, and channel estimation is done in the DD domain. Conversely, known time-domain sequences, such as pseudo-noise (PN) sequences, can be sent as pilot sequences, and the estimation issue can be resolved as a time-frequency shift problem [20].

4.1 Channel Estimation Method

The OTFS system differs from the traditional OFDM system in that the pilot symbols are assigned in the DD domain rather than the TF domain. Pilot symbols are supplied in the DD domain at locations using Doppler and delay indexes of (p, q), where $1 \leq p \leq M$ and $1 \leq q \leq M$. Figure 2 shows an example of the pilot allocation [16].

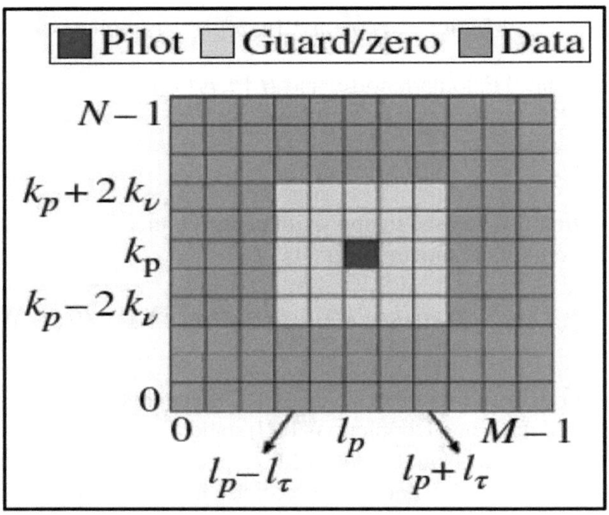

Fig. 2. Pilot placement in the DD domain [20]

First, the channel response is evaluated at pilot points in the receiver's TF domain. Then, these values are projected to other data positions. Careful consideration of channel characteristics should guarantee the quantity and distribution of pilot symbols to maximize channel estimation accuracy while maintaining a manageable proportion of pilot symbols in the total transmission [22].

The DD domain pilot-based methods of estimating channels are classified to four general classes determined by how the data and pilot symbols are multiplexed in an OTFS frame. Figure 3 shows this classification, consisting of (i) a PN pilot approach, (ii) an exclusive pilot approach, (iii) an embedded pilot approach, and (iv) a superimposed pilot (SP) approach [19].

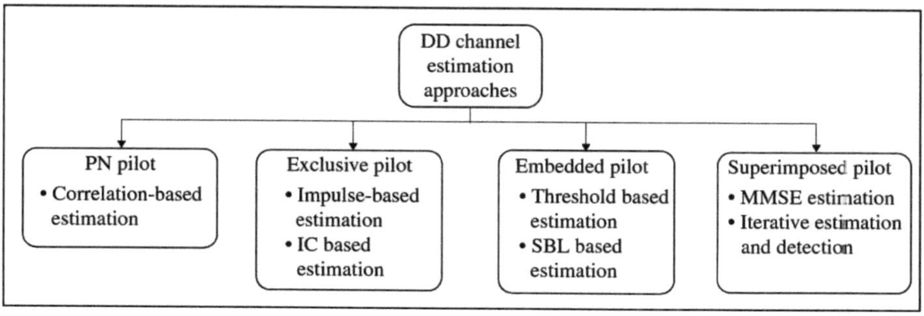

Fig. 3. OTFS channel estimate methods based on DD domain pilots [20]

Sending PN sequences as pilot sequences allows the receiver to do correlation-based estimation in the PN pilot method. For channel estimation, the exclusive pilot method sends out OTFS frames with just pilot symbols. Detection in the following data frames is based on the estimated channel matrix acquired in the pilot frame. The embedded pilot method separates the pilot and data symbols using guard bins and inserts them into a frame. The superimposed pilot method does not use guard bins and instead superimposes pilot symbols on top of data symbols [20].

Incorporation of Pilot-Based Channel Estimation into the System: In the above-explained OTFS (or OFDM) system, the estimation of the channel is carried through a pilot system in the sense that the preassigned pilot symbols are placed inside the delay-Doppler grid (for OTFS) or in the time-frequency plane (for OFDM). The adoption of the above procedure into the overall system is presented below:

Pilot Insertion: At the transmitter stage of OTFS and OFDM transmissions, while the data symbols are transmitted, known pilot symbols are transmitted at specific places in the grid. The specific pilot symbol insertion depends on the specific placement design (for example, a single impulse pilot with scattered pilots, or it could take on structured pilot placements) that gives a balance between the accuracy of the channel estimation and spectral efficiency.

Channel Probing: As the frame propagates through the doubly selective fading channel, the data and pilot symbols are both distorted (generally, delay spreading and Doppler spreading). The pilot symbols are a known value and represent benchmarking points for probing the channel.

Pilot Extraction at Receiver: When receiving the signal, the receiver will extract the pilot symbols from the received signal after performing OTFS (or OFDM) demodulation. The transmitted pilot symbols are given, and so the variance in the received pilot symbols is indicative of the channel response.

Channel Estimation Algorithm: Once the receivers create their pilots for extraction, they input those received pilots to the iterative path estimation algorithm to generate the effective channel matrix in the delay-Doppler domain. The effective channel estimation may include interpolation or iterative refinements for elements of stronger and weaker taps that are driven by multipath and Doppler shifts.

Equalizer incorporation (MMSE): The estimated channel coefficients are used by the equalizer (e.g., MMSE) to reduce the distorted data symbols.

Data Detection: Ultimately, after processing by the equalizer using refined channel estimates, the equalizer gives better symbol decisions, and symbol decisions are passed off to the detector, in the traditional way, then to the demapper to recover bits.

In conclusion, pilot-based estimation is still not a separate block but is integrated into the transceiver chain; pilots are inserted at the transmitter, removed and extracted at the receiver, and their estimates are fed directly into the equalizer to facilitate data detection [23].

4.2 Linear Equalization

When the (CSI) is obtained through channel estimation, channel equalization can be applied to mitigate the effects of fading channels on the received signals. In this discussion, we primarily concentrate on linear equalization for OTFS, which is a method that is effective and at the same time relatively challenging. In the context of OTFS, it is irrelevant whether linear equalization is executed within the delay Doppler (TF) domain or (TD); the same type of equalization consistently yields the same results. For linear equalization, the ZF equalizer represents the simplest form. It is possible to rebuild the estimated (TD) channel matrix, denoted as $\hat{\mathrm{H}}$ and sized $MN \times MN$, using the estimated channel parameters obtained from the channel estimation. The received TD signal vector is denoted by the symbol r, where $\mathrm{r} = [\mathrm{r}[0]; \mathrm{r}[1]; \mathrm{r}[2]; \ldots; \mathrm{r}[\mathrm{MN} - 1]]^{\mathrm{T}}$. A straightforward method to derive ZF equalization involves multiplying T by the length of MN.

A simple ZF equalizer formula in the time domain removes the channel effect without taking into account noise, as represented in Eq. (12):

$$\begin{aligned} \tilde{\mathrm{r}} &= \hat{\mathrm{H}}^{-1}\mathrm{r} - \hat{\mathrm{H}}^{-1}\tilde{\mathrm{w}} \\ &\approx \hat{\mathrm{H}}^{-1}\mathrm{r} \end{aligned} \tag{12}$$

where $\tilde{\mathrm{r}}$ represents the received signal that is equalized and may be utilized directly for symbol detection. The AWGN noise vector (w) is neglected. While this enables ZF equalization to maintain minimal complexity, it results in a loss of performance due to neglecting the impact of AWGN noise.

In this scenario, a linear minimum mean square error (LMMSE) was used to guarantee effective equalization. Unlike zero forcing (ZF), LMMSE considers AWGN, enabling it to achieve better performance than ZF. LMMSE is executed in TD, as indicated by Eq. (13):

$$\tilde{\mathrm{r}} = (\hat{\mathrm{H}}^{H}\hat{\mathrm{H}} + N_0\mathrm{I})^{-1}\hat{\mathrm{H}}^{H}\mathrm{r} \tag{13}$$

LMMSE is more complex than ZF, where $(.)^H$ refers to the Hermitian transposition, and I denote an $MN \times MN$ identity matrix.

Then, using the matrix form, we may change the equalized TD received signal $\tilde{r}$ to the DD domain using Eq. (14):

$$\tilde{y} = \tilde{R}F_N \tag{14}$$

where $\tilde{y}$ is the received symbol matrix for the equalized DD domain, its $[l, k]$-th entry is the DD domain symbol found on the l-th and k-th delay indices and it may be utilized for PSK/QAM demodulation. $\tilde{R}$ is the matrix version of $\tilde{r}$, which is $M \times N$ in size, and F_N is an $N \times N$ FFT matrix [24].

Figure 4 provides a schematic of the signal detection and channel estimator that the equalization uses:

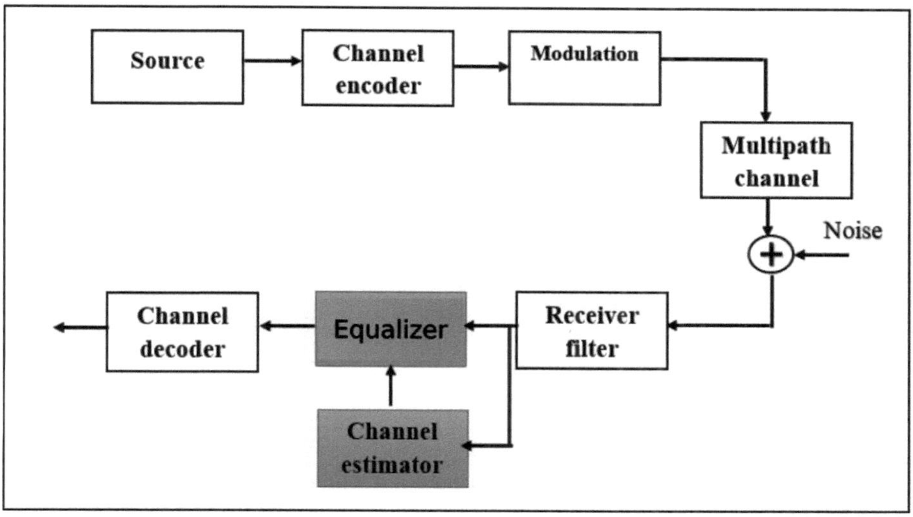

Fig. 4. Block representation of the channel estimator and equalizer in a wireless system [25].

Figura 5a–d shows the effect of SNR on the accuracy and reliability of a channel estimation algorithm:

The estimator is limited by noise at low signal-to-noise ratio (SNR), making it more arduous to identify the true channel topology, and, therefore, generating many erroneous path detections, as demonstrated in Fig. 5a and b. Nonetheless, given a higher SNR, the estimator can more readily discern the real and pertinent paths from noise, as seen in Fig. 5c, where it begins noting the delay, the Doppler, and the gain on the dominant path, most likely a line-of-sight (LOS) or robust early reflection. Once we reach a high SNR, the estimator accurately captures the strongest channel path(s), with minimal noise distortion (Fig. 5d). The performance generally increases as the SNR is increased. It generally provides more reliable results, and this is the case for many of the signal processing techniques to discover signals within noise. The figures above illustrate an

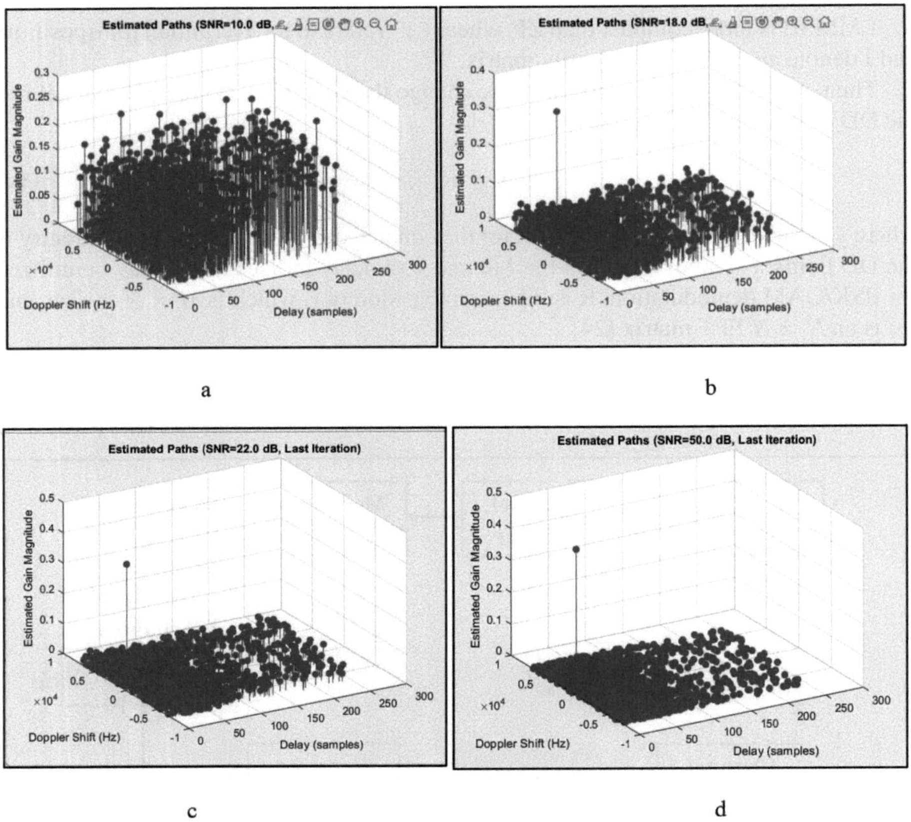

Fig. 5 Estimated Channel Paths at Different SNRs (10, 18, 22, and 50 dB)

example of how well a sparse channel estimation technique performs, which seeks to characterize a low number of dominating channels in a highly congested environment.

The pilot estimating sequence of (*τi, vi, hi*) can be chosen as a PN sequence of the time domain. Let the impulsive response of the delay-Doppler channel be assumed by Eq. (15):

$$h(\tau, \nu) = \sum_{i=0}^{p} hi\ \delta(\tau - \tau_i)\delta(\nu - \nu_i) \tag{15}$$

A relationship between the channel and the input signal x(t) can be expressed as in Eq. (16):

$$\begin{aligned} y(t) &= \sum\nolimits_{i=0}^{p} h_i x(t - \tau_i) e^{j2\pi \nu_i (t-\tau_i)} + v(t) \\ &= \sum\nolimits_{i=0}^{p} h_i'\ e^{j\pi \nu_i^t x(t-\tau_i)} + v(t) \end{aligned} \tag{16}$$

This entails the estimation of $= h_i' e^{-j2\pi v i \tau i}$, $\tau_i \in \mathbb{R}+$, and $v_i \in \mathbb{R}$. The discrete-time channel model is obtained by converting the continuous-time channel model in (16). Upon converting the waveforms to sequences in the discrete channel model, channel estimation becomes easier. The procedure of discretization will be explained here in detail as follows:

With multiplication and addition modulo Np, let $\mathfrak{H}$ be the complex-valued functions vector space over the set of the finite integers $\mathbb{Z}_{Np} = \{0, 1,\ldots, Np - 1\}$. The inner product definition in $\mathfrak{H}$ is expressed in Eq. (17):

$$\langle g1,\ g2\rangle = \sum\nolimits_{n\in\mathbb{Z}Np} g_1[n]g_2^*[n],\ g_1,\ g_2 \in \mathfrak{H}$$

Begin by transmitting the following analog signal in Eq. (18) with a bandwidth of W, starting with a sequence S $\in \mathfrak{H}$:

$$S_{\mathrm{A}}(t) = \sum_{n=0}^{M-1} S\left[n \bmod N_p\right] \mathrm{sinc}\ (Wt - n) \quad (18)$$

When M is at or above N_p. Let M be the sum of N_p plus K, with K as the highest value of W. The analog signal S_{A}(t) must be communicated from the time t = 0 until the time t = M/ W. Associated with S_{A}(t) by the relation Eq. (16) is the received signal $\mathrm{R_A}$(t). The sequence R[n] = $\mathrm{R_A}$ (K + n/n/W) is derived from the sampled $\mathrm{R_A}$(t) with the sampling interval T_s = 1/W from the time K/W onwards for any value of n between 0 to $N_p - 1$. [20].

5 Simulation Results

Extensive simulations were conducted under various high-mobility channel conditions in order to assess how well the proposed OTFS system functions, which incorporates joint channel estimation and MMSE equalization. The scenarios for the simulation consisted of EVA, ETU, UAV, and TDL-C (5G) channel conditions. To take into account the modulation order effects on Bit Error Rate (BER) performance, several channel scenarios were analyzed utilizing various modulation techniques (e.g., QPSK, 16-QAM, and 64-QAM). The main objective was to examine the performance capability and resilience of the proposed receiver design in the presence of high levels of Doppler dispersion and multipath fading. The results, illustrated as BER versus Signal-to-Noise Ratio (SNR) curves, offer a comparative overview of the system's performance in realistic conditions. Table 1 lists the parameters used in the simulation.

The four-channel models, including EVA (Extended Vehicular A), ETU (Extended Typical Urban), UAV (a Drone channel), and TDL-C (Tapped Delay Line C) were specifically selected to provide diverse realistic simulations of wireless propagation environments. The EVA model is capable of preserving the nature of high mobility vehicular applications with the vital Doppler influences; it is best applied in verifying the robustness of OTFS and OFDM in rapidly changing channel conditions. The ETU model captures highly dense urban deployments characterized by multipath fading at a high level. Exponential scattering can produce frequency selectivity, which directly hinders

Table 1. Simulation Parameters

Name of the Parameters	Current Value	Unit/Options	Explanation
n Subcarriers	8	–	Number of active subcarriers (M in OTFS)
n Symbols Per Block	10	–	Number of OTFS symbols per frame (N in OTFS, represents Doppler bins)
f Subcarrier Spacing	15×10^3	Hz	Subcarrier spacing
nFft	256	–	Fast Fourier Transform (FFT) size
n Cyclic Prefix	17	–	CP length in samples
Mod Order	4 16 64	4 (QPSK) (16QAM) (64QAM)	Modulation order (number of points in the QAM constellation)
Velocity _kmph	500	km/h	User velocity in kilometers per hour
F Center	0.8e9	Hz	Center carrier frequency
Channel Estimation algorithm		Pilot-based iterative path estimation	Channel estimation algorithm
Equalizer Algorithm	–	MMSE	Type of equalizing algorithm
Channel Model		'EVA', 'ETU', 'UAV', 'TDLC'	The channel model is used for simulation
SNR Range	0:2:30	dB	Variation in Signal-to-Noise Ratio (SNR) values for simulation

equalization performance. The UAV channel model has gained momentum with the rise of drone-assisted communication systems in addition to wireless system channel models. It represents unique channel characteristics, including rapid altitude modification and disparate line-of-sight versus non-line-of-sight channel scenarios. The last channel model, TDL-C (Tapped Delay Line C) (5G channel), represents delay taps explicitly, which is standardized by 3GPP and widely adopted. It establishes a baseline tapped-delay representation of multipath fading and is used primarily in benchmarking of advanced modulation schemes in regulated yet realistic wireless environments. Collectively, the four channels cover vehicular, urban, aerial, and standardized multipath environments, reasonably making the evaluation framework holistic and relevant to the present usage of next-generation wireless systems.

Table 2. Algorithm Sequence

Stage	Step	Description
1	Begin	Starting the algorithm
2	Parameter Initialization	Assigning values or setting up system parameters (e.g., M, N, CP, QAM order)
3	Algorithm Selection	Deciding about the estimation, equalization, and channel model
4	SNR-Check range	Checking whether all SNR values are set
5	Load Previous Simulation	If plot or results are found in storage
6	Pilot Symbols Generation	Generating pilot symbols to be used for channel estimation
7	SNR Loop	Looping over all SNR values
8	Variable Initialization	Preparing variables for SNR
9	loop Iterations	Continuing loop iteration over the number of iterations
10	Transmitter Chain	Bits on carrier = Bit generation → Encode → Map → OTFS/OFDM Modulation
11	Channel model	Transmitting the signal through channel (EVA, ETU, UAV…)
12	Receiver Chain	OTFS/OFDM Demodulation
13	Channel Estimation	Pilot-based iterative path estimation
14	Equalization	Applying the MMSE equalizer
15	Symbol Detection	Detecting symbols
16	Bit Damping/Bit Stream Decoding	Translating or converting symbols back into a bitstream
17	Error Calculation	Computing BER/SER and updating new results
18	Iteration End Check	If not finished → go to the iteration end
19	Iteration Results Store	Storing results for this loop
20	Final Aggregation	Computing average or final metrics
21	Save Results	Saving all the parameters and simulation results
22	Check the GUI availability	If a GUI is available, the next step is to prepare plots
23	Plot Curves	Generating curves for BER/SER performance
24	End	Ending algorithm and any other necessary call functions

The simulation results for BER were calculated using Monte Carlo simulations, with each SNR point being run for 20 Monte Carlo runs. The number of Monte Carlo runs was reduced due to processing power and time; however, it gives us a general sense of performance. The statistical variability with the limited number of runs at higher SNR could be quite significant. Future work can include additional runs to minimize the variability and provide statistically significant answers.

Table 2 explains the algorithm sequence used in this research:

5.1 EVA Channel

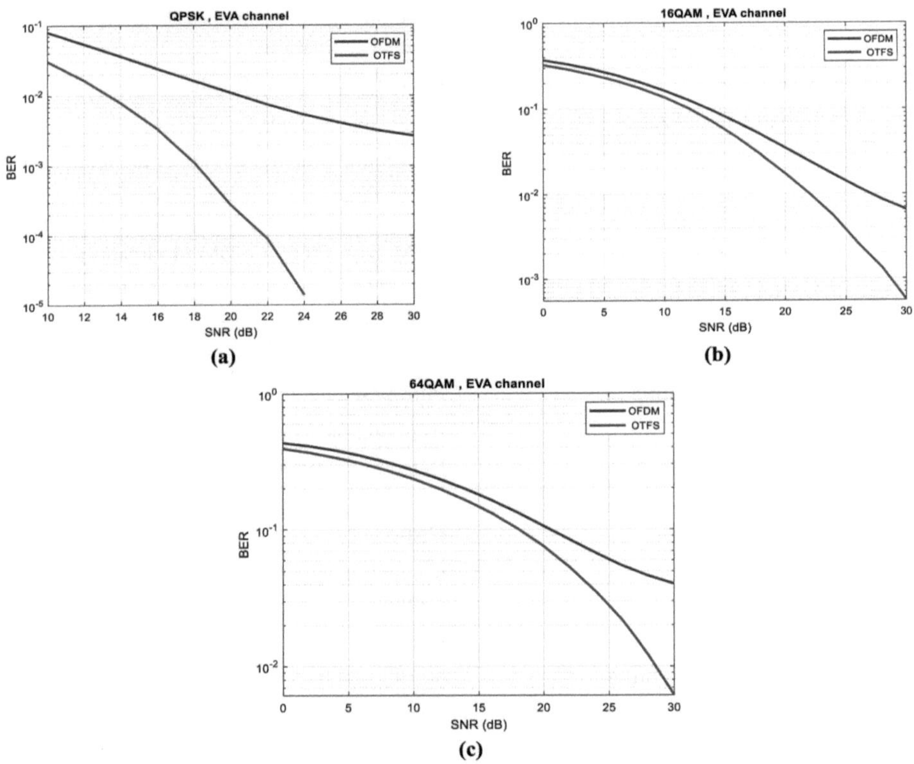

Fig. 6. BER for OTFS & OFDM in EVA channel

Figure 6a–c shows plots of BER versus SNR performance of QPSK, 16QAM, and 64QAM modulations in the EVA channel model. For the same signal-to-noise ratio (SNR), QPSK provides a better quality of performance (lower BER) than 16QAM and 64QAM because it encodes symbols within bandwidths that are less demanding and provides a larger distance between symbols. This increases its ability to tell noise from changes in the signal.

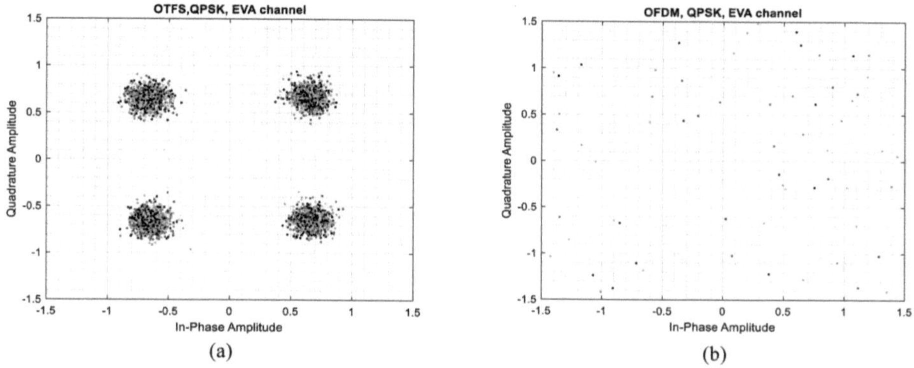

Fig. 7. Constellation diagram for OTFS & OFDM over the EVA channel using a QPSK modulation scheme

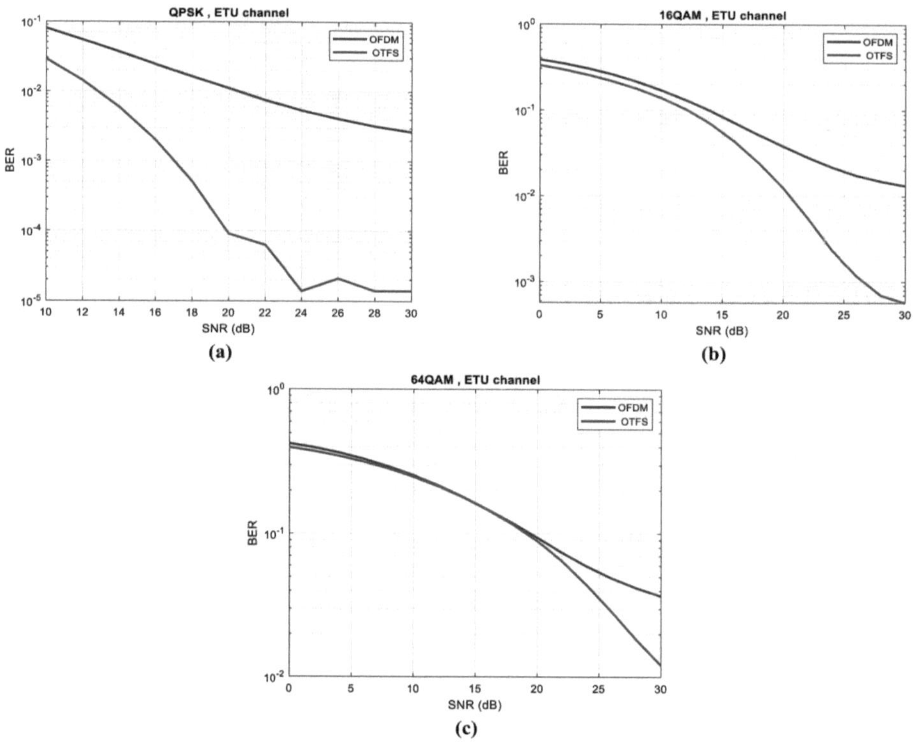

Fig. 8. BER for OTFS & OFDM under ETU channel

Figure 7a–b presents a comparison between the OTFS and OFDM performances in doubly dispersive channels like EVA, which are temporally and frequency selective. Unlike OFDM, the OTFS constellation is able to maintain its structure and integrity in the presence of channel imperfections. This demonstrates that OTFS is an excellent choice for the newest generations' wireless communication networks, particularly in situations involving high mobility.

5.2 ETU Channel (High-Speed Train)

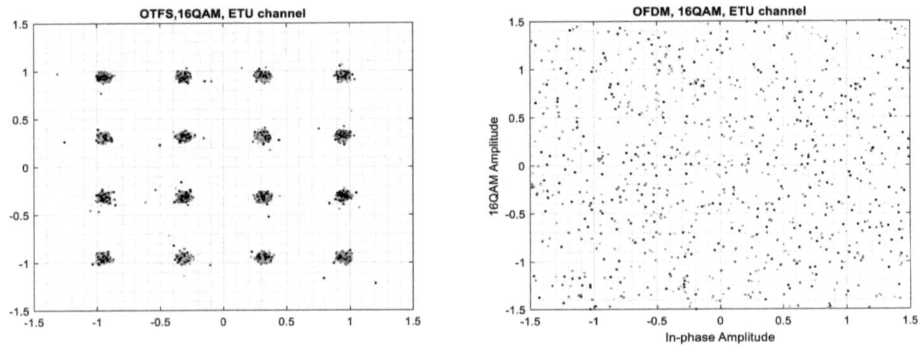

(a) (b)

Fig. 9. Constellation diagram for OTFS & OFDM using 16QAM & under ETU channel

Compared to the EVA model, the Extended Typical Urban (ETU) model exhibited more significant multipath and Doppler effects. In both scenarios, the bit error rate (BER) performance was lower than that of EVA conditions, as illustrated in Fig. 8a–c. The analysis revealed that higher-order modulations were more susceptible to Doppler spread and delay dispersion; consequently, QPSK outperformed 16QAM and 64QAM, as observed in the EVA case.

Figure 9a–b showcases the effectiveness and robustness of the OTFS modulation scheme with 16QAM under distributed wireless environments. Clearly, OTFS modulation supports effective symbol clusters, and it is efficient in recovering usable signal in an urban multipath fading environment. The received symbols in OFDM exhibit a significant distortion due to their extensive dispersion and ambiguous organization. The transmitted 16QAM symbols are notably incorrect compared to their optimal positions in the constellation.

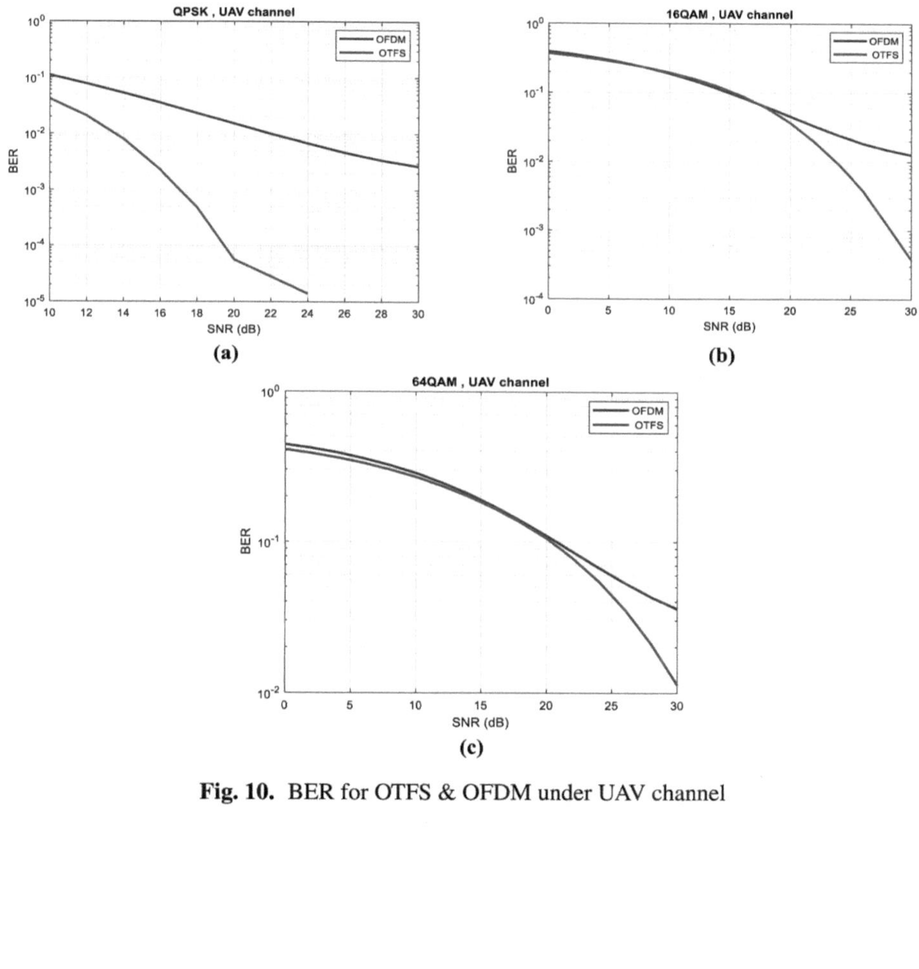

Fig. 10. BER for OTFS & OFDM under UAV channel

5.3 UAV Channel (Drone)

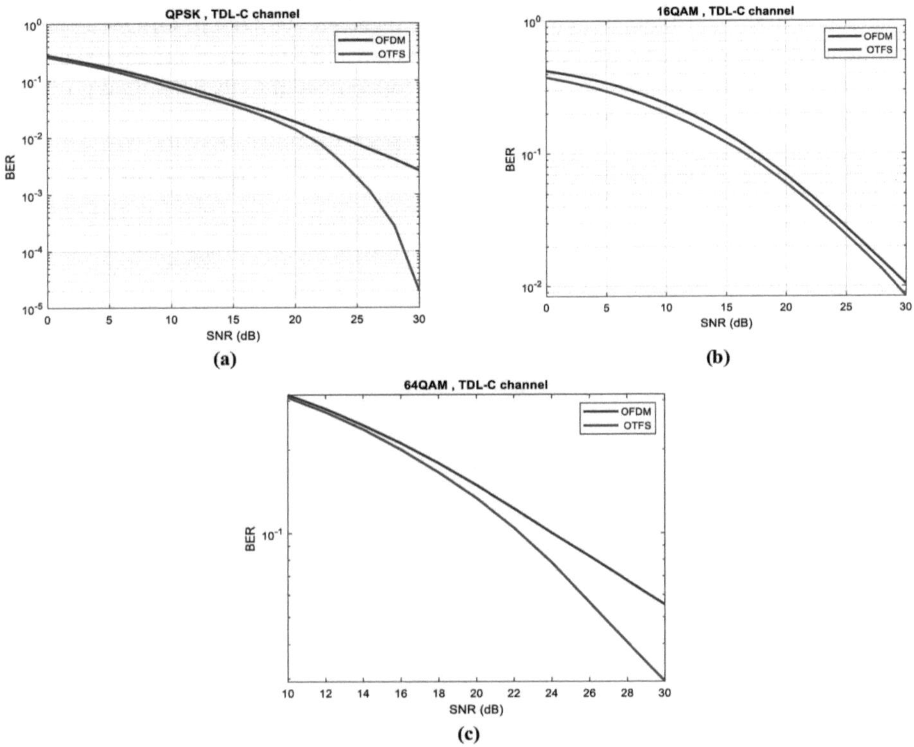

Fig. 11. BER for OTFS & OFDM under TDL-C channel

Figure 10a–c shows that the decrease in BER is more pronounced, particularly for 64QAM, as illustrated in these plots. The result underscores the difficulty of maintaining a reliable connection with high spectral efficiency with mobile UAVs. It also emphasizes the advantages of using simpler modulation schemes like QPSK in such scenarios.

5.4 TDL-C Channel (5G)

The Tapped Delay Line Channel Model C, or TDL-C, is known for its significant delay spreads and a rich multipath environment. As illustrated in Fig. 11a–c, QPSK achieves the best bit error rate (BER) performance using the least number of constellations. In contrast, 64QAM achieves the worst BER performance, particularly at the low signal-to-noise ratios (SNR), illustrating the trade-off between spectral efficiency and robustness, with 16QAM just behind. Table 3 summarizes the simulation results.

Table 3. Channel Estimation & Equalization Results

Channel type	SNR	Modulation Order	OTFS BER	OFDM BER
Extended Vehicular A (EVA)	24 dB	QPSK	1.39×10^{-5}	0.005
	30 dB	16 QAM	0.5×10^{-3}	0.006
	30 dB	64 QAM	0.006	0.04
Drone (UAV)	24 dB	QPSK	1.38×10^{-5}	0.006
	30 dB	16 QAM	0.3×10^{-3}	0.012
	30 dB	64 QAM	0.011	0.035
Extended Typical Urban (ETU)	30 dB	QPSK	1.39×10^{-5}	0.002
	30 dB	16 QAM	0.5×10^{-3}	0.013
		64 QAM	0.012	0.036
Tapped Delay Line C (TDL-C)	30 dB	QPSK	1.95×10^{-5}	0.002
	30 dB	16 QAM	0.008	0.01
	30 dB	64 QAM	0.02	0.05

6 Discussion

The outcomes definitively confirmed the superiority of OTFS over OFDM for various orders of modulations, SNR levels, and channel models. At lower order modulations, such as QPSK, OTFS consistently offers very low BER values in the order of 10^{-5}, regardless of the type of channel (EVA, UAV, ETU, or TDL-C). This highlights the significant robustness of OTFS against strong time-frequency selectivity and impairments caused by mobility, when combined with pilot-based channel estimation and MMSE equalization methods. With the order of modulation rising to 16-QAM and 64-QAM, OTFS and OFDM both displayed worse BER due to higher symbol density and lower Euclidean distance between constellation points. OTFS, however, tended to maintain a higher position among OFDM for the most part, and its BER values were either lower or equal to those for all tested cases. In the case of the EVA channel at 30 dB, for example, OTFS achieved 0.5×10^{-3} with 16-QAM, emphasizing almost an order-of-magnitude gain. In high-mobility UAV channels, the gap slightly decreased at higher modulations, yet OTFS also exhibited superior reliability, especially for QPSK and 16-QAM. In ETU and TDL-C channels, for which multipath delay spreading is considerable, OTFS exhibited superior performance over OFDM, particularly at moderate levels of modulation, yet both systems degrade at 64-QAM. In general, these results verify that OTFS is superior to OFDM in treating high-Doppler and highly dispersive systems and has a strong potential for next-generation high-mobility wireless systems, especially for applications involving reliable communication for difficult channel cases.

As for the complexity of the pilot-based channel estimation and equalization solution, we need to discuss complexity from both the algorithmic execution point of view and from a hardware implementation standpoint.

Algorithmic Complexity: Pilot-based channel estimation has a relatively high algorithmic complexity as a result of the matrix manipulations that are typical of Minimum

Mean Square Error (MMSE) and Least Squares (LS) type algorithms. Most of this type of algorithm relies on an iteration scheme whereby matrix multiplication, inversion, and solving linear equations are usually the most computationally intensive. Estimation is done at OTFS receivers in a delay-Doppler grid that is on the order of $M \times N$. The resulting complexity is directly proportional to the number of delay-Doppler bins, that is, MN. Specifically, MMSE estimation is typically an inverse of the $(MN) \times (MN)$ matrix and is therefore typically of order $O((MN)^3)$ computation-wise, while LS is cheaper with a typical order of $O((MN)^2)$.

In other words, with an increase in the number of delay-Doppler bins, pilot-based channel estimation also incurs a corresponding increase in computation complexity by way of matrix expansion. The complexity for an LS estimator generally has a complexity of $O(MN)$, where M & N are the respective delay and Doppler grid sizes. The MMSE estimation includes matrix inversion, which increases the complexity to roughly $O(MN)^3$. Given the iterative equalization step of e.g., message passing or MMSE equalizers, we also need to consider the cost of each iteration, which results in the overall complexity being linearly dependent on the number of iterations. Overall, the proposed solution is more computationally intensive than conventional OFDM-based estimators; however, it has a significantly increased accuracy in doubly selective channels.

Hardware Implications: From a hardware perspective, the concern is the necessity to carry out a significant number of operations and to have sufficient memory to accommodate large delay-Doppler matrices. To implement MMSE estimation and equalization on hardware, the challenge is to have high-throughput matrix multipliers and a mechanism by which memory accesses are both fast and highly optimized. In addition, inherent in the problem of hardware implementations are power consumption and latency. Iterative algorithms might realistically require multiple passes of operations until convergence is reached. Note that there is the potential for hardware parallelization (i.e., exploitation of the 2D FFT/ISFFT modalities in using OTFS modulation) that can considerably limit processing time, rendering real-time performance realizable. However, with respect to hardware constraints, pilot-based estimation offers pilot overhead reductions compared to fully training-based systems, thus slightly relaxing hardware demands in transmitting and receiving pilot symbols.

In conclusion, the described solution offers a trade-off: It is algorithmically more challenging than 'traditional' single-carrier or OFDM-based estimation because of the need to iteratively invert the matrix; however, with the proper hardware build and parallelization, the extra complexity can be handled. It allows for practical use in high-mobility 6G use cases, where the additional computational and hardware burden is justified by greater robustness against Doppler spread.

7 Conclusion

In speed dynamic situations, the present work provides a comprehensive performance analysis of OTFS systems, utilizing joint channel estimation and MMSE equalization. The presented method effectively mitigates the effects of Doppler spread and multipath fading through a combination of pilot-assisted delay-Doppler channel estimation and linear MMSE equalization. Under challenging conditions, OTFS outperformed traditional OFDM, as demonstrated by detailed simulations using real-world channel models such as EVA, ETU, UAV, and TDL-C. The data indicated that bit error rates were consistently lower for lower-order modulations like QPSK and 16QAM, particularly at higher user velocities. These findings indicated that the OTFS modulations have a bright future with regard to 5G and 6G wireless communications, especially when combined with practical receiver designs. Further research into hardware-efficient implementations, hybrid equalization techniques, and the optimization of pilot placement could enhance the feasibility of OTFS for commercial deployment.

It is notable that this research did not include the creation of a new algorithm, nor did it include attempts to compare various pilot placement design methods. The iterative estimation scheme of paths was based on fixed pilot points. It is used frequently and has become a standard in OTFS systems as it provides reliable channel estimation in high mobility scenarios. The main focus of this work was to benchmark the OTFS and OFDM performance in terms of Bit Error Rate (BER) as a function of EVA, ETU, UAV, and TDL-C channel models. Therefore, this research filled a crucial and important gap in the literature by the scientific evaluation of OTFS in real propagation environments.

8 Future Work

As it would be a crucial research path to validate its robustness and usability, the proposed OTFS system should be investigated in various Doppler environments. Researchers need to specifically investigate its robustness by evaluating it across a broad spectrum of Doppler frequencies - very low to extremely high - simulating different mobile situations, like walking, driving a car, and high mobility platforms (high speed trains and/or airborne). Key performance measures are BER, channel estimation accuracy, and degradation in overall throughput. The benefits of OTFS need to be highlighted compared to other modulation schemes (like OFDM) under the same high-Doppler scenarios. Such studies can provide not only evidence of the theoretical advantages of OTFS in time-variant channels, but also a great deal of new information on how OTFS can be utilized in actual wireless communication systems. Deep learning-based estimators could be investigated as a future endeavor to enhance pilot-based schemes, particularly in non-stationary or UAV channels.

References

1. Vahidi, V., Saberinia, E.: OFDM high speed train communication systems in 5G cellular networks. In: 2018 15th IEEE Annual Consumer Communications & Networking Conference (CCNC), pp. 1–6. Las Vegas, NV, USA (2018). https://doi.org/10.1109/CCNC.2018.8319172
2. Jamel, T.M., Khadum, S.H., Khazaal, H.F.: Comparative analysis of orthogonal time frequency space in mobile communications: a review and simulation study. In: IEEE 22nd International Multi-Conference on Systems, Signals & Devices (SSD) (2025)
3. Hadani, R., et al.: Orthogonal time frequency space modulation. In: 2017 IEEE Wireless Communications and Networking Conference (WCNC), pp. 1–6. San Francisco, CA, USA (2017). https://doi.org/10.1109/WCNC.2017.7925924
4. Raviteja, P., Phan, K.T., Hong, Y., Viterbo, E.: Interference cancellation and iterative detection for orthogonal time frequency space modulation. IEEE Trans. Wireless Commun. **17**(10), 6501–6515 (2018). https://doi.org/10.1109/TWC.2018.2860011

5. Li, Z., Yuan, W., You, C., Cui, Y.: Efficient channel estimation for OTFS systems in the presence of fractional Doppler. In: 2023 IEEE Wireless Communications and Networking Conference (WCNC), pp. 1–5. Glasgow, United Kingdom (2023)
6. Jamel, T.M., Khadum, S.H., Khazaal, H.F.: A performance and evaluation of OTFS modulation systems using different high mobility channels. Int. J. Electron. Telecommun. **71**(2), 505–512 (2025)
7. Thaj, T., Viterbo, A.E.: Low complexity iterative rake decision feedback equalizer for zero-padded OTFS systems. IEEE Trans. Vehicul. Technol. **69**(12) (2020)
8. Li, H., Yu, Q.: Doubly-iterative sparsified MMSE turbo equalization for OTFS modulation. IEEE Trans. Commun. **71**(3), 1336–1351 (2023)
9. Surabhi, G.D., Chockalingam, A.: Low-complexity linear equalization for OTFS modulation. IEEE Commun. Lett. **24**(2), 330–334 (2020). https://doi.org/10.1109/LCOMM.2019.2956709
10. Wu, H., Chen, H., Peng, Q., Luo, Q., Ou, J.: Performance analysis of BEM-based channel estimation for OTFS WITH HARDWARE IMPAIRMENTS. IEEE Commun. Lett. **29**(7), 1719–1723 (2025). https://doi.org/10.1109/LCOMM.2025.3572905
11. Li, Y., Stuber, G.L.: Orthogonal frequency division multiplexing for wireless communications. Springer Publisher (2006). https://doi.org/10.1007/0-387-30235-2
12. Edfors, O., Sandell, M., van de Beek, J.J., Wilson, S.K., Ola Borjesson, P.: OFDM channel estimation by singular value decomposition. In: Proceedings of Vehicular Technology Conference - VTC, vol. 2, pp. 923–927. Atlanta, GA, USA (1996). https://doi.org/10.1109/VETEC.1996.501446
13. Raviteja, P., Phan, K.T., Hong, Y.: Embedded pilot-aided channel estimation for OTFS in delay-doppler channels. IEEE Trans. Veh. Technol. **68**(5), 4906–4917 (2019). https://doi.org/10.1109/TVT.2019.2906357
14. Surabhi, G.D., Chockalingam, A.: Low-complexity linear equalization for OTFS modulation. IEEE Commun. Lett. **24**(2), 330–334 (2020)
15. Shadangi, A.: Analyzing the BER of OTFS compared To OFDM in a multipath fading channel. IAPQR Trans. **50**(1), 2025 (2025). https://doi.org/10.13140/RG.2.2.13360.26889
16. Chong, R., Mohammadi, M., Quoc Ngo, H., Cotton, S.L., Matthaiou, M.: Hybrid OTFS/OFDM design in massive MIMO. IEEE Trans. Commun. **73**(3), 1575–1590 (2025). https://doi.org/10.1109/TCOMM.2024.3454688
17. Zhang, X., Ni, Z., Yuan, W., Zhang, J.A.: Deep Learning-based OTFS channel estimation and symbol detection with plug and play framework (2025). https://arxiv.org/abs/2503.11102
18. Rather, I.H., Kumar, S., Gandomi, A.H.: Breaking the data barrier: a review of deep learning techniques for democratizing AI with small datasets, vol. 57. Springer, Artificial Intelligence Review (2024). https://doi.org/10.1007/s10462-024-10859-3
19. Zhen, Q., et al.: Adaptive implicit-based deep learning channel estimation for 6G communications. IEEE Commun. Magaz. **63**(8) (2025)
20. Mohammed, S.K., Hadani, R., Chockalingam, A.N.: OTFS modulation, theory and applications Wiley-IEEE Press (2024)
21. Raviteja, P., Hong, Y., Viterbo, E., Biglieri, E.: Practical pulse-shaping waveforms for reduced-cyclic-prefix OTFS. IEEE Trans. Vehic. Technol. **68**(1), 957–961 (2019). https://doi.org/10.1109/TVT.2018.2878891,2019
22. Liu, Y., Tan, Z., Hu, H., Cimini, L.J., Li, G.Y.: Channel estimation for OFDM. IEEE Commun. Surv. Tutor. **16**(4), 1891–1908, Fourth quarter (2014)
23. Ye., Li: Pilot-symbol-aided channel estimation for OFDM in wireless systems. IEEE Trans. Veh. Technol. **49**(4), 1207–1215 (2000)
24. Padaganur, S.K., Mallapur, J.D.: A neural network-based resource allocation scheme for 4G LTE heterogeneous networks. In: 2017, the 2nd International Conference for Convergence in Technology (I2CT), pp. 250–254. Mumbai, India (2017)

Wireless Communication

Enhancing 5G Network Capacity Through Integrated mmWave and Carrier Aggregation Technologies

Zuhor M. Ismail[1] and Saad Ahmed Ayoob[2](✉)

[1] Department of Electrical, College of Engineering, University of Mosul, Mosul, Iraq
zohor.23enp16@student.uomosul.edu.iq
[2] Department of Communications and Intelligent Digital Systems Engineering, University of Mosul, Mosul, Iraq
sa_ah_ay@uomosul.edu.iq

Abstract. Millimeter wave (mmWave) frequencies are gaining significant attention in 5G communications due to their wide bandwidth compared to lower frequency cellular bands. This wider bandwidth helps meet the significant increase in data demand. However, there is a drawback of significant path losses. A 5G network was modeled using the SIMU5G framework within the OMNeT++ simulator to show carrier aggregation (CA) behavior and mmWave technology on network capacity. There were clear improvements in overall throughput with 10 carriers compared to a single-carrier configuration. There was also an increase in capacity with larger resource blocks (RBs). However, this increased computational complexity due to subcarrier spacing and greater transmission power requirements at the gNB (i.e. response for connecting user equipment like smart phones and other devices to the 5 G network). Negative impacts on system capacity included Doppler shift (as low as 3%), reduced bandwidth allocated to each user in the network given the higher number of users, and user distance from the base station. The findings provided valuable insight into the positive and negative effects of mmWave carrier aggregation on cellular network performance.

Keywords: mmWave · 5G · Capacity · Carrier Aggregation

1 Introduction

The number of global telecommunications users has grown rapidly, with many individuals using multiple network connected devices simultaneously. As a result, user data rates have increased dramatically in recent years, driven by increased demand for video streaming, widespread adoption of diverse communication platforms, and increase in the use of intelligent home devices requiring remote management [1, 2]. These trends require technologies that enhance spectrum efficiency, enable spectrum reuse, and expand bandwidth and capacity to address the challenges posed by heavy network loads. Fifth generation (5G) networks are designed to meet these demands by supporting emerging applications such as smart healthcare, vehicle to everything (V2X) communications,

W. A. Mahmoud et al. (Eds.): ACDN 2025, CCIS 2798, pp. 69–85, 2026.
https://doi.org/10.1007/978-3-032-15448-4_5

and autonomous vehicles. Key enablers of these applications include millimeter wave (mmWave) communications, carrier aggregation (CA), and massive MIMO technology [3–6]. New Radio (NR) standard in 5G, defined by (3GPP), supports peak data rates (DR) to 10 Gbps with 1ms latency [7, 8]. The 5G system uses two main deployment configurations: non-standalone (NSA) mode, which leverages the existing 4G core network for control plane functions while 5G NR utilizes the user plane, and standalone (SA) mode, which operates entirely on the 5G core [7, 8]. In 5G New Radio (NR), the spectrum allocation is categorized into two primary ranges including FR1, extending approximately from 450 MHz up to 6 GHz and FR2 (millimeter-wave spectrum) covering frequencies between 24.25 GHz and 52.6 GHz. In addition, newer regulations have expanded the accessible spectrum beyond 52.6 GHz, which also includes the license-free 60 GHz range [9, 10]. As shown in Fig. 1, the mmWave spectrum offers much larger frequency bands compared to lower frequencies, which is essential for enabling high capacity and high speed transmissions, which are essential for 5G technology [11]. This shows improvement of the overall throughput through the integrated application of mmWave and CA technologies.

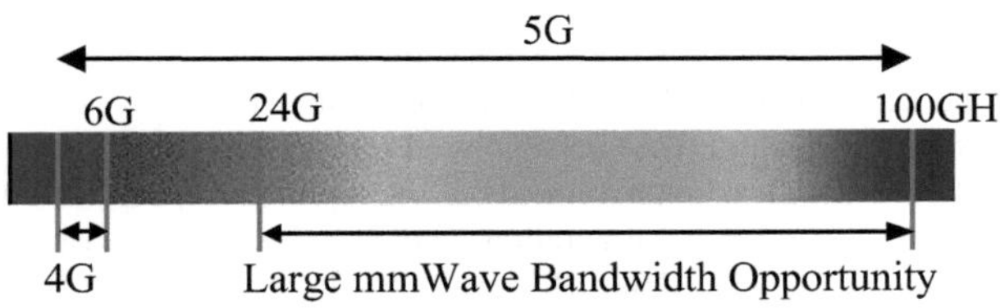

Fig. 1. Large mmWave bandwidth opportunity.

All these developments pave the way for exploring how CA and mmWave technology can be combined to overcome 5G limitations and further improve network capacity.

The paper is organized to provide a logical flow of ideas. After outlining the most relevant studies in Sect. 2, the discussion in Sect. 3 introduces the fundamental technologies underpinning 5G systems. Section 4 describes the developed carrier aggregation model. The obtained results and the interpretations are reported in Sect. 5, and the study is concluded in Sect. 6 with the key insights.

2 Related Work

To address capacity constraints in hotspot areas, researchers have proposed a coordinated multipoint (CoMP) transmission scheme utilizing millimeter wave (mmWave) aerial base stations (mAeBS). They have introduced a dual timescale framework combining large timescale user association (via proximity diffusion aggregation) with small timescale 3D beamforming. Simulation results have demonstrated significant network throughput gains over traditional methods, with MADDPG outperforming centralized deep reinforcement learning (DRL) in terms of deployment efficiency [12]. The effective capacity of a reconfigurable intelligent surface (RIS) assisted mmWave downlink network, operating under statistical quality of service (QoS) constraints, was analyzed in [13]. It was observed that the effective capacity can be preserved within acceptable limits [13]. Authors in [14] investigated capacity enhancement by mmWave within a self-organizing network (SON). They proposed a framework featuring a closed-loop optimization procedure. This procedure addressed hotspot detection and optimal 3D mAeBS deployment using the clustering based on Gaussian mixture model. A use case study validated the approach, showing significant load reduction in hotspot areas and substantial user throughput gains [14]. The benefits of CA technology were explored in [15] by combining TDD 2.3 GHz and FDD 0.85 GHz carriers. Aggregating these operators' resources increased per user system capacity. Scenario based results indicated lower Physical Resource Block (PRB) utilization and improved average radio frequency performance metrics, such as throughput [15]. A comprehensive review of 5G wireless communication systems was presented in [16], focusing on enabling technologies for high capacity, scalable, and reliable networks. The study systematically examined system evolution, performance metrics, frequency standardization, use cases, and critical design challenges. The key findings highlighted the crucial role of mmWave, CA, and massive MIMO in enhancing spectral efficiency and wireless capacity. The study serves as a comprehensive reference point for future investigations focused on enhancing 5G and beyond networks [16]. A key strategy in this context is the joint utilization of Frequency Range 1 (FR1) and Frequency Range 2 (FR2, also known as mmWave). FR1 is characterized by its wide-area coverage, whereas FR2 provides substantially higher capacity; however, it is limited by significant propagation losses and sensitivity to blockages. According to [17], CA enables the concurrent use of both bands, significantly increasing aggregate network throughput. Simulation results in [17] revealed that substantial disparities in link quality between FR1 and FR2 can lead to performance challenges, such as uneven user experience, in certain deployment scenarios. Although studies have offered important perspectives on the features and opportunities of mmWave and CA in enhancing network capacity, there is a noticeable gap to fill. Few works have comprehensively explored the integrated performance of these technologies within standalone (SA) 5G networks under the combined influence of critical real world factors. These factors include variable numerology (adapting subcarrier spacing and symbol duration), Doppler shift effects (especially relevant for mobility), user mobility patterns, and variations in gNB transmit power levels.

The present work seeks to bridge the gap in the literature through an in-depth assessment of how integrating CA with mmWave technology affects critical performance measures, focusing on SINR capacity subjected to realistic and varying operational environments.

3 Overview of Some 5G Technologies

3.1 Carrier Aggregation Technology

One of the most important techniques used in 5G to expand the spectrum and improve data rates is CA from different spectrums. The key purpose is to provide operators with the capability to utilize multiple spectrum segments in combination, which supports capacity growth under different radio conditions and strengthens system performance [18]. 5G allows for wave aggregation in the mmWave bands. The CA aggregation can extend the cell coverage area for time division duplex (TDD) (Nidhi, 2022). This technology was used in the 4G (LTE) with limited capabilities and it is expanded in the new generation. CA is divided into three types [19]:

- Intra-Band Contiguous CA: Aggregating adjacent, equal sized channels.
- Intra-Band with Non-Contiguous CA: Aggregating non-adjacent, different sized channels.
- Inter-Band with non-contiguous carrier aggregation, which is regarded as the most practical option, since wide contiguous spectrum blocks are rarely available for supporting high data rates. In this approach, channels belonging to different and separate spectrum bands can be combined.

3.2 The mmWave Technology

The use of millimeter frequencies is very important in 5G, as it has witnessed widespread interest and rapid growth in use due to its available bandwidth and enormous data rates [4, 20, 21]. It is more important when used along with MIMO or CA technology, among others [22, 23]. Despite its high losses including path loss in the atmosphere, radiation loss, and others [24, 25] 3GPP has identified several mmWave subbands (Table 1) [20, 26]. The bandwidth used by these systems ranges from 500 MHz to 2 GHz, resulting in significant cell capacity of up to several gigabits per second [27].

Table 1. FR2 NR operating bands.

Frequency Band	Uplink (GHz)	Downlink (GHz)
n 257	26.5–29.5	26.500–29.5
n 258	24.25–27.5	24.250–27.5
n 259	39.5–43.5	39.500–43.5
n 260	37–40	37.000–40
n 261	27.5–28.35	27.500–28.35
n 262	47.2–48.2	47.2–48.2
n 263	57–71	57–71

After NR standardization, it was deployed by operators on a global scale. However, deployment in the mmWave range, which is expected to provide high data rates, is hampered by several challenges, including propagation difficulties and obstruction of the line of sight. This causes frequent interruptions, leading to service degradation. The 3GPP has a set of solutions to address this problem [1, 28].

3.3 Numerology Index

Compared to 4G, which supports Numerology (μ) $=$ 0 that represents 15 kHz wave spacing, 5G supports multiple types of subcarrier spacing, as shown in Table 2. Each is classified as 0 representing 15 kHz, which is similar to 4G [29].

Table 2. 5G Numerology index values.

Numerology index	Subcarrier spacing
$\mu = 0$	15 kHz
$\mu = 1$	30 kHz
$\mu = 2$	60 kHz
$\mu = 3$	120 kHz
$\mu = 4$	240 kHz

Simulations were performed for all values of μ available in 5G to show their effects on cellular capacity with the technologies used in this study.

4 System Model

The Simu5G framework was used to simulate a 5G network in this study. OMNet++ simulated discrete events and model any type of wired, wireless, optical, sensor networks, etc. The primary elements in the system include NrUe and gNodeB, corresponding to the UE and gNB with 5G functionality. Their internal architectures are illustrated in Fig. 2 [30].

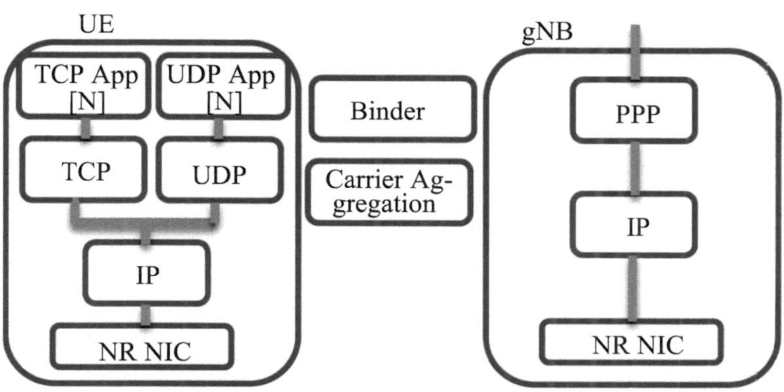

Fig. 2. Main modules of the Simu5G model library

The PPP represents the telecommunications layer protocol in the gNB complex unit, which is a layer 3 (IP) communication protocol. Any number of gNBs and UEs can be added as needed by the settings for designing and testing different networks [30, 31].

4.1 Modelling and System Layout

In the modeled system, one 5G base station (gNB) is placed at the cell center, providing coverage over an area of 500 × 500 m. Since mmWave signals attenuate rapidly with distance [24], four users are distributed across the cell in proximity to the gNB. CA is used to group together 10 mmWave frequency carriers [20], and study their impact on capacity when users are present, when they move, when the numerology value changes from 0 to 4 [29], and other conditions that will be explained in the next paragraph.

4.2 Modelling Assumptions

One of the most important assumptions on which the model was designed is shown in Fig. 5.

1. Network type, Stand-Alone (SA) [32].
2. Number of gNB = 1.
3. Number of User = 4.
4. Model area = 500 *500 m [33].
5. Inter-Band Non- Contiguous

4.3 Simulation Parameters

Table 3 lists the most important simulation parameters in this model.

Table 3. Important simulation parameters.

Components	Description
gNB tx power (dBm)	40, 42, 44, 46, 48, 50 [12]
gNB height	25 m
Use height	1.5 m [28]
Building height	20 m
Distance from gNB (m)	Ue[0] = 50, Ue[1] = 200, Ue[2] = 150, Ue[3] = 10, [24]
User Status	Mobility
Mobility Type	Circle
Users Speed (Km/h)	220, 340, 460, 580
User Status	Mobility
Mobility Type	Circle
Number of CC's	10 [20]
Operating Band	n257, n258, n259, n260, n261, n262 [20, 26]
Duplex Mode	TDD [26]
Propagation Model	Rayleigh Model [26]
Path loss exponent	3 [26]

The network diagram that was studied and modelled in the Simu5G framework is shown in Fig. 3. The locations of the users and the base station, in addition to the important icons in the proposed model are illustrated.

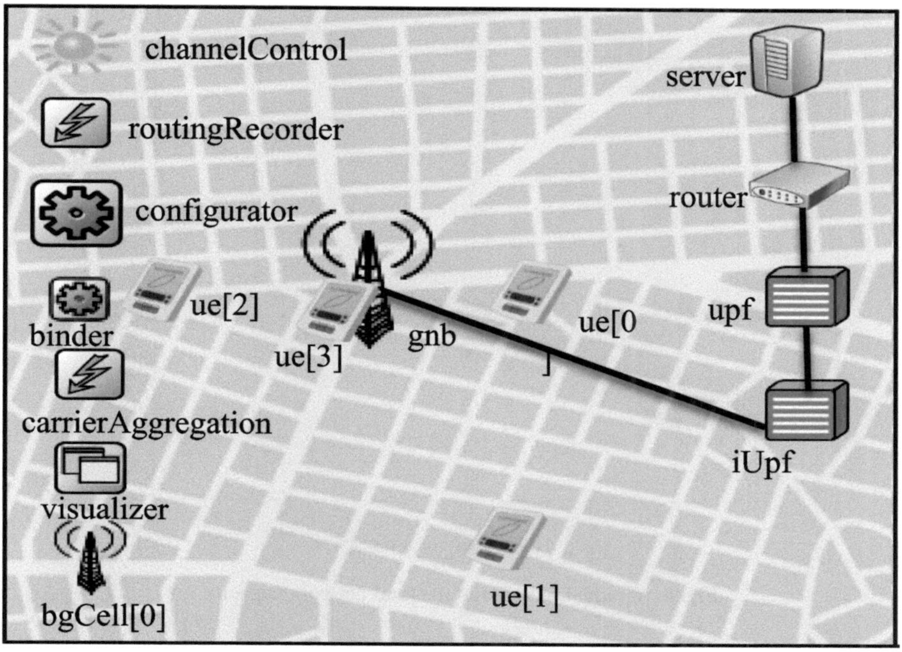

Fig. 3. 5G network simulation model in SIMU5G simulator with 1 gNB, 4 users, and carrier aggregation technology to aggregate 10-mm frequency carriers.

5 Results and Discussion

After configuring the network and adding users, it was operated using carrier aggregation technology to combine carrier waves. The impact of these two technologies on cellular communications was studied with several factors and the results are as follows:

5.1 Effects of the Number of Carriers

When working with CA technology, it is necessary to first study the effect of increasing the number of carriers on the SINR in the cell. According to Eq. 1, the SINR increases with increasing the number of carriers.

$$SINR_{CA} = \sum\nolimits_{k=1}^{N_c} SINR_k \tag{1}$$

where: $SINR_{CA}$: Total SINR for multiple carriers.

$SINR_k$: SINR for single carrier.

N_c: Number of carriers.

This observation is validated by the simulation outcomes illustrated in Fig. 4. Where the dots represent the results in the OMNet++ simulator, while the solid line represents the curve matching to represent the points as a curve in the MATLAB program.

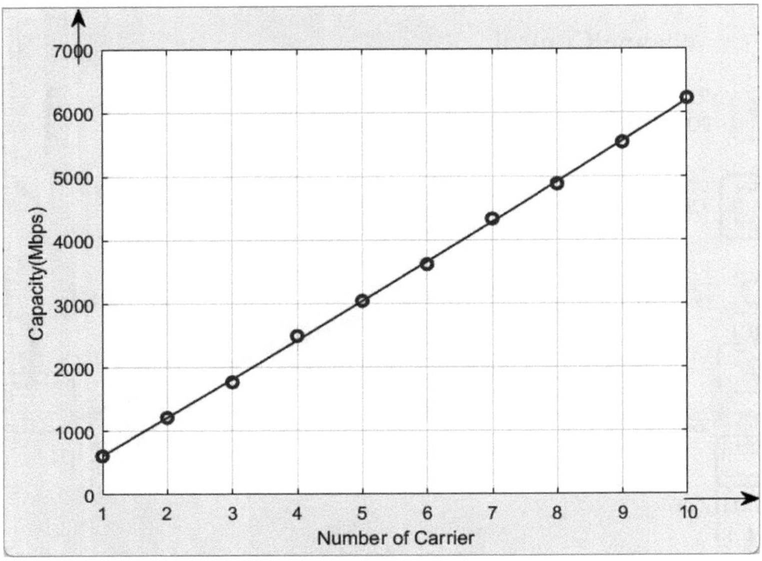

Fig. 4. Gradual increase in the total network capacity.

According to Eq. 2 (Shannon's Equation), the capacity increases with increasing SINR.

$$C = B_{total}.log_2(1 + SINR) \tag{2}$$

where: B_{Total}: bandwidth in hertz (Hz), and the total bandwidth is equal to:

$$B_{total} = \sum\nolimits_{k=1}^{Nc} B_k \tag{3}$$

B_k: B for carrier number k.

This indicates that the channel capacity increases in direct proportion to the available bandwidth. When multiple carriers are combined in the millimeter wave band, the total available bandwidth increases significantly, resulting in a logarithmic increase in cell capacity. As confirmed by the simulation results, capacity increases with the number of carriers, improving by 90% when the number increases from 1 to 10 (Fig. 5). This should not be interpreted as a quasi-linear increase that contradicts Shannon's law, but rather as a special case in which the trends appear quasi linear under constant SINR conditions compared to reality. It should be noted that increasing the number of carriers had no significant effect on the average cell delay (Fig. 6).

As depicted in Fig. 7, a higher number of carriers leads to a noticeable rise in the packets delivered to users.

5.2 Resource Blocks Effect

Given the effects of increasing the resource blocks (RBs) that directly affects the bandwidth, the capacity increases as the RBs increase (Fig. 8). As the number of RBs increases

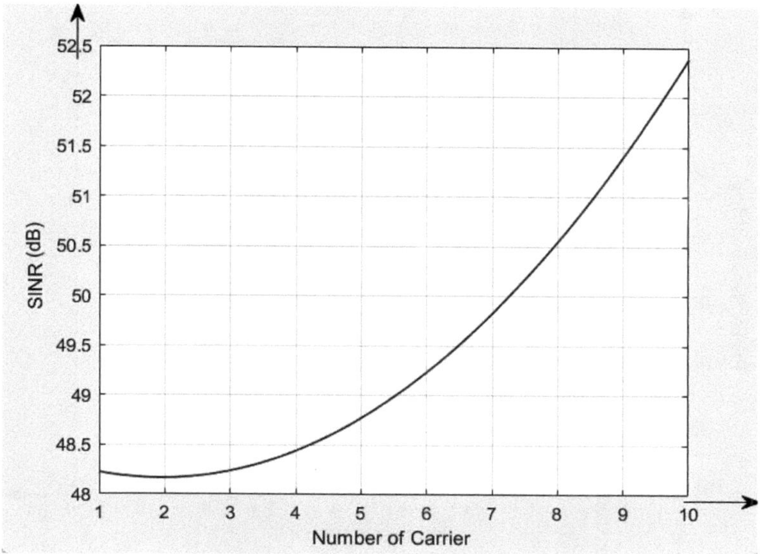

Fig. 5. Increase in the SINR as the number of wave carriers increases.

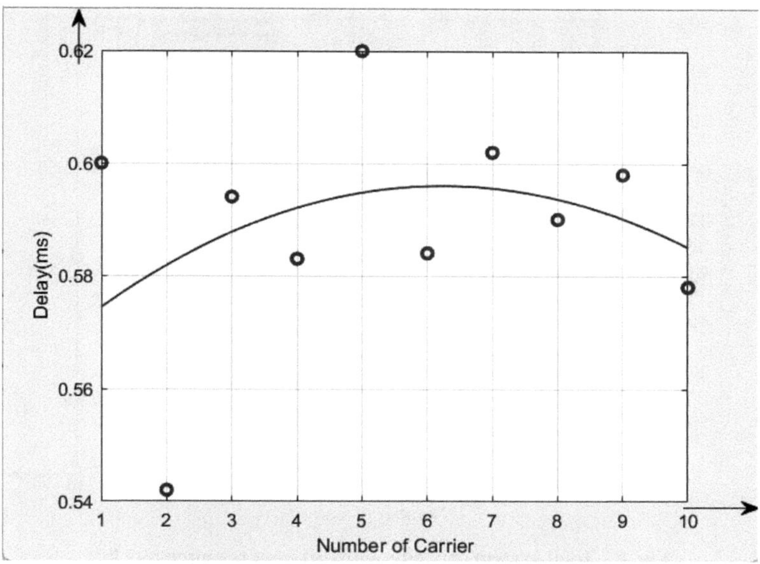

Fig. 6. Network delay rate is affected differently by increasing the number of carriers.

from 50 to 75, the system capacity improves by 32.3%, whereas expanding from 75 to 100 RBs results in a 25% gain.

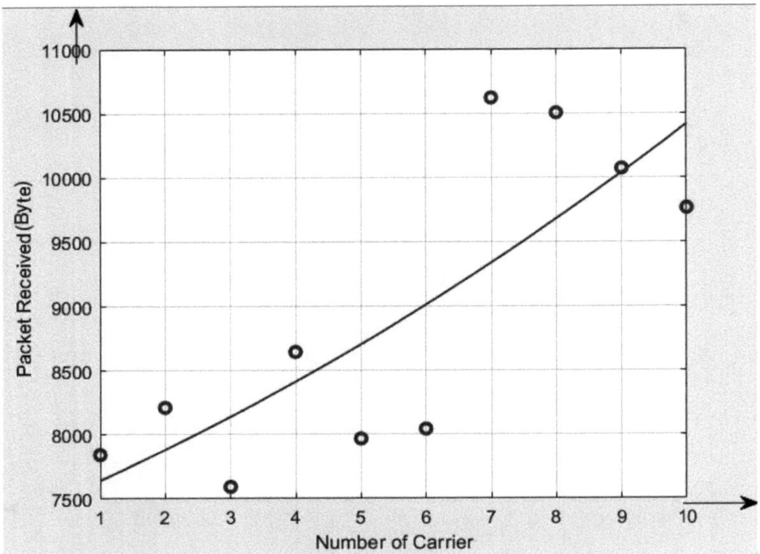

Fig. 7. Variation in received packets as a function of carrier quantity.

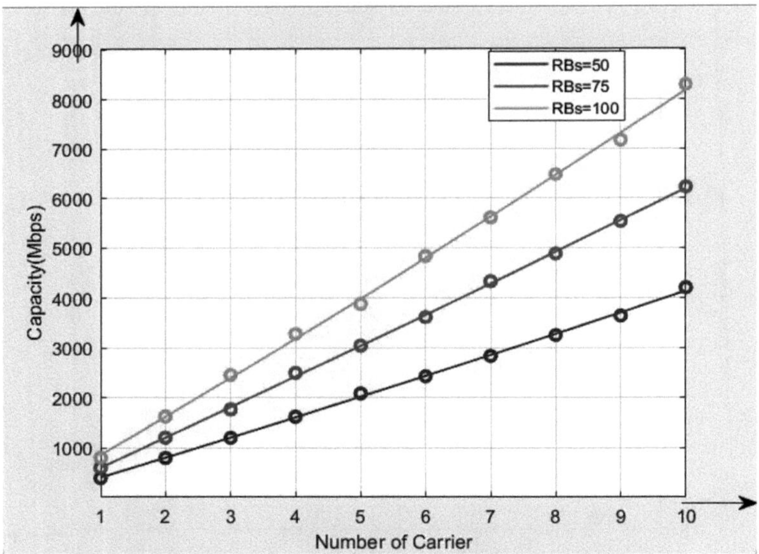

Fig. 8. Total system capacity with different resource blocks.

5.3 Increase in User's Number

With an increase in the number of users within the cell, the mutual interference among their signals intensified, which in turn reduced the SINR values. This affected the total capacity, which decreased by 21.4% (Fig. 9).

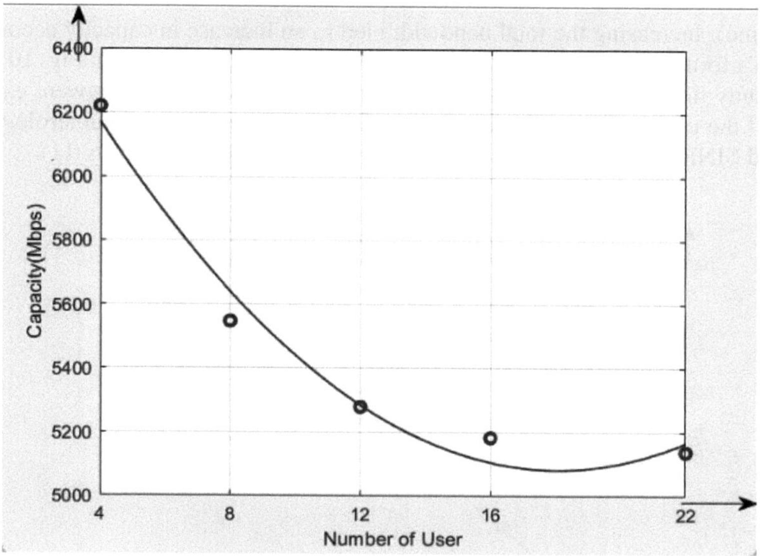

Fig. 9. Effects of user number on capacity performance.

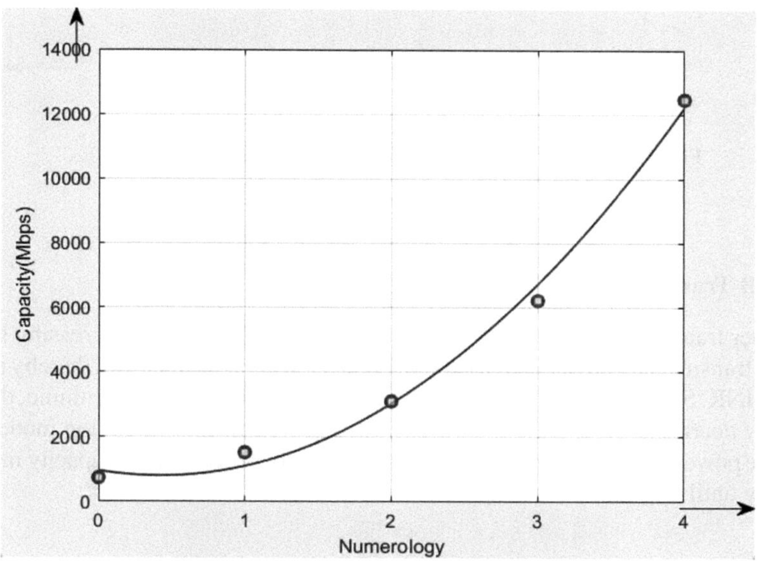

Fig. 10. The effects of numerology on total capacity.

5.4 The Impact of Numerology Index

Increasing numerology index from 0 to 4 directly reduced the symbol duration and increased the carrier bandwidth, which led to a shorter transmission interval (i.e., lower access time). Increasing the total bandwidth led to an increase in capacity according to Shannon's formula, as demonstrated by the simulation results shown in Fig. 10.

To study the effects of some factors on capacity more clearly, they were examined on one of the users in the cell (user 0). It is noted that increasing the numerology value increased SINR of user0 and thus increased the capacity by 51.4% (Fig. 11).

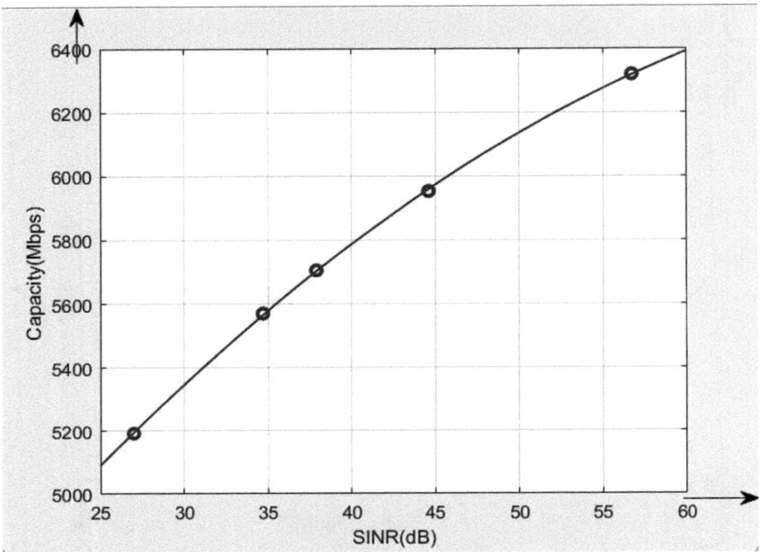

Fig. 11. Cellular capacity increases by increasing network SINRs.

5.5 gNB Transmit Power

The power transmitted by a GNB affected the overall cell capacity. Increasing the base station's transmission power increased the signal strength at the receiver, thereby improving the SINR. Since the relationship between capacity and SINR is logarithmic, the gains gradually decreased with increasing transmitted power. In the simulation model under study, the power was gradually increased from 40 dB to 50 dB, and the capacity increased gradually until it reached 5% (Fig. 12).

5.6 Doppler Shift Effect

Doppler shift introduces frequency shifts into the signals received by the receiver. This affects systems with large frequency separations between subcarriers. In turn this affects the carriers and causes interference between them (ICI). The Doppler shift is expressed by Eq. 4 [34].

$$f_d = \frac{V}{\lambda} cos\Theta \tag{4}$$

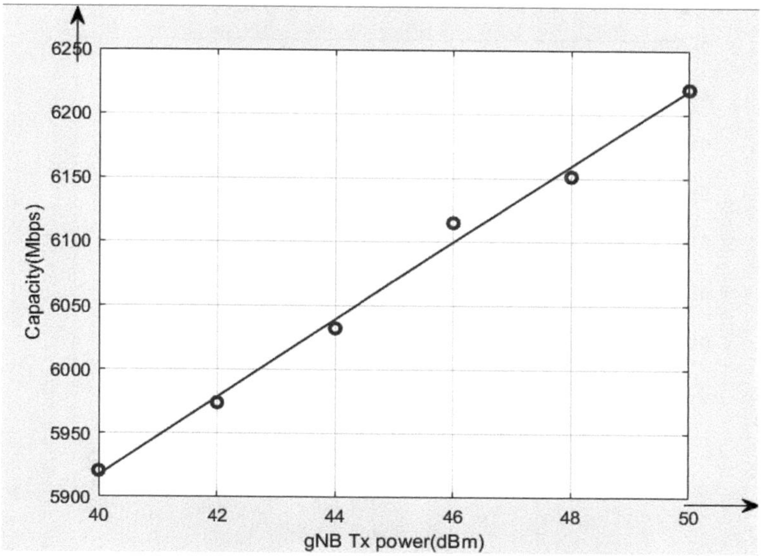

Fig. 12. The capacity increases with the increase of the transmit power of the gNB.

where: f_d: Doppler frequency shift (Hz).

V: Velocity of the user/receiver relative to the signal source, in m/s.

λ: Wavelength of the carrier wave.

The results showed that the Doppler effect negatively affected the capacity by only 3% when the speed increased from 0 to 580 km/h, as shown in Fig. 13. This is consistent with theoretical expectations for systems with high SINR.

5.7 The Effects of User Distance from gNB

A representative user was considered to examine how varying the distance from the gNB influences the system capacity. At first, the user was stationary and 50 m away from the base station. Then, gradually moved away, and measurements were taken while the user was stationary until he reached a distance of 250 m. The capacity decrease rate was 52%, and the simulation results are shown in Fig. 14.

As the user moved farther from the base station, the VoIP Mean Opinion Score (MOS), ranging from 1 to 5, indicated a 2.7% reduction in call audio quality (Fig. 15).

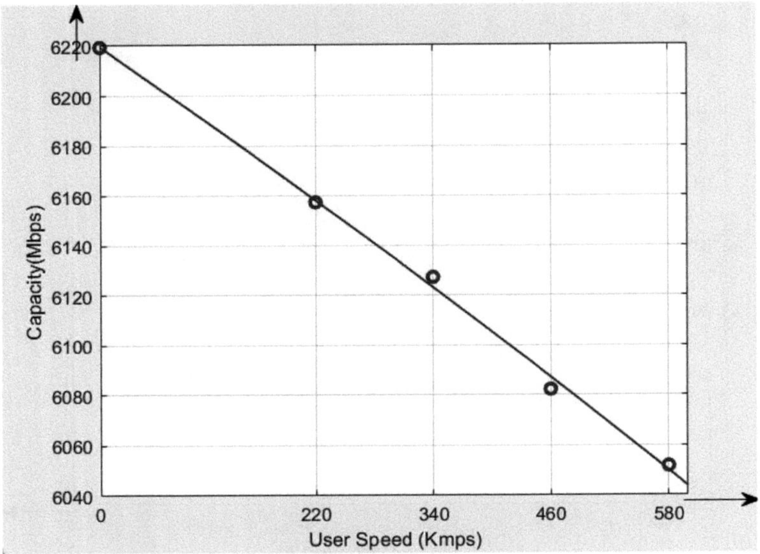

Fig. 13. Total user capacity is negatively affected by the Doppler shift.

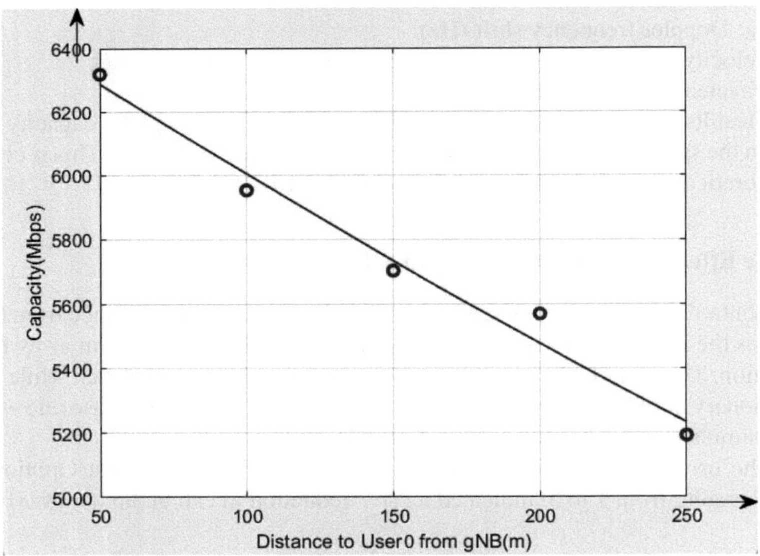

Fig. 14. User capacity decreases as the user moves away from the gNB.

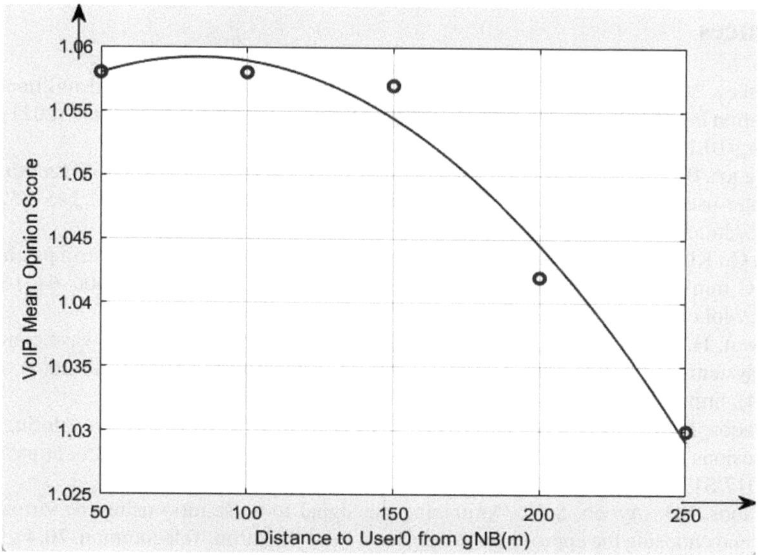

Fig. 15. Average user opinion score decreases as gNB distance increases.

6 Conclusion

When used in conjunction with other technologies, such as CA, wireless network operators are keen to leverage mmWave frequency bands to achieve a better performance and ultra-fast data transmission speeds. The results confirmed the capacity improvement resulting from the combination of mmWave and CA technologies. The simulations were conducted on a standalone 5G network within the SIMU5G framework. The results indicated a clear and significant capacity improvement as the number of carriers increased from 1 to 10. Resource blocks and increased transmitted power from the gNB significantly improved the overall network capacity, while other factors, such as Doppler shift stability, the accumulation of additional users inside the cell coverage, and the distance between the receiver and the gNB negatively impacted capacity and caused capacity degradation. Capacity improved by 90% with 10 carriers compared to a single carrier, and by 49.3% with increasing resource blocks (RBs) from 50 to 100. Cellular capacity increased by 21.4% when the number index increased, as new users joined the network, the total capacity decreased by 21.4% when the number increased from 4 to 22 users. The Doppler shift at 580 km/h resulted in a 3% capacity reduction. Increasing the user's distance to the cell edge resulted in a 52% capacity reduction. Unlike other studies that relied on abstract modeling or fixed configurations, this study used a programmable simulation environment (SIMU5G) with user customized control plane behavior to evaluate capacity under realistic conditions. These results highlight the potential of mmWave CA simulations to address capacity challenges in future 5G networks. However, this model is limited to simulation environments and does not take into account multipath fading in practical applications, size constraints in small stations, and high-power consumption. Future research works need to investigate adding MIMO technology to the current configuration and its impact on system performance under complex mobility scenarios and the constraints mentioned above.

References

1. Begishev, V., et al.: Performance analysis of multi-band microwave and millimeter-wave operation in 5G NR systems. IEEE Trans. Wirel. Commun. **20**(6), 3475–3490 (2021). https://doi.org/10.1109/TWC.2021.3051027
2. Qeryaqos, B.J., Ayoob, S.A.: Proposed multiple reconfigurable intelligent surfaces to mitigate the inter-user-interference problem in NLOS. J. Commun. Softw. Syst. **20**(3), 245–252 (2024). https://doi.org/10.24138/jcomss-2024-0039
3. Kim, G., Kim, S.: Design and analysis of dual polarized broadband microstrip patch antenna for 5G mmWave antenna module on FR4 substrate. IEEE Access **9**, 64306–64316 (2021). https://doi.org/10.1109/ACCESS.2021.3075495
4. Alsawaf, H.A., Ayoob, S.A.: Optimized wideband beamforming for mm-wave communication systems with intelligent reflecting surfaces. J. Commun. Softw. Syst. **20**(4), 350–360 (2024). https://doi.org/10.24138/jcomss-2024-0090
5. Qeryaqos, B.J., Ayoob, S.A.: Improving SINR with smart RIS solutions: exploring optimal dimensions and sizes. Int. J. Microw. Wirel. Technol. **70**(4), 909–914 (2025). https://doi.org/10.1017/S1759078725000169
6. Qeryaqos, B.J., Ayoob, S.A.: Optimizing the signal-to-noise ratio using the virtual line of sight and choosing the appropriate dimensions. Int. J. Electron. Telecommun. **70**(4), 909–914 (2024). https://doi.org/10.24425/ijet.2024.152077
7. Aldalbahi, A., Shahabi, F., Jasim, M.: Instantaneous beam prediction scheme against link blockage in mmWave communications. Appl. Sci. **11**(12) (2021). https://doi.org/10.3390/app11125601
8. Liu, G., Huang, Y., Chen, Z., Liu, L., Wang, Q., Li, N.: 5G deployment: standalone vs. non-standalone from the operator perspective. IEEE Commun. Mag. **58**(11), 83–89 (2020). https://doi.org/10.1109/MCOM.001.2000230
9. Pinheiro, B., Silva, D., Andrade, F., Ribeiro, R.: Comparison of current consumption and data rates in 5G NSA over FR2 and FR1 bands. J. Commun. Inf. Syst. **39**(1), 109–112 (2024). https://doi.org/10.14209/jcis.2024.10
10. Nidhi, Khan, B., Mihovska, A., Prasad, R., Velez, F.J.: A study on cross-carrier scheduler for carrier aggregation in beyond 5G networks. URSI Atl. Asia Pac. Radio Sci. Meet. (AT-AP-RASC), 3–6 (2022). https://doi.org/10.23919/AT-AP-RASC54737.2022.9814320
11. Alsharbaty, F.S., Ayoob, S.A.: Intra-site CoMP operation effect of fifth generation techniques on 802.16e downlink stream. Int. J. Eng. Trends Technol. **67**(4), 12–17 (2019). https://doi.org/10.14445/22315381/IJETT-V67I4P204
12. Zhao, Y., Zhou, F., Feng, L., Li, W., Yu, P.: MADRL-based 3D deployment and user association of cooperative mmWave aerial base stations for capacity enhancement. Chin. J. Electron. **32**(2), 283–294 (2023). https://doi.org/10.23919/cje.2021.00.327
13. Haider Shah, S.W., Pavan Deram, S., Widmer, J.: On the effective capacity of RIS-enabled mmWave networks with outdated CSI. In: IEEE INFOCOM (2023). https://doi.org/10.1109/INFOCOM53939.2023.10229028
14. Yu, P., et al.: Capacity enhancement for 5G networks using mmWave aerial base stations: self-organizing architecture and approach. IEEE Wirel. Commun. **25**(4), 58–64 (2018). https://doi.org/10.1109/MWC.2018.1700393
15. Kusuma, F., Putri, H.: Increasing the LTE-advanced network capacity using inter-band carrier aggregation (downlink side) method. J. Commun. **12**(2), 52–59 (2020). https://doi.org/10.20895/infotel.v12i2.474
16. Imam-Fulani, Y.O., et al.: 5G frequency standardization, technologies, channel models, and network deployment: advances, challenges, and future directions. Sustainability **15**(6) (2023). https://doi.org/10.3390/su15065173

17. Lai, K., Mao, J., Zhang, P., Li, Z.: Challenges and analysis of combining FR1 and FR2 bands using 5G carrier aggregation. J. Phys. Conf. Ser. **2906**(1) (2024). https://doi.org/10.1088/1742-6596/2906/1/012005
18. Adamu, P.U., Lopez-Benitez, M.: Performance evaluation of carrier aggregation as a diversity technique in mmWave bands. IEEE Vehicular Technology Conference (VTC-Spring) (2021). https://doi.org/10.1109/VTC2021-Spring51267.2021.9448984
19. Wulandari, A., Hasan, M., Hikmaturokhman, A., Ashamdono, Damayanti, L., Damelia: 5G stand alone inter-band carrier aggregation planning in Kelapa Gading Jakarta Utara. In: International Conference on ICT for Rural Development (IC-ICTRuDev) (2021). https://doi.org/10.1109/IC-ICTRuDev50538.2021.9656497
20. Azari, A., Skrivervik, A., Aliakbarian, H.: A mmWave low complexity and low-cost super wideband dual-polarized aperture coupled antenna for 5G applications. IEEE Access **12**, 85601–85607 (2024). https://doi.org/10.1109/ACCESS.2024.3415167
21. Ayoob, S.A., Alsharbaty, F.S., Alhafid, A.: Enhancement the heavy file application of 802.16 e cell using intra-site CoMP in uplink stream. J. Eng. Sci. Technol. **17**(3), 1721–1733 (2022)
22. Zidour, A., et al.: Wideband endfire antenna array for 5G mmWave mobile terminals. IEEE Access **12**, 39926–39935 (2024). https://doi.org/10.1109/ACCESS.2024.3375811
23. Ayoob, S.A., Alsharbaty, F.S., Hammodat, A.N.: Design and simulation of high efficiency rectangular microstrip patch antenna using artificial intelligence for 6G era. TELKOMNIKA **21**(6), 1234–1245 (2023). https://doi.org/10.12928/telkomnika.v21i6.25389
24. Cheng, Y., Dong, Y.: Wideband circularly polarized planar antenna array for 5G millimeter-wave applications. IEEE Trans. Antennas Propag. **69**(5), 2615–2627 (2021). https://doi.org/10.1109/TAP.2020.3028213
25. Huang, A., Lin, K.H., Wei, H.Y.: Beam-aware cross-layer DRX design for 5G millimeter wave communication system. IEEE Access **8**, 77604–77617 (2020). https://doi.org/10.1109/ACCESS.2020.2989625
26. Taylor, C.: 3GPP MCC: Adding channel bandwidth to existing NR bands (2022). https://www.3gpp.org
27. Lu, X., et al.: Integrated use of licensed-and unlicensed-band mmWave radio technology in 5G and beyond. IEEE Access **7**, 24376–24391 (2019). https://doi.org/10.1109/ACCESS.2019.2900195
28. Beschastnyi, V., Ostrikova, D., Moltchanov, D., Gaidamaka, Y., Koucheryavy, Y., Samouylov, K.: Balancing latency and energy efficiency in mmWave 5G NR systems with multiconnectivity. IEEE Commun. Lett. **26**(8), 1952–1956 (2022). https://doi.org/10.1109/LCOMM.2022.3175663
29. Mihovska, A., Prasad, R.: Overview of 5G new radio and carrier aggregation: 5G and beyond networks, pp. 2–7 (2020). https://doi.org/10.1109/WPMC50192.2020.9309496
30. Nardini, G., Sabella, D., Stea, G., Thakkar, P., Virdis, A.: SiMu5G–An OMNeT++ library for end-to-end performance evaluation of 5G networks. IEEE Access **8**, 181176–181191 (2020). https://doi.org/10.1109/ACCESS.2020.3028550
31. Simu5G: A system-level simulator for 5G networks. https://www.researchgate.net/publication/340874792_Simu5G_A_System-level_Simulator_for_5G_Networks
32. Hakegard, J.E., Lundkvist, H., Rauniyar, A., Morris, P.: Performance evaluation of an open source implementation of a 5G standalone platform. IEEE Access **12**, 25809–25819 (2024). https://doi.org/10.1109/ACCESS.2024.3367120
33. Joda, R., et al.: Carrier aggregation with optimized UE power consumption in 5G. IEEE Netw. Lett. **3**(2), 61–65 (2021). https://doi.org/10.1109/LNET.2021.3076409
34. Zhang, C., Wang, G., Jia, M., He, R., Zhou, L., Ai, B.: Doppler shift estimation for millimeter-wave communication systems on high-speed railways. IEEE Access **7**(c), 40454–40462 (2019). https://doi.org/10.1109/ACCESS.2018.2861889

Enhancing 6G NOMA Performance with HRL-Driven mMIMO, CR, and RIS Integration

Ibrahim Khider[1(✉)], Mohamed Hassan[2], Khalid Hamid[2], and Elmuntaser Hassan[3]

[1] Department of Electronics and Communication Engineering, Uruk University, Baghdad, Iraq
ibrahim.kh.altahir@uruk.edu.iq

[2] Department of Electrical Engineering, Omdurman Islamic University, Omdurman, Sudan
khalid.bilal@oiu.edu.sd

[3] Department of Computer Science, Al-Neelain University, Khartoum, Sudan

Abstract. The study addresses the critical challenge of improving downlink performance, namely average throughput, latency, and packet loss in ultra-dense 6G networks. The issue intensifies when the number of users increases and traditional resource allocation methods fail under high-bandwidth (BW) mmWave settings. To solve this, a novel framework that integrates massive MIMO (mMIMO), Cognitive Radio (CR), and Reconfigurable Intelligent Surfaces (RIS) with Power-Domain (PD) NOMA was proposed. The approach includes a Hierarchical Reinforcement Learning (HRL) algorithm for adaptive power allocation, leveraging a logarithmically-scaled reward function to promote training stability. The system was tested using several Monte Carlo simulations in a 30 GHz mmWave environment with 512-QAM modulation. This study utilized bespoke simulations in MATLAB, including realistic channel models to authenticate the proposed system. The results showed that the HRL-optimized combined mMIMO-CR-RIS system worked much better than the baseline setups. At a user density of 100 and a signal-to-noise ratio of 30 dB, the HRL-driven solution produced a peak average throughput of 4.99 Gbps, a latency of 2.91 ms, and a packet loss rate of 4.67%. These numbers are 18.5%, 32.6%, and 6.16% better than non-HRL benchmarks, respectively. The synergistic combination of RIS and CR, dynamically regulated by HRL is a profoundly successful technique for minimizing interference and boosting QoS in 6G networks.

Keywords: NOMA · CR · RIS · mMIMO · Hierarchical Reinforcement Learning (HRL)

1 Introduction

Earlier generations of communication were mostly built utilizing multiple antennas and orthogonal multiple access (OMA) methods, such as time-domain and frequency-domain multiple access. Currently, power-domain (PD) non-orthogonal multiple access (NOMA) has gained a great deal of interest in 5G and post-5G communication systems.

W. A. Mahmoud et al. (Eds.): ACDN 2025, CCIS 2798, pp. 86–99, 2026.
https://doi.org/10.1007/978-3-032-15448-4_6

Unlike traditional OMA systems, NOMA lets several users access the same orthogonal resource blocks (RBs) at the same time, which makes it much easier for them to communicate with one another. Superposition coding (SC) at the transmitter facilitates communications. Systems with more serious channel problems usually have more power in the supply chain than those with better channel conditions. This power distribution system ensures that all customers are treated fairly and makes it easier to apply the sequential interference cancellation (SIC) method [3]. SIC reads and removes content suited for less skilled users from messages meant for more skilled users [4].

The combination of NOMA with other tried-and-true multiple access methods, such as hybrid NOMA-OMA systems and multi-antenna NOMA systems [5, 6], improves its performance. These connected technologies provide users more options by letting them use different domains at the same time. Moreover, these hybrid systems make it easier to use NOMA in networks with a lot of people and make sure that latency requirements are met [7]. Cognitive radio (CR) technology provides opportunistic and on-demand connection and is known as a good way to manage spectrum that can handle the bandwidth problems in standard licensed wireless communication networks [8, 9]. There are two types of users in cognitive radio-based networks: primary (licensed) users (PUs) and secondary (unlicensed) users (SUs). Primary users have the most access to the spectrum, whereas secondary users try to make the most of the available spectrum when they can [10]. Because of this, CR technology is expected to be very important for the growth of large networks and meeting the fast needs of new wireless networks [11].

The CR runs mostly on Software Defined Radios (SDRs), which are more flexible hardware that can be modified by software. CR can adapt for best spectrum usage by being both flexible and aware of its operating radio environment, hence preserving the performance of main users. Due to its potential benefits over other approaches, the integration of CR with NOMA, also referred to as "CR-based NOMA," has attracted much interest within the scholarly community. The reason for this is that CR-based NOMA systems fit IoT-based network requirements. In particular, CR enables the opportunistic use of bandwidth whereas NOMA lets more IoT devices concurrently use the same resource block [12, 13].

As shown in [14] and [15], there have been many studies on how to construct CR-based NOMA systems and how to best use their resources. Millimeter Wave (mmWave) communication is quite popular right now since it can transport data at speeds of gigabits per second and uses a wide range of frequencies (30–300 GHz). However, it has a lot more route loss than lower frequency bands [16, 17]. Using additional antennas in a limited area to combine massive MIMO with mmWave reduces route loss [18]. The primary idea behind large MIMO is to employ a lot of antennas (N) to connect a lot of people (M) at once. The reconfigurable intelligent surface (RIS) has attracted significant attention owing to its cost-effectiveness and straightforward installation on building exteriors. The RIS is a two-dimensional meta surface that is constructed to modify the direction of wireless signals and reflect them in a specific way. RIS uses passive reflecting elements (REs). The reflection coefficient (amplitude and phase) reveals that each RE may reflect electromagnetic waves that hit it [19]. Changing the reflection coefficients adds the reflected signal in the right direction (the receiver) and breaks it down in other directions (to cut down on interference). Unlike other technologies like relays and MIMO beamforming [6], RIS does not need its own power supply. This means that RIS can help the wireless system utilize less energy and wider spectrum. The RIS in the mmWave mMIMO system enhances channel performance.

Authors in [20] looked at the differences between active and passive RIS-aided systems. To make a fair comparison, they assumed that both the base station and the RIS had the same amount of power. The system was graded based on their top seed. The results showed that active RIS worked best when there was not much power or numerous RIS parts. As the number of RIS parts grows, the power amplifiers need more power to work, which makes the active RIS's thermal noise level rise. In [21], an energy-efficient RIS replaced the usual hybrid precoder to drive the analogue precoder. Authors in [22] explained how active and passive RIS-assisted procedures were different from one other. To make the comparison, both the base station and the RIS received the same amount of electricity overall. The system was rated based on the highest overall rate it can attain. The results revealed that active RIS works best when there are not too many RIS pieces and the power budget is large. Adding extra RIS elements makes the power amplifiers use a lot of power, which increases the thermal noise in active RIS. In [23], an energy-efficient RIS substituted a normal hybrid precoder with an analog precoder.

The RIS partitioning method is discussed in [24]. The base station only needs one antenna, and each sub-surface is for one user. Authors in [25] examined a RIS system employing NOMA with only two users. They compared RIS-NOMA and RIS-OMA and demonstrated that NOMA helped users consume less energy. Neither [24] nor [25] included the mmWave spectrum and instead they both focused on passive RIS. Additionally, [23] investigated the benefits of RIS in a parasitic radio system. The authors came up with both passive and active RIS and BS beamforming methods to use less power while sending signals from the BS. There were two restrictions that the designs had to follow: the fastest speed for core communication and the signal-to-interference-plus-noise ratio (SINR) for decoding data that bounced back. The system models in [26, 27] examined networks in which users utilized a single antenna, hence constraining the performance of the network equipment. Most of the early studies on RIS-enabled NOMA systems assumed a wholly stable channel, which is unrealistic in practice. Additional research on enhancing performance in the NOMA process is essential. The findings compel us to examine QoS performance in a hybrid system.

This paper highlights key contributions, including a comprehensive simulation framework comparing mMIMO-NOMA with CR and RIS, development of simplified mmWave channel and RIS models, and a customized Hierarchical Reinforcement Learning framework for adaptive power allocation to enhance SINR, throughput, latency, and packet loss. The framework was validated through extensive Monte Carlo simulations with realistic assumptions, including 30 GHz bandwidth, 256-antenna mMIMO, and 512-element RIS. Section 2 outlines the mathematical formulation techniques and the attributes of the network model. Section 3 delineates the suggested system parameters, findings, and debates. Section 4 offers closing insights and recommendations for further research.

2 System Model

This study focuses on a wireless network. Figure 1 illustrates that the network consists of many user groups employing mMIMO DL NOMA, CR integration, and mmWave technologies. The differing distances of users from the base station (BS) result in a broad spectrum of received power levels. The network transmits signals using 512-quadrature amplitude modulation (QAM). There are u users and NOMA functions within the PD.

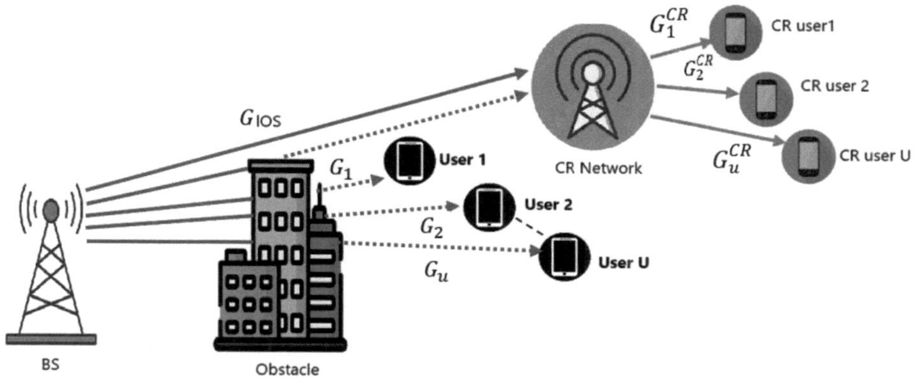

Fig. 1. Two networks with U users

Each channel is produced as a complicated Gaussian distribution (Rayleigh fading), as shown in Eq. (1) [28, 29].

$$H_{u,a} = \frac{1}{\sqrt{2}}(N(0, 1) + j \cdot N(0, 1)) \tag{1}$$

Where $H_{u,a}$ is detailed channel coefficient between user u and antenna a.

The amount of transmit power given to user u is a proportion of the overall system power, as stated in Eq. (2).

$$P_u = \alpha_u P_{total}, u = 1, 2, ..., U \tag{2}$$

where, P_u is Permitted power for user u, α_u is a user-specific power allocation factor that shows how important or fair the user is, and P_{total} is system power.

To make sure that the overall power given out does not go beyond the system power available, the allocation factors must meet the normalization condition in Eq. (3).

$$\sum\nolimits_{u=1}^{U} \alpha_u = 1 \tag{3}$$

In downlink (DL) PD-NOMA with successive interference cancellation (SIC), user u first decodes and cancels signals from users with indices $i < u$. This means that when user u decodes its own signal, the only residual interference originates from users with indices $i > u$. Therefore, the SINR after SIC is given by Eq. (4).

$$SINR_u = \frac{P_u|h_u|^2}{\sum_{i=u+1}^{U} P_i|h_u|^2 + N_0 + \epsilon} \tag{4}$$

Where $|h_u|^2$ is the channel gain (the strength of the channel coefficient) for user u, $P_u|h_u|^2$ is the usable signal power that user u receives, N_0 is the power of the noise at the receiver, and ϵ is a tiny positive number that is added to avoid difficulties with dividing by zero and to show the noise floor.

From the channel matrix $H \in C^{K \times N}$, total number of transmit antennas (N) and total number of users (U) are obtained [30].

Equation (5) yields the channel gain (G_u) for user u.

$$G_u \triangleq \|h_u\|^2 \tag{5}$$

Where h_u is the channel vector for user u in the channel matrix H's $u - th$ row.

Equation (6) indicates the capacity (C_u) of user u [30],

$$C_u = B \cdot log_2(1 + SINR_u \cdot G_u) \tag{6}$$

where B is bandwidth.

The total throughput (T) for mMIMO is given in Eq. (7)

$$\mathcal{T}_{mMIMO} = \sum_{u=1}^{U} C_u \tag{7}$$

Assuming the CR user utilizes the spectrum through an underlay/overlay paradigm, its SINR expression must align with SIC. The CR user u experiences residual NOMA interference only from users $i > u$ and, if present, interference from primary users (PUs). Equation (8) provides a general, precise CR SINR.

$$SINR_{CR,u} = \frac{P_u|g_u|^2}{\sum_{i>u} P_i\left|g_{i,u}\right|^2 + \sum_{p \in P} P_p\left|g_{p,u}\right|^2 + \sigma^2 + \epsilon} \tag{8}$$

Where P is the set of PUs (empty if there are none), P_p is the power of the PU transmitters, and $g_{p,u}$ is the gain of the PU $\rightarrow$ SU channel.

Figure 2 demonstrates how the reflective elements of the intelligent RIS device may improve communication quality by modifying the phase of incoming electromagnetic waves.

The SINR for CR [31] integration with RIS user is defined in Eq. (9) [32],

$$SINR_u^{CR+RIS} = \frac{\left|\left(h_{d,u}^T + h_{r,u}^T \Theta G\right) w_u\right|^2 P_u}{\sum_{i>u}\left|\left(h_{d,u}^T + h_{r,u}^T \Theta G\right) w_i\right|^2 P_i + \sum_{p \in P}\left|g_{p,u}\right|^2 P_p + \sigma^2 + \epsilon} \tag{9}$$

where $h_{d,u}^T$ is the direct channel vector that goes from the BS to user u, $h_{r,u}^T$ is the channel vector that connects the RIS to user u, Θ RIS is reflection matrix (diagonal), where each

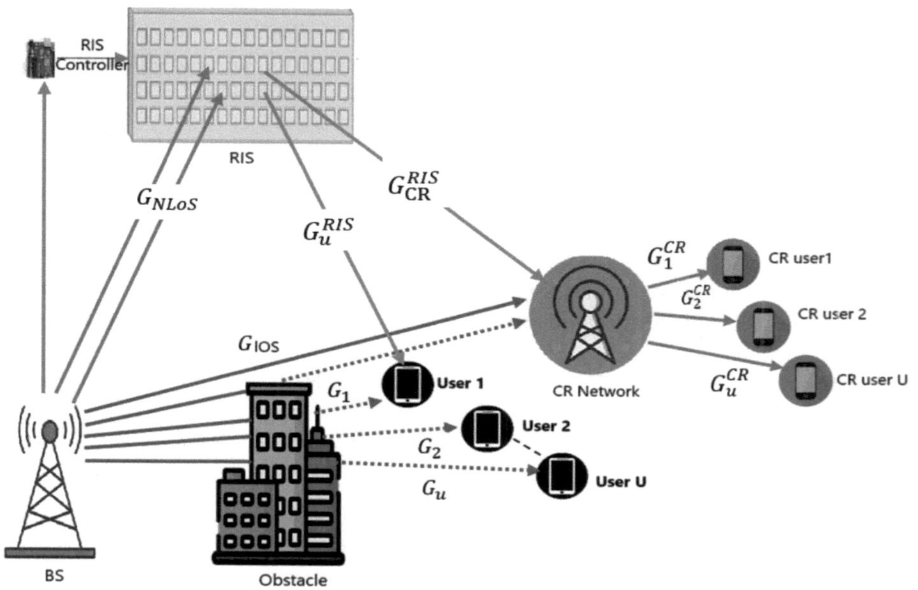

Fig. 2. Two networks with U users and RIS method

member is a phase shift that a RIS element applies. The G Channel matrix goes from the BS to the RIS. Beamforming vector w_u is sent to user u.

The channel matrix with RIS assistance $H_{RIS} \in C^{U \times N_{RIS}}$, where the channel gain [32] is:

$$G_u^{RIS} \triangleq \|h_{d,u}^T + h_{r,u}^T \Theta G\|^2 \tag{10}$$

$$C_u^{CR+RIS} = B\left(1 + SINR_u^{CR+RIS}\right) \tag{11}$$

The throughput is calculated in a manner analogous to Eq. (12)

$$\Gamma_{mMIMO-CR-RIS} = \sum\nolimits_{u=1}^{U} C_u \tag{12}$$

The latency (L) of the user u is:

$$L_u = \frac{R_u}{C_u} \tag{13}$$

Then the Packet Loss (PL) is expressed in Eq. (14).

$$PL = \sum\nolimits_{u=1}^{U} 1(SINR_u < SINR_{threshold}) \tag{14}$$

The indicator function, denoted as 1, equals 1 if the specified condition is satisfied, and 0 if it is not.

The logarithm HRL in many reinforcement learning difficulties, rewards vary substantially. Logarithmic transformations compress the reward scale to avoid big rewards from impacting learning [33]. Equation (15) shows how to utilize HRL to allocate power to user u.

$$P_u = \frac{u^{\delta}}{\sum_{i=1}^{U} i^{\delta}} \cdot P_{total} \tag{15}$$

The user index for power allocation is u and i is the user index in the summation used to normalise overall power allocation. The shaping factor δ affects power distribution among consumers. This formulation enables HRL to determine δ adaptively in response to channel feedback.

Equation (16) shows the SINR that user u gets when HRL power allocation is used.

$$SINR_u = \frac{P_u \cdot \gamma_u}{\sum_{i=1}^{u-1} P_i \cdot \gamma_u + \sigma^2} \tag{16}$$

Where P_i represents the power assigned to user i, γ_u represents the channel gain between user u and the receiver, σ^2 represents noise power, and P_u represents user i's power. This fits with PD-NOMA SIC, user u cancels signals from users $i < u$ and yet has some interference from users $i > u$.

In a CR setting, using the RIS increases the SINR, as shown in Eq. (17),

$$SINR_u^{CR+RIS} = SINR_u \cdot (\alpha + \beta \cdot u) \cdot log_2(1 + u) \tag{17}$$

The goal of HRL is to maximize cumulative reward. The benefits may vary greatly, making it hard for the user to balance exploration and exploitation, as shown in the algorithmic (1) steps. Logarithmic functions compress reward space and prevent big values from dominating learning. The goal of the HRL agent is to achieve the most cumulative throughput. Equation (18) defines the immediate reward signal as follows,

$$R(s, a) = Throughput(s, a) \tag{18}$$

Where $R(s, a)$ is the reward, particularly the throughput attained by performing action a in state s.

As demonstrated in Eq. (19), the reward is compressed using a logarithmic function since raw throughput numbers might be quite large and make training unstable.

$$R(s, a) = log(1 + Throughput(s, a)) \tag{19}$$

To encourage $H(\pi)$ exploration, HRL uses an entropy term in its policy $\pi(a \mid s)$. The entropy of the policy distribution is given in Eq. (20).

$$\mathcal{H}(\pi) = -\sum_a \pi(a \mid s) log\pi(a \mid s) \tag{20}$$

Where $\pi(a \mid s)$ represents the probability of performing action in state s.

Equation (21) gives the total goal function that finds the right balance between maximizing throughput and exploration,

$$J(\theta) = E_{\pi_\theta}[Reward] - \lambda H(\pi_\theta) \tag{21}$$

Where π_θ is policy parameters, E_{π_θ} is expected cumulative reward for policy π_θ, (π_θ) is policy entropy, indicating action selection uncertainty or unpredictability. The Entropy coefficient (λ) balances reward and exploration (entropy).

The Kullback-Leibler (KL) divergence, described in Eq. (22), was used to compare learnt policies to a reference distribution.

$$D_{KL}(P\|Q) = \sum_x P(x)log\left(\frac{P(x)}{Q(x)}\right) \tag{22}$$

where $P(x)$ is the true distribution (observed or real) and $Q(x)$ is predicted or approximate distribution

Algorithm (1): HRL-based Power Allocation in PD-NOMA

Input:

State space s, action space a, P_{total} , B, α, γ, λ, KL β, E, steps T.

Initialize:

Policy network $\pi_\theta(a \mid s)$, value function $V\phi(s)$, experience buffer D.

For E =1 to E:

1. Observe initial state s_0.
2. **For** $t = 0$ to $T - 1$:
   - Select action $a_t \sim \pi_\theta(a \mid s_t)$.
   - Allocate powers / RIS phases accordingly.
   - Compute throughput (s_t, a_t).
   - Reward: $R(s_t,a_t)$
   - Observe next state s_{t+1}, store (s_t,a_t,R_t,s_{t+1}) *in D*.
3. **End For**

Policy Update:

- Estimate return.
- Update critic.

End For

3 Simulation Results and Discussion

Table 1 delineates the simulation parameters for several models of network. The mMIMO NOMA device graphs illustrate the variations in average throughput, latency, and packet loss in relation to user density across many configurations. The results indicate that prior to and following the introduction of RIS, the challenges posed by the heightened user density in 6G networks are addressed.

Average throughput and user density for mmWave mMIMO NOMA, mmWave mMIMO CR NOMA, and mmWave mMIMO DL CR with RIS on the 6G network are shown in Fig. 3. The users have channels with differing power distribution and distance. The average throughput for mMIMO NOMA is 2.8 Gbps, 2.91 Gbps for mMIMO NOMA + CR; and 3.43 Gbps for mMIMO + CR + RIS at a user density of 100. Using RIS improves average throughput for experienced users above their performance without RIS.

Table 1. Parameters of the simulators employed to replicate the models.

Parameter	Value
Number of User	100
Number of Antennas	256 × 256
RIS	512 × 512
Modulations	512 QAM
Bandwidth	GHz30
SNR	0 to 30 dB

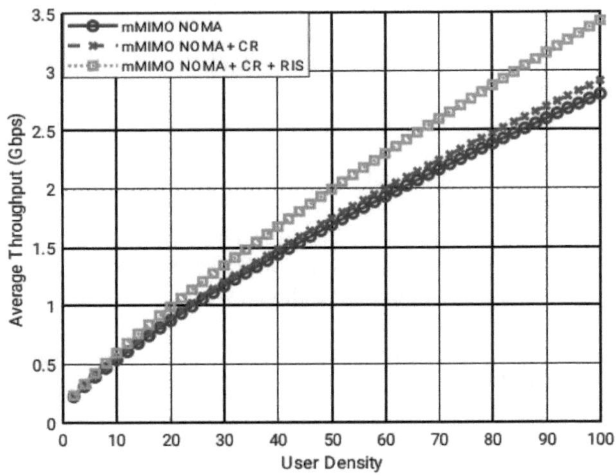

Fig. 3. Average throughput versus user density for three models.

Figure 4 shows the correlation between average throughput and user density for mmWave mMIMO NOMA, mmWave mMIMO CR NOMA, and mmWave mMIMO DL CR with RIS within the context of 6G network integration utilizing HRL logarithm. At a user density of 100, the average throughput for HRL mMIMO NOMA is 3.13 Gbps, 4.04 Gbps for HRL mMIMO NOMA + CR, and 4.99 Gbps for HRL mMIMO + CR + RIS. The use of HRL logarithm across the three models results in a notable enhancement in average performance throughput, increasing by 5.6%, 12.7%, and 18.5%, respectively, compared to their performance without HRL at SNR of 30 dB.

The latency and user density for mmWave mMIMO NOMA, mmWave mMIMO CR NOMA, and mmWave mMIMO DL CR with RIS on the 6G network are illustrated in Fig. 5. The latency for mMIMO NOMA is 2.13 ms, 2.73 ms for mMIMO NOMA + CR, and 1.48 ms for mMIMO + CR + RIS at a user density of 100. Utilizing RIS enhances latency for proficient users compared to their performance without RIS.

Figure 6 illustrates the relationship between latency and user density for mmWave mMIMO NOMA, mmWave mMIMO CR NOMA, and mmWave mMIMO DL CR with

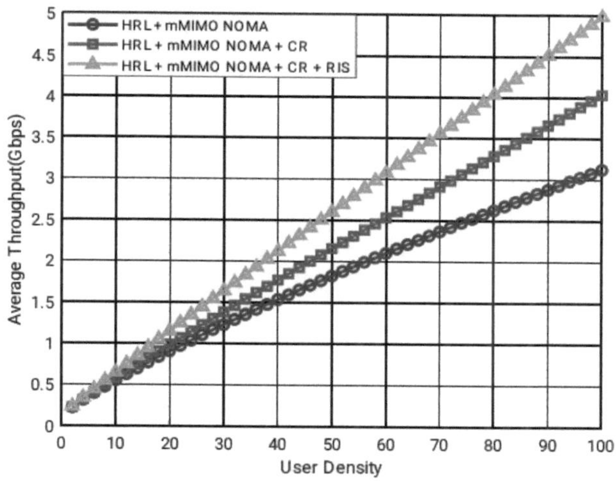

Fig. 4. Average throughput in relation to user density across three models with the HRL logarithm.

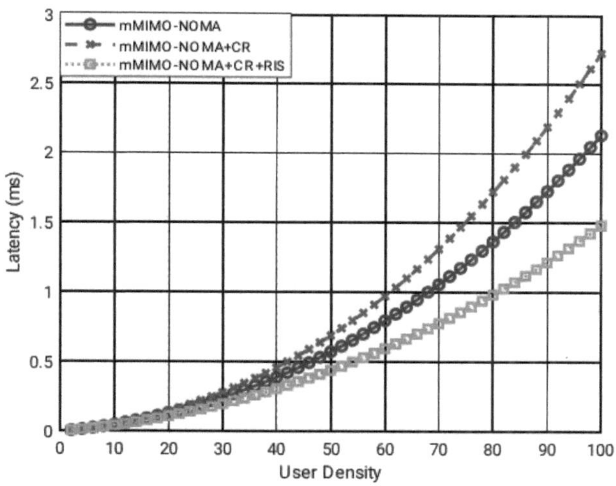

Fig. 5. Latency in relation to user density for three models.

RIS in the framework of 6G network integration with HRL logarithm. At a user density of 100, the latency for HRL mMIMO NOMA is 3.5 ms, 3.64 ms for HRL mMIMO NOMA + CR, and 2.91 ms for HRL mMIMO + CR + RIS. The use of HRL logarithm across the three models yields a significant improvement in latency performance, with increases of 24.3%, 14.3%, and 32.6%, respectively, relative to their performance without HRL, with 30 dB SNR.

Figure 7 shows the packet loss and user density for mmWave mMIMO NOMA, mmWave mMIMO CR NOMA, and mmWave mMIMO DL CR with RIS the 6G network. With a user density of 100 the packet loss rates are 12.17% for mMIMO NOMA, 12.83%

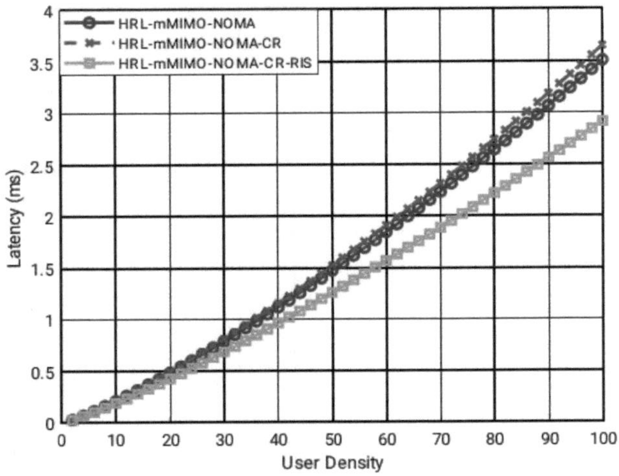

Fig. 6. Latency in proportion to user density across three models utilizing the HRL logarithm.

for mMIMO NOMA + CR, and 10.83% for mMIMO + CR + RIS. Using RIS improved the packet loss rate for experienced users to some extent relative to their performance without RIS.

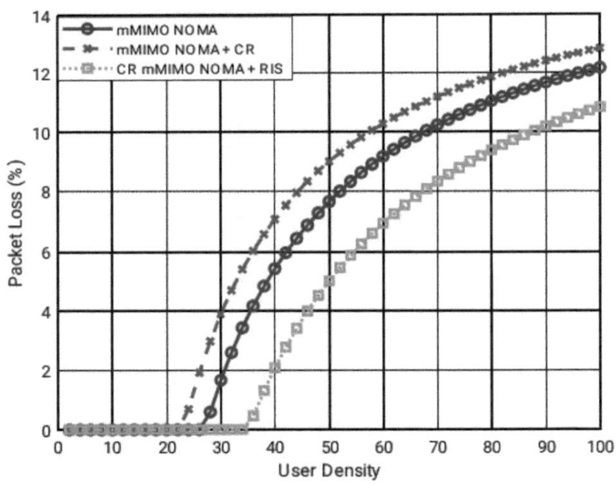

Fig. 7. Three models' packet loss rate with respect to user density.

Figure 8 depicts the correlation between packet loss rate and user density for mmWave mMIMO NOMA, mmWave mMIMO CR NOMA, and mmWave mMIMO DL CR with RIS within the context of 6G network integration utilizing HRL logarithm. At a user density of 100, the packet loss rate for HRL mMIMO NOMA is 7.83%, 9.17% for HRL mMIMO NOMA + CR, and 4.67% for HRL mMIMO + CR + RIS. The application of HRL logarithm in the three models yields a straightforward enhancement in packet loss rate performance, with improvements of 4.34%, 3.66%, and 6.16%, respectively, compared to their performance without HRL at SNR of 30 dB.

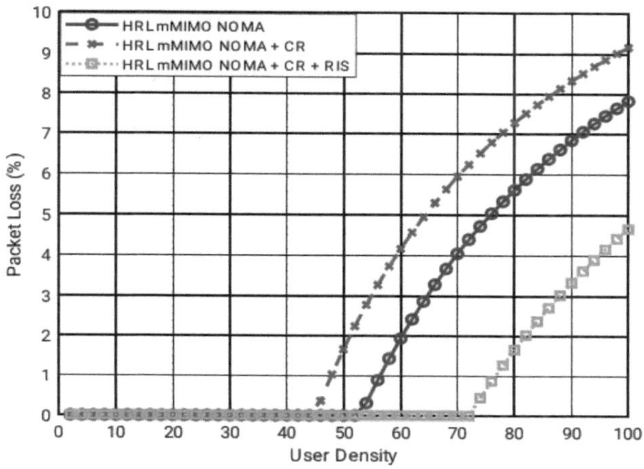

Fig. 8. Packet loss rate relative to user density across three models employing the HRL logarithm.

4 Conclusion

The results indicated that the integrated mMIMO-NOMA-CR-RIS architecture, dynamically optimized using a hierarchical reinforcement learning (HRL) framework, outperformed other alternatives. The proposed system (HRL mMIMO + CR + RIS) achieved a data rate of 4.99 Gbps, a latency of 2.91 ms, and a packet loss rate of 4.67% at high traffic density. This is a clear indication of significant performance benefits. These results are significantly superior to those of other settings. The HRL optimizer alone improved throughput by up to 18.5%, latency by 32.6%, and packet loss rate by 6.16% compared to static allocation. The main contribution of this work is demonstrating how HRL can be used to address the complex interactions between these advanced technologies. Clearly, HRL technology is capable of shifting resources as needed and improving quality of service under congested network conditions. The significant changes in the fully integrated system demonstrate how efficiently CR and RIS work together when controlled by a single intelligent system. The results revealed an improvement in packet loss; however, not as much as expected. This suggests that this parameter may require more precise approaches to optimization. A key challenge with the study was its exclusive focus on fixed-channel scenarios, which set a performance limit and ignored mobility challenges. Therefore, further research should validate these encouraging results in alternative scenarios and enhance HRL to enable real-time operation.

References

1. Gamal, S., Rihan, M., Hussin, S., Zaghloul, A., Salem, A.A.: Multiple access in cognitive radio networks: from orthogonal and non-orthogonal to rate-splitting. IEEE Access **9**, 95569–95584 (2021)

2. Liu, Y., Xing, H., Pan, C., Nallanathan, A., Elkashlan, M., Hanzo, L.: Multiple-antenna-assisted non-orthogonal multiple access. IEEE Wirel. Commun. **25**(2), 17–23 (2018)
3. Liu, Y., et al.: Evolution of NOMA toward next generation multiple access (NGMA) for 6G. IEEE J. Sel. Areas Commun. **40**(4), 1037–1071 (2022)
4. Gurugopinath, S., Al-Hammadi, Y., Sofotasios, P.C., Muhaidat, S., Dobre, O.A.: Non-orthogonal multiple access with wireless caching for 5G-enabled vehicular networks. IEEE Netw. **34**(5), 127–133 (2020)
5. Hassan, M., Singh, M., Hamid, K.: Survey on NOMA and spectrum sharing techniques in 5G. In: 2021 IEEE International Conference on Smart Information Systems and Technologies (SIST), Nur-Sultan, Kazakhstan (2021)
6. Hassan, M., et al.: BER improvement of cooperative spectrum sharing of NOMA in 5G network. In: 2023 IEEE 3rd International Maghreb Meeting of the Conference on Sciences and Techniques of Automatic Control and Computer Engineering (MI-STA), Benghazi, Libya (2023)
7. Hassan, M., et al.: NOMA cooperative spectrum sharing average capacity improvement in 5G network. In: 2023 IEEE 3rd International Maghreb Meeting of the Conference on Sciences and Techniques of Automatic Control and Computer Engineering (MI-STA), Benghazi, Libya (2023)
8. Hassan, M., et al.: Overview of cognitive radio networks. J. Phys. Conf. Ser. **1831**. International Conference on Robotics and Artificial Intelligence (RoAI) 2020 28-29 December 2020
9. Bhattacharjee, S., Acharya, T., Bhattacharya, U.: Cognitive radio based spectrum sharing models for multicasting in 5G cellular networks: a survey. Comput. Netw. **208** (2022)
10. Ostovar, A., Zikria, Y.B., Kim, H.S., Ali, R.: Optimization of resource allocation model with energy-efficient cooperative sensing in green cognitive radio networks. IEEE Access **8**, 141594–141610 (2020)
11. Loghin, D., et al.: The disruptions of 5G on data-driven technologies and applications. IEEE Trans. Knowl. Data Eng. **32**(6), 1179–1198 (2020)
12. Do, D.-T., Le, A.-T., Lee, B.M.: NOMA in cooperative underlay cognitive radio networks under imperfect SIC. IEEE Access **8**, 86180–86195 (2020)
13. ElHalawany, B.M., El-Banna, A.A.A., Pham, Q.-V., Wu, K., Mohamed, E.M.: Spectrum sharing in cognitive-radio-inspired NOMA systems under imperfect SIC and cochannel interference. IEEE Syst. J. **16**(1), 1540–1547 (2022)
14. Salameh, H.B., Abdel-Razeq, S., Al-Obiedollah, H.: Integration of cognitive radio technology in NOMA-based B5G networks: state of the art, challenges, and enabling technologies. IEEE Access **11**, 12949–12962 (2023)
15. Tseng, S.-M., Chen, Y.-F., Tsai, C.-S., Tsai, W.-D.: Deep-learning-aided cross-layer resource allocation of OFDMA/NOMA video communication systems. IEEE Access **7**, 157730–157740 (2019)
16. Wang, X., et al.: Millimeter wave communication: a comprehensive survey. IEEE Commun. Surv. Tutor. **20**(3), 1616–1653 (2018)
17. Zrar Ghafoor, K., et al.: Millimeter-wave communication for Internet of Vehicles: status, challenges, and perspectives. IEEE Internet Things J. **7**(9), 8525–8546 (2020)
18. Elmezughi, M.K., Afullo, T.J.: An efficient approach of improving path loss models for future mobile networks in enclosed indoor environments. IEEE Access **9**, 110332–110345 (2021)
19. Liu, Y., et al.: Reconfigurable intelligent surfaces: principles and opportunities. IEEE Commun. Surv. Tutor. **23**(3), 1546–1577 (2021)
20. Zhang, Z., et al.: Active RIS vs. passive RIS: which will prevail in 6G? IEEE Trans. Commun. **71**(3), 1707–1725 (2023)

21. Daghari, N.K., Elganimi, T.Y., Rabie, K.M.: Energy-efficient hybrid precoding schemes for RIS-assisted millimeter-wave massive MIMO. In: 2021 IEEE International Mediterranean Conference on Communications and Networking (MeditCom), Athens, Greece (2021)
22. Lv, W., Bai, J., Yan, Q., Wang, H.M.: RIS-assisted green secure communications: active RIS or passive RIS? IEEE Wirel. Commun. Lett. **12**(2), 237–241 (2023)
23. Sun, Y., et al.: Energy-efficient hybrid beamforming for multilayer RIS-assisted secure integrated terrestrial-aerial networks. IEEE Trans. Commun. **70**(6), 4189–4210 (2022)
24. Ren, J., Lei, X., Peng, Z., Tang, X., Dobre, O.A.: RIS-assisted cooperative NOMA With SWIPT. IEEE Wirel. Commun. Lett. **12**(3), 446–450 (2023)
25. Liu, R., et al.: Resource allocation for NOMA-enabled cognitive satellite–UAV–terrestrial networks with imperfect CSI. IEEE Trans. Cognitive Commun. Netw. **9**(4), 963–976 (2023)
26. Zhao, B., Zhang, C., Yi, W., Liu, Y.: Ergodic rate analysis of STAR-RIS aided NOMA systems. IEEE Commun. Lett. **26**(10), 2297–2301 (2022)
27. Karim, F., Singh, S.K., Singh, K., Flanagan, M.F.: STAR-RIS aided full duplex communication system: performance analysis. In: GLOBECOM 2022 - 2022 IEEE Global Communications Conference, Rio de Janeiro, Brazil (2022)
28. Ding, Z., Lei, X., Karagiannidis, G.K., Schober, R., Yuan, J., Bhargava, V.K.: A survey on non-orthogonal multiple access for 5G networks: research challenges and future trends. IEEE J. Sel. Areas Commun. **35**(10), 2181–2195 (2017)
29. Björnson, E., Hoydis, J., Sanguinetti, L.: Massive MIMO has unlimited capacity. IEEE Trans. Wirel. Commun. **17**(1), 574–590 (2018)
30. Wang, M., Gao, F., Jin, S., Lin, H.: An overview of enhanced massive MIMO with array signal processing techniques. IEEE J. Sel. Top. Signal Process. **13**(5), 886–901 (2019)
31. Jameel, F., Wyne, S., Kaddoum, G., Duong, T.Q.: A comprehensive survey on cooperative relaying and jamming strategies for physical layer security. IEEE Commun. Surv. Tutor. **21**(3), 2734–2771 (2019)
32. Wu, Q., Zhang, R.: Towards smart and reconfigurable environment: intelligent reflecting surface aided wireless network. IEEE Commun. Mag. **58**(1), 106–112 (2020)
33. Xiong, Z., Zhang, Y., Niyato, D., Deng, R., Wang, P., Wang, L.-C.: Deep reinforcement learning for mobile 5G and beyond: fundamentals, applications, and challenges. IEEE Veh. Technol. Mag. **14**(2), 44–52 (2019)

Spectral Efficiency Improvement Using Joint Non-orthogonal Multiple Access and Spatial Modulation NOMA-SM

Khalifa Abboud Salim[1(✉)] and Maryam K. Abboud[2]

[1] URUK University, Baghdad, Iraq
dr.khalifaabboud@uruk.edu.iq
[2] Electrical Engineering Technical College, Middle Technical University, Baghdad, Iraq
maryam.khalifa@mtu.edu.iq

Abstract. SM-MIMO system refers to the Spatial Modulation-transmission technique that was introduced as an energy efficient Multiple Input-Multiple Output systems. Only single transmit antenna is activated in SM at a time. Therefore, the activated antenna and constellation size of Amplitude Phase modulated data are used for the indexing of the information bits. In the SM, the Inter-Channel-Interference (ICI) is avoided, which reduces hardware complexity, and power consumption. Non-Orthogonal-Multiple-Access (NOMA) is a hopeful technique which is used as a multiple access scheme over power domain for 6G era wireless networks. A novel approach to improve spectral efficiency and performance enhancement for 5G systems and beyond was presented by combining NOMA with SM. The spatial domain utilization in NOMA systems enables them to simultaneously serve a number of users using different communication resources, time, frequency, or space without the need for full MIMO complexity. This joint approach enables the development of a scalable and energy efficient communication system that enhances user capacity and efficient resource utilization. Improved performance enhancement of NOMA was carried through jointly applying NOMA-SM schemes to enhance total sum rate in addition to Inter User Interference cancellation and SIC.

Keywords: NOMA · SM · 5G · SIC

1 Introduction

To meet the increasing demand for high traffic in wireless-communication, two basic limiting factors should be handled will be faced; congested spectrum allocation and energy consumption. To improve spectral efficiency for 5G communication systems a new dimension of multiple access has been adopted. NOMA superposes multi-users simultaneously in a non-orthogonal way such as the PD-power domain or CD-code domain [1, 19]. The power-domain NOMA system has been presented to be a promising technique for 5G to achieve high spectral efficiency. NOMA provides users with the same time frequency resources, so that users' data are integrated in the power domain while

W. A. Mahmoud et al. (Eds.): ACDN 2025, CCIS 2798, pp. 100–111, 2026.
https://doi.org/10.1007/978-3-032-15448-4_7

traditional Orthogonal Multiple Access used in 4G allocates different time-frequency resources for each user. At the receiver side, Successive Interference Cancellation SIC should be employed in order to recover the inter user interference [2, 20]. The NOMA power allocation criteria for different users are based on channel state conditions. That means, users or subscribers with good channel conditions are allocated less power while others with poor channel conditions are allocated more power to facilitate the discovery of users with less power through SIC [3, 4]. Spatial Modulation SM emerged to overcome the energy consumption of traditional MIMO schemes, where the number of radio frequency channels is the same as the transmit antennas number [5, 6].

The data stream in SM is divided into two-part groups where one part is mapped to a symbol which represents one of the constellation diagrams used in the transmission, and the other part is used to activate one of the transmit antennas. Hence, one RF chain is required at each slot of time which results in high energy efficient technique compared to MIMO technique.

This paper presents a power domain NOMA which can be used for downlink multiuser wireless communication systems combined with SM in order to mend the spectral efficiency, hardware complexity reduction, and inter channel interference avoidance.

The rest of this paper discusses the fundamental principles of the NOMA system in Sect. 2. In Sect. 3, power domain NOMA is discussed. Section 4 demonstrates the modelling of the NOMA-SM system. Finally, simulation results of BER performance of 2 users is presented in Sect. 5 over Rayliegh fading channel. While, Sect. 6 remarks main conclusions and future works.

2 NOMA with SIC Basics

Different from the current 4G which uses orthogonal radio access scheme, NOMA uses an additional power domain for multiuser separation which can be achieved through Successive Interference Cancellation SIC at sender's side. At the destination side, SIC may be viewed as a drawback due to receiver complexity as shown in Fig. 1. This complexity is because the receiver performs its own data demodulation in addition to other user equipment's data and processing latency. NOMA's performance highly depends on channel gain differences between users or user equipment's UE's [7].

The most important principle of power-domain NOMA which is adopted in this work is that it multiplexes diverse users through the same (time/frequency) resources simultaneously via assigning each user a different transmit power level. This can be done due to the path loss variation of each user [2, 8, 22]. Superposition coding is the basic coding scheme used to transmit signals simultaneously. Where, high-power is assigned to the signal with bad channel-conditions or low SINR while low-power is assigned to the signal with good-channel condition or high SINR. This ensures less interference between users at the final signal destination. Successive-Interference-Cancellation SIC was found to be effective when the difference in the channel state information or power level between users is large. Therefore, if two users are considered then SIC is used only at the receiver with lowest power or good channel state because a user with large power or poor channel condition interferes with the user with lowest power. Thus, high power signal must be removed from the multiplexed signal before data detection. However, signals associated with poor channel conditions or assigned with higher power are decoded without the need for SIC.

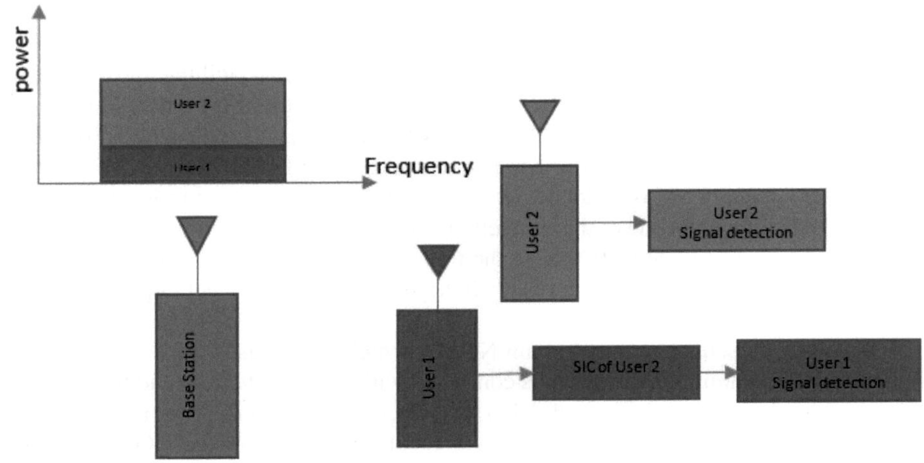

Fig. 1. Two user power domain down-link NOMA with SIC

3 Power-Domain-NOMA (PD-NOMA)

Using power-domain NOMA, users can be served using the same communication resources by allocating different power to different users with a controllable interference. In this article only power domain was considered, where multiple users were accommodated through allocation within the same time, and frequency at various power levels. The power-level allocation to each user depends on the user's channel state and signal variation [2, 8].

The transmitted signal consists of the multiplexed signals with superposition coding where SIC is applied at the user end to recover the different signals. The key idea behind power-domain NOMA is that the signals of the nearest subscriber (user) with good channel-condition are encoded with low power assignment whereas the other farthest user or the user with bad channel conditions is assigned high power levels. Let $x_1, x_2, \ldots\ldots x_N$ denotes messages to be transmitted, then the NOMA signal may be written as:

$$x_{NOMA} = \sqrt{p}\sum\nolimits_{1}^{K} \sqrt{\alpha_i}x_i \tag{1}$$

Where α_i, is the fractional power coefficient of the transmitted signal, $i \in \{1,2, \ldots .N\}$ and p refers to the total power, $\alpha_1 > \alpha_2 > \ldots\cdots > \alpha_N$ of the received signal:

$$y_i^{NOMA} = h_i x_{NOMA} + w_i \tag{2}$$

Where h_i is the Rayleigh fading channel, w_i is the AWGN vector of zero-mean, and σ^2 variance, $w_i = \mathcal{N}(0, \sigma^2)$. The received-signal may be rewritten as:

$$y_i^{NOMA} = h_i\sqrt{p}\sum\nolimits_{i=1}^{N} \sqrt{\alpha_i}x_i + w_i \tag{3}$$

For a two-user down link PD-NOMA where the two users are served via the base-station BS, the received-vector at first far user may be written as:

$$y_1^{NOMA} = h_1\sqrt{p}\left(\sqrt{\alpha_1}x_1 + \sqrt{\alpha_2}x_2\right) + w_1 \tag{4}$$

From the above equation, x_1 can be estimated directly because the signal is dominating due to high power allocated to user 1 ($\alpha_1 > \alpha_2$), the rest of the signal or user 2's message is treated as a noise. Subsequently, the obtainable rate of user 1 equals to:

$$R_1^{NOMA} = log2\left(1 + \frac{|h_1|^2 p\alpha_1}{|h_1|^2 p\alpha_2 + \sigma^2}\right) \tag{5}$$

While, at the second user, the acknowledged or received vector is as follows:

$$y_2^{NOMA} = h_2\sqrt{p}\left(\sqrt{\alpha_1}x_1 + \sqrt{\alpha_2}x_2\right) + w_2 \tag{6}$$

Based on the process of SIC, the signal of user1 is subtracted and yields the following signal:

$$y{'}_2^{NOMA} = h_2\sqrt{p}\left(\sqrt{\alpha_1}x_1 + \sqrt{\alpha_2}x_2\right) + w_2 - h_2\sqrt{p}\sqrt{\alpha_1}x_1 \tag{7}$$

Achievable rate of second user is:

$$R_2^{NOMA} = log2\left(1 + \frac{|h_2|^2 p\alpha_2}{\sigma^2}\right) \tag{8}$$

In general, the achievable rate of any user for NOMA the throughput is given by [2]:

$$R_k^{NOMA} = log_2\left(1 + \frac{\alpha_k \rho |h_k|^2}{1 + \alpha_{k+1}\rho |h_k|^2}\right) \tag{9}$$

The sum-rate of all users is:

$$R_{sum}^{NOMA} = \sum\nolimits_{i=1}^{N} R_i^{NOMA} \tag{10}$$

This means that the terminal user with poor-channel-conditions can extract their signal directly without-SIC, while the terminal user with good-channel-condition should apply SIC to recover their signal. In conclusion, users with good channel condition can take advantage of communication resources which cannot be utilized by users with bad channel condition without performance degradation and hence overall system throughput improves.

However, OMA schemes can be used only by the user with good channel condition, which leads to inefficient spectral usage. For two-user OMA system, the throughput due to Shannon channel capacity for user1 and 2 is given by [2]:

$$R_1^{OMA} = \beta log2\left(1 + \frac{|h_1|^2 p}{\beta\sigma^2}\right) \tag{11}$$

$$R_2^{OMA} = (1-\beta) log2\left(1 + \frac{|h_2|^2 p}{(1-\beta)\sigma^2}\right) \tag{12}$$

Where β is a normalized resource allocation coefficient and p is the allocated-power if no power control is used. As a result, the sum-rate of all subscribers in OMA may be written as:

$$R_{sum}^{OMA} = \sum_{i=1}^{N} R_i^{OMA} \tag{13}$$

In case of two users the sum-rate-achieved by OMA may be represented as follows:

$$R_{sum}^{OMA} = R_1^{OMA} + R_2^{OMA} = \frac{1}{2} log2\left(1 + \gamma|h_1|^2\right) + \frac{1}{2} log2\left(1 + \gamma|h_2|^2\right) \tag{14}$$

Where γ refers to the transmit Signal-to-Noise- Ratio SNR. For very high SNR equation, (14) and (10) can be reduced to [2]:

$$R_{sum}^{NOMA} \approx log2\left(\gamma|h_2|^2\right) \tag{15}$$

$$R_{sum}^{OMA} \approx log2\left(\gamma\sqrt{|h_1|^2|h_2|^2}\right) \tag{16}$$

$$\therefore R_{sum}^{Gain} = R_{sum}^{NOMA} - R_{sum}^{OMA} = \frac{1}{2} log2\left(\frac{|h_2|^2}{|h_1|^2}\right) \tag{17}$$

It can be concluded that the value of throughput gain varies according to the difference of channel gain between users. However, power domain NOMA has the following advantages;

1. Different users may be served-simultaneously by dedicating the same communication time, and frequency-resources. However, different power levels are assigned to each user such that multiple access can be realized [9–12].
2. Fairness: In OMA technique users with bad channel conditions do not take advantage of the transmitted power while users with good channel conditions do. In this case weak users cannot take the opportunity to transmit for a long time. However, using power domain NOMA both users are given the chance to transmit information data with controlled interference.
3. In NOMA, various users can be served simultaneously by controlling the allocated power for each user using the same time and frequency communication resources. This means bandwidth efficient utilization whereas OMA assigns each user with its own resource which resulted in inefficient bandwidth utilization [2, 13, 14, 21].

Power domain NOMA disadvantages:

1. The use of power domain NOMA requires a receiver equipped with SIC which can be a drawback due to its complexity. User separation in such receivers requires demodulation, and detection for other user's equipment, in addition to the specified user equipment. All this increases the processing delay.
2. When the signal detection using SIC is done with error, this error will affect the other remaining signals such that the useful signal may be recovered erroneously. This means error propagation and to overcome or minimize error propagation, sufficient power must be allocated to the first user [15].
3. Performance degradation depends mainly upon the increased number of users. The increased number of users results in co-channel interference due to minimized power level difference between users. Therefore, the power domain NOMA will be better for two users.

4 NOMA-SM System Modelling

By increasing the demands of wireless data communication due to the increased applications like Internet-of-Things IOT, smart cities, mobile voice, and video transmission, these requirements nictitate the need to enhance the spectral efficiency [16, 17]. However, time energy consumption of the base station should be minimized. The application of traditional MIMO techniques where the number of power amplifiers should equals the number of transmit antennas.

Conventional MIMO techniques suffer from high Inter Channel Interference ICI. Therefore, two challenging problems arise to accommodate beyond 5G communications, first is the spectral efficiency and the second is the ICI.

A non-orthogonal multiple Access NOMA has been recommended to improve spectral-efficiency, where different subscribers are allocated the same-time-frequency communication resources. However, SM can reduce power consumption where only one antenna is chosen among N_t transmit antennas, thus one power amplifier can be used.

4.1 Transmitter

In this work a multiuser down link transmission was used, where transmitting and receiving antennas are denoted by $N_t \times N_r$ with k users [16, 17]. With SM, the information data bits will be conveyed by activated antenna index in addition to the constellation bits used in the adopted modulation such as QPSK or QAM. Thus the kth user data rate could be:

$$R_k^{NOMA-SM} = log_2 M + log_2 N_t \quad bps/Hz \tag{18}$$

Where R_k is the data rate of the kth user, N_t is the number of transmitting antennas, and M denotes the constellation size of the modulation type under consideration. Figure 2 shows the block diagram of the proposed system; it is clear that all users share the equal number of transmit-antennas used in the base-station. Care must be taken with power allocation for different users.

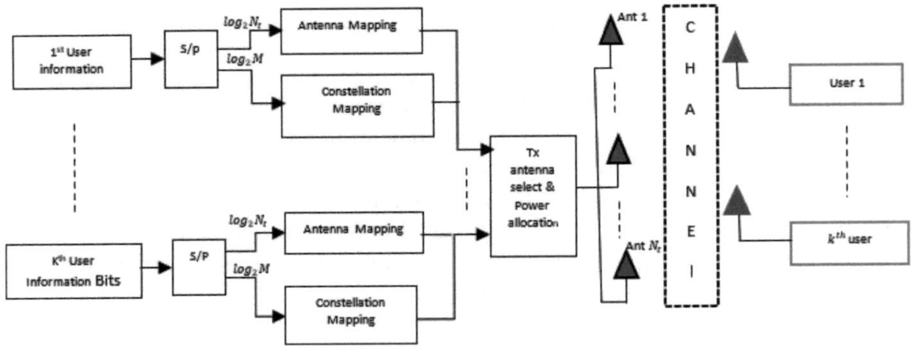

Fig. 2. Block diagram of multi-user NOMA-SM Transmitter and Receiver system

The transmitted signal vector over the channel is represented as:

$$x_{j,m}^{k} = \sqrt{p}\left[0 \cdots \sqrt{\alpha_k}S_m \cdots 0\right]^T \tag{19}$$

Where p denotes the total transmit power, α_k denotes the kth user fractional coefficient of the total transmitted power, j denotes the selected transmit antenna index $1 \leq j \leq N_t$, S_m represents the data symbol selected where $m \in M$ the M-ary constellation size. It should be noted that $\alpha_1 > \alpha_2 > \cdots > \alpha_K$ and $\sum_1^K \alpha_k = 1$

It is clear that NOMA-SM support better data rate than that can be supported by orthogonal with spatial modulation OMA-SM which may be expressed as:

$$R_k^{OMA-SM} = \frac{1}{\beta}\left(log_2M + log_2N\right) \quad bps/Hz \tag{20}$$

Where $\frac{1}{\beta}$ denotes the time frequency resource allocated to each user so that no interference can occur.

4.2 Receiver

At the receiver side, a single user detection scenario can be used directly provided that a complicated SIC procedure is employed before data detection to overcome inter-user interference. The user1 which is assigned the highest power is directly decoded without complex processing involved with SIC. Maximum-likelihood ML detection method can be used [6] for estimating transmitted symbols and antenna index. Note that other detection techniques such as Maximum Ratio Combining MRC may be applied for transmitted symbols detection. The transmitted signal is:

$$x_{NOMA} = \sqrt{p}\sum_{i=1}^{K}\sqrt{\alpha_i}x_i \tag{21}$$

The received vector is:

$$y_{i,NOMA} = h_i x_{NOMA} + w_i \tag{22}$$

For the case of two users, the received vector at the first user $y_{1,NOMA}$ was used to directly estimate the transmitted signal x_1. That is because SIC is not necessary since the first user is subjected to the highest power.

$$[\hat{j}_1, \hat{x}_1] = \underbrace{argmax}_{j,m} \left\| y_{1,NOMA} - \sqrt{p}\sqrt{\alpha_1}\, h_1 S_m \right\|_2^2 \quad (23)$$

Where $\left(\sqrt{p}\sqrt{\alpha_1}h_1 S_m\right)$ is the hypothesis of the received symbol, and $\hat{J}_1, \hat{x}_1$ represent the detected data and antenna index of 1st user terminal. However, at the 2nd user terminal, it becomes much more complicated due to SIC which should be applied for interference cancelation from the previous user. At the second user, the SIC concept is applied to estimate the x_2 signal.

$$\hat{y}_2 = h_2\sqrt{p}\left\{\sqrt{\alpha_2}x_2 + \sum\nolimits_{i\neq 1,2}^{K} \sqrt{\alpha_i}x_i\right\} + w_2 - \sqrt{p}\sqrt{\alpha_1}h_2\hat{x}_1 \quad (24)$$

The same procedure should be applied in a sequential way [2, 18] to remove the interference caused by the previous users. It is clear that no inter-user interference occurs in case of OMA-SM, which is because the communication resources; time and frequency are allocated exclusively to various users. On the other hand, for NOMA-SM a complicated interference mitigation SIC technique must be deployed to overcome the interference. Compared to OMA-SM, SIC complexity increases as the number of users increases. In addition to the spectral efficiency advantage of NOMA-SM application, its hardware complexity is more than OMA-SM where it required only one radio frequency RF chain to support multi-user communication in the base station. In NOMA-SM, RF-chains required equal the number of users. In addition, the power-allocation system is required at the transmitter side and SIC is needed at the end user's device.

5 Simulation Results

The proposed NOMA-SM BER performance was examined to test the system over Rayleigh fading channel assuming fixed power allocation and perfect channel estimation. Figure 3. Shows the BER performance of a two-user downlink. The simulation was carried out under the consideration that the SNR at both ends of user1 and 2 were the same. It is clear that, error-performance of the-second user is worse as compared to that of user1. This is because of the SIC criterion where the first user's interference cannot be completely removed (i.e. error propagation due to SIC). Figure 4 Shows the BER performance with different power allocation coefficients $\alpha_1 = 0.25, \alpha_2 = 0.75$.

Figure 5 presents the outage-probability of two-user fixed power allocation of NOMA-SM system, where the user may be inaccessible if the gained-rate is less than a specified target-rate. The simulation was carried under fixed power allocation coefficients thus neither instantaneous channel variations nor target rate variations were taken into consideration.

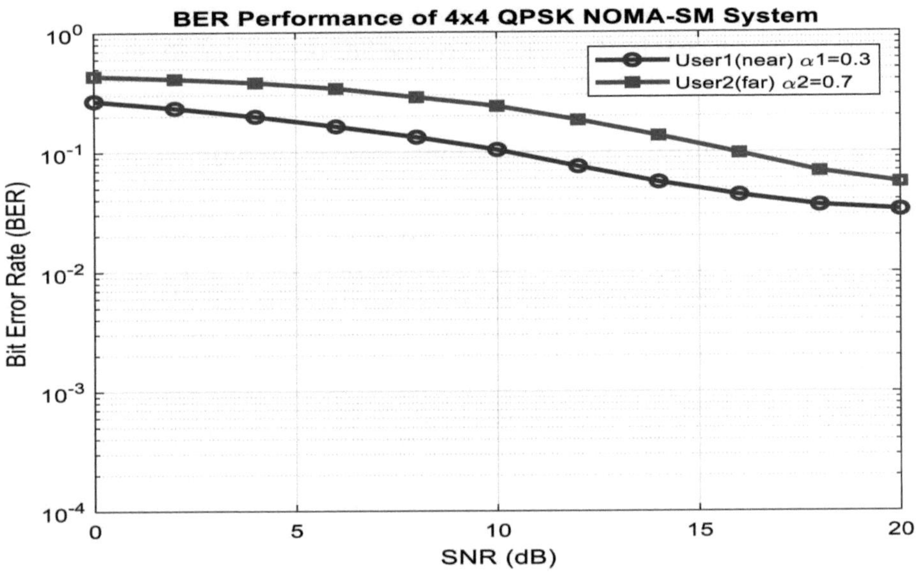

Fig. 3. Bit-Error-Rate Vs Signal-To-Noise-Ratio for NOMA-SM system $\alpha_1 = 0.3, \alpha_2 = 0.7, N_t = 4, N_r = 4$

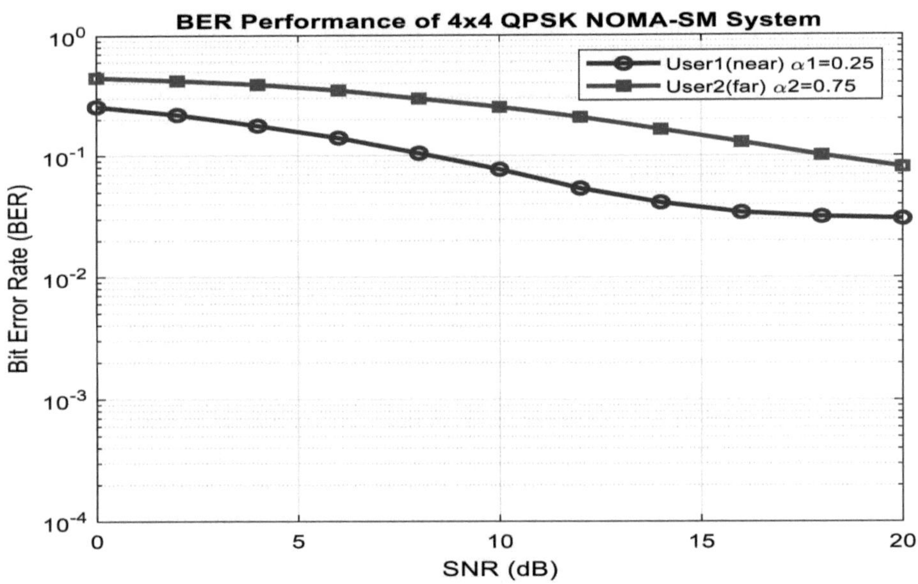

Fig. 4. Bit-Error-Rate Vs Signal-To-Noise-Ratio for NOMA-SM system $\alpha_1 = 0.25, \alpha_2 = 0.75, N_t = 4, N_r = 4$

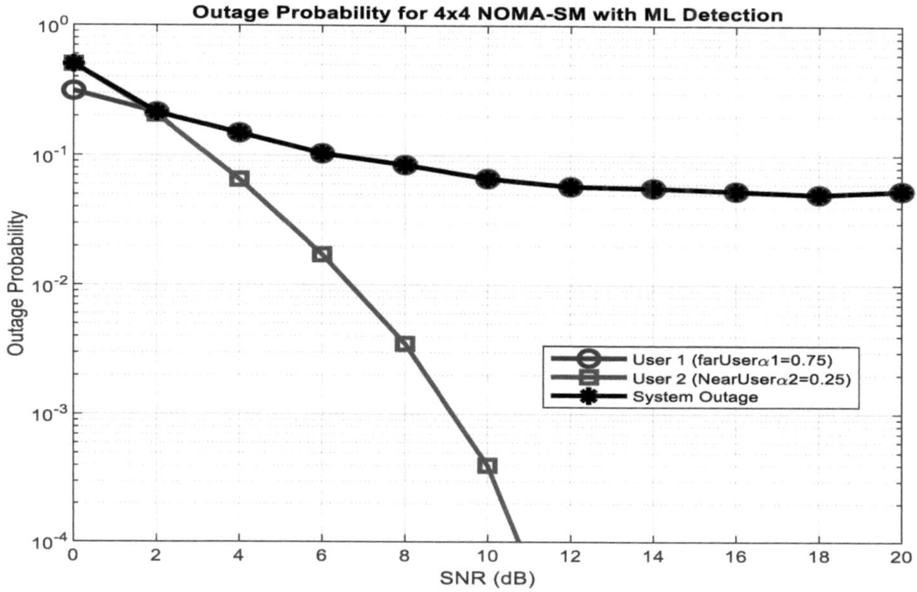

Fig. 5. Outage-probability Vs Signal-to-Noise-Ratio for NOMA-SM system $\alpha_1 = 0.25, \alpha_2 = 0.75, N_t = 4, N_r = 4$

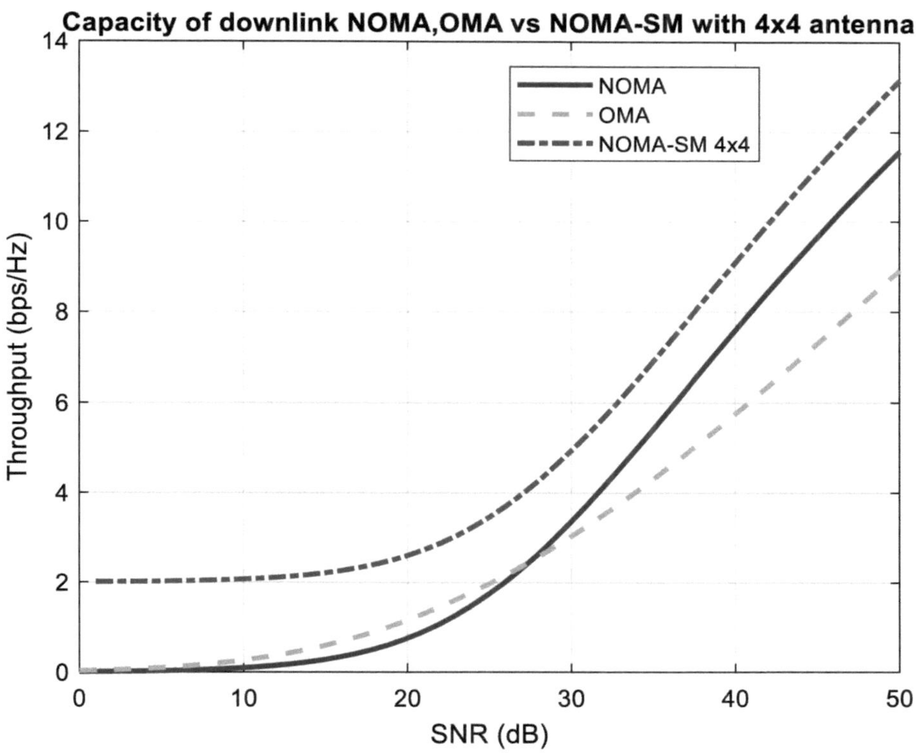

Fig. 6. Downlink throughput comparison NOMA, OMA, and NOMA-SM with 4 –transmit antenna

Figure 6 presents the spectral efficiency of conventional NOMA, OMA, and NOMA-SM with four transmit antennas.

6 Conclusions

A NOMA-SM arrangement was proposed to accommodate the requirement of spectral-efficiency maximization which is linearly proportional to the number of transmit antennas used. By applying NOMA-SM techniques, an achievable trade-off was gained between inter carrier interference and spectral efficiency when MIMO and OMA were used respectively. There are some challenges for successful realization of NOMA. The main challenge or drawback of NOMA is the detection process which requires a complicated SIC algorithm specifically when the number of users are greater than two. Power allocation is another challenge especially when the channel variations are highly changing i.e. fast fading which requires sophisticated channel estimation algorithms. The SIC receiver is sensitive to errors which contribute to the added noise. Further investigations about increasing the number of users >2 is required for dynamic power allocation to overcome outage probability, which requires estimation of user channels with high mobility.

References

1. Dai, L., Wang, B., Yuan, Y., Han, S., Chih-lin, I., Wang, Z.: Non-orthogonal multiple access for 5g: solutions, challenges, opportunities, and future research trends. IEEE Commun. Mag. **53**(9), 74–81 (2015)
2. Saito, Y., Kishiyama, Y., Benjebbour, A., Nakamura, T., Li, A., Higuchi, K.: Non-orthogonal multiple access (NOMA) for cellular future radio access. In: IEEE Vehicular Technology Conference (VTC Spring), Dresden, pp. 1–5 (2013)
3. Timotheou, S., Krikidis, I.: Fairness for non-orthogonal multiple access in 5G systems. IEEE Signal Process. Lett. **22**(10), 1647–1651 (2015)
4. Ding, Z., Fan, P., Poor, H.V.: Impact of user pairing on 5G nonorthogonal multiple-access downlink transmissions. IEEE Trans. Veh. Technol. **65**(8), 6010–6023 (2016)
5. Jeganathan, J., Ghrayeb, A., Szczecinski, L., Ceron, A.: Space shift keying modulation for MIMO channels. IEEE Trans. Wirel. Commun. **8**(7), 3692–3703 (2009)
6. Jeganathan, J., Ghrayeb, A., Szczecinski, L.: Spatial modulation: optimal detection and performance analysis. IEEE Commun. Lett. **12**(8), 545–547 (2008)
7. Higuchi, K., Kishiyama, Y.: Non-orthogonal access with successive interference cancellation for future radio access. In: APWCS2012, August 2012
8. Liu, Y., Oin, Z., Elkashlan, M., Ding, Z., Nallanathan, A., Hanzo, L.: Non-orthogonal multiple access for 5G and beyond, August 2018
9. Saito, Y., Benjebbour, A., Kishiyama, Y., Nakamura, T.: System level performance evaluation of downlink non-orthogonal multiple access (NOMA). In: Proceedings of the IEEE International Symposium on Personal, Indoor and Mobile Radio Communications, London, UK, September 2013
10. Ding, Z., Yang, Z., Fan, P., Poor, H.V.: On the performance of non-orthogonal multiple access in 5G systems with randomly deployed users. IEEE Signal Process. Lett. **21**(12), 1501–1505 (2014)

11. Choi, J.: Power allocation for max-sum rate and max-min rate proportional fairness in NOMA. IEEE Commun. Lett. **20**(10), 2055–2058 (2016)
12. Choi, J.: Non-orthogonal multiple access in downlink coordinated two point systems. IEEE Commun. Lett. **18**(2), 313–316 (2014)
13. Higuchi, K., Kishiyama, Y.: Non-orthogonal access with random beamforming and intra-beam SIC for cellular MIMO downlink. In: IEEE 78th Vehicular Technology Conference (VTC Fall), Las Vegas, NV, USA, IEEE, September 2013
14. Zhang, N., Wang, J., Kang, G., Liu, Y.: Uplink nonorthogonal multiple access in 5G systems. IEEE Commun. Lett. **20**(3), 458–461 (2016)
15. Tabassum, H., Ali, M.S., Hossain, E., Hossain, M.J., Kim, D.I.: Non-orthogonal multiple access (NOMA) in cellular uplink and downlink challenges and enabling techniques (2016). http://arxiv.org/abs/1608.05783
16. Andrews, J.G., et al.: What will 5G be? IEEE J. Sel. Areas Commun. **32**(6), 1065–1082 (2014)
17. Boccardi, F., Heath, R.W., Lozano, A., Marzetta, T.L., Popovski, P.: Fivedistruptive technology directions for 5G. IEEE Commun. Mag. **52**(2), 74–80 (2014)
18. Benjebbour, A., Saito, Y., Kishiyama, Y., Li, A., Harada, A., Nakamura, T.: Concept and practical considerations of non-orthogonal multiple access (NOMA) for future radio access. In: IEEE Intelligent Signal Processing and Communications Systems (ISPACS), pp.770–774 (2013)
19. Wang, F., Zuo, T., Zhang, J., Shi, S., Li, Y.: SM and NOMA joint assisted indoor multi-user VLC downlink. IEEE Trans. Green Commun. Netw. **9**(1), 15–28 (2025). https://doi.org/10.1109/TGCN.2024.3409080
20. Hendraningrat, D.K., Narottama, B., Shin, S.Y.: Non-orthogonal multiple access in downlink coordinated multipoint transmissions. Phys. Commun. **39**, 101017 (2020). ISSN 1874-4907. https://doi.org/10.1016/j.phycom.2020.101017
21. Jadhav, K.P., Mahor, A., Bhowmick, A., Anveshkumar N.: A detailed review on non-orthogonal multiple access based spatial modulation systems. Int. J. Pervasive Comput. Commun. **16**(2), 143–164 (2020). https://doi.org/10.1108/IJPCC-10-2019-0078
22. Kumar, M.H., Kumar, A., Sharma, S., Kumar, M.V.: Performance analysis of a spatial modulation aided cooperative NOMA system. IEEE Commun. Lett. **28**(10), 2273–2277 (2024). https://doi.org/10.1109/LCOMM.2024.3452127

Deep Q-Network Based Multi-service Resource Scheduling for 5G Networks

Zainulabdeen A. Alsaeedi(✉) and Haider D. Al-janabi

Department of Automation and Artificial Intelligence Engineering, College of Information Engineering, Al-Nahrain University, Baghdad, Iraq
zainulabdeen.msei23@ced.nahrainuniv.edu.iq,
dr.haider.aljanabi@nahrainuniv.edu.iq

Abstract. The explosive expansion of heterogeneous services in Fifth Generation (5G) wireless networks necessitates intelligent resource scheduling techniques that can optimize numerous conflicting performance objectives simultaneously. Traditional scheduling techniques fail to explore the full capabilities of intelligent resource allocation due to static parameter configurations and single objective optimization, leading to poor performance in dynamic network environments. A Deep Q-Network (DQN) based framework was proposed for multi-service resource scheduling in 5G networks. The DQN framework addresses resource allocation problems for Voice over Internet Protocol (VoIP), Video, and File Transfer Protocol (FTP) services. The proposed approach implemented a four-dimensional state space consisting of normalized system throughput, head-of-line packet delay, packet loss rate, and an index for fairness in packet scheduling, with a twelve-action space for dynamically adapting scheduling parameters. The reward function implemented multi-objective optimization through the simultaneous maximization of throughput and fairness, while minimizing delay and packet loss. Extensive simulation results showed the advantages of the DQN-based approach over the traditional Proportional Fair, Modified Largest Weighted Delay First, and Exponential Proportional Fair algorithms. Performance evaluation with 10 UEs and 25 resource blocks over 150 Transmission Time Intervals showed considerable gains: 22.7% gain in throughput, 31.5% total delay reduction and 10.5% fairness improvement. The framework obtained an overall reward score of 0.9471, indicating 109.7% superiority to the best performing traditional algorithm. The findings supported the usefulness of deep reinforcement learning in solving multi-service resource allocation problems for 5G networks.

Keywords: 5G · Deep Q-Network · Resource Scheduling · Multi-Service Optimization · Reinforcement Learning

1 Introduction

Fifth Generation (5G) wireless communication is a breakthrough in mobile network technology, transforming how digital services are provided across a variety of applications. 5G networks can reach peak download rates of 10 gigabits per second and

W. A. Mahmoud et al. (Eds.): ACDN 2025, CCIS 2798, pp. 112–135, 2026.
https://doi.org/10.1007/978-3-032-15448-4_8

have considerably less latency than 4G, thereby facilitating almost instantaneous communication via cellular base stations [1]. This technology is especially suited for new services with stringent requirements, such as Ultra-Reliable Low-Latency Communication (URLLC), which requires up to 1 ms latency and up to 99.999% reliability [2]. Fifth-generation communication technology is tailored to offer higher data rates, better user experience, lower power utilization, and extremely low latency while supporting multi-layered infrastructures such as device-to-device, macro-cells, and various types of small cells [3].

In the context of fifth-generation (5G) networks, the necessity to dynamically allocate resource blocks in real-time depends on service demands such as Enhanced Mobile Broadband (eMBB), Ultra-Reliable Low-Latency Communication (URLCC), and Massive Machine Type Communication (mMTC) [4]. This environment of multiple services may ultimately affect many facets of the research about interference management and resource allocation methodologies and schemes in 5G networks [3]. Scheduling is the term that refers to the process of resource component assignment according to various service types. The most basic resource component for scheduling is the Physical Resource Block (PRB) or Resource Block (RB) [5]. 5G NR architecture supports a more adaptable way of resource scheduling in the frequency domain to more effectively assist in wide bandwidth activities [6], along with expanding in the frequency domain and contracting in the time domain compared to LTE. 5G NR resource blocks comprise 12 contiguous subcarriers, and their bandwidth is a function of the subcarrier spacing rather than the frequency band. When LTE introduced the fixed bandwidth of 180 kHz per resource block, the NR resource block bandwidth was different from LTE. NR resource block bandwidths are: 180 kHz for 15 kHz subcarrier spacing, 360 kHz for 30 kHz subcarrier spacing, and in-band n78 as high as 720 kHz for a 60 kHz subcarrier spacing [7]. In addition, each resource block traditionally corresponds to one slot in the time domain [8]. Resource blocks are further divided into smaller units known as resource elements (REs), and each RE is an intersection of one subcarrier and one OFDM symbol in the time-frequency grid [9]. Scheduling algorithms dictate how much time and space is shared between the base station and mobile UEs, i.e., bandwidth allocation, time slot assignment, and fair sharing of limited resources among network UEs [10]. During each scheduling period, User Equipment (UE) gathers and sends buffer status information in the form of scheduling requests to the base station over dedicated physical uplink control channels [11]. The base station, therefore, assigns Resource Blocks (RBs) to UEs based on scheduling algorithms received in the form of physical downlink control channels [12].

Problem formulation illustrates the scalability of utility functions to address different use-cases like eMTC, URLLC, and eMBB with LTE to facilitate Fifth-generation 5G NSA architecture. Various services with different quality of service demands are expected in 5G networks to be accommodated in a common physical infrastructure in an efficient way [13]. Small-sized resource blocks are allocated to user equipment to support variations of traffic demands and link failure, providing the capability of low-latency communication while ensuring the performance of eMBB user equipment and prioritizing URLLC user equipment [14].

2 Background and Related Work

The development of resource scheduling in wireless networks has undergone tremendous growth, spanning classical algorithmic solutions to contemporary artificial intelligence-based solutions. This section provides an exhaustive review of the literature, assessing the transition from classical scheduling methods to state-of-the-art deep reinforcement learning solutions, and determining important research gaps that drive the present study.

2.1 Traditional Scheduling Approaches

Studies on wireless network scheduling are typically aimed at algorithms for throughput optimization in trade-off with fairness concerns. Kwan et al. [15] laid the groundwork by demonstrating that Proportional Fair (PF) scheduling in LTE cellular networks was able to attain better fairness outcomes with small losses in throughput, especially when average Signal-to-Interference-plus-Noise Ratios (SINRs) among UEs are similar. Their work concluded that PF achieved a good trade-off between network efficiency and resource equity, and it was a gold standard for future generations of scheduling research. Their performance evaluation was, nevertheless, confined to scenarios with quite homogeneous SINR conditions, which renders it less relevant to heterogeneous network contexts.

Recent research works on 5G NR scheduling have been on the optimization of certain criteria. Mamane et al. [16] put forth a multi-criterion scheduling solution for 5G eMBB communication in a very dense urban environment. Their solution merged weighted sum multi-objective optimization with perceptron weight control implemented through neural networks, thereby optimizing 5G eMBB's conflicting demands comprising higher data rates, effective spectrum utilization, improved fairness levels, and smaller buffer sizes. Although their study provided perceptive results on multi-objective scheduling optimization, the evaluation was directed primarily at eMBB scenarios without complete analysis of heterogeneous service coexistence.

2.2 Deep Reinforcement Learning in Network Resource Management

The use of artificial intelligence, particularly deep reinforcement learning (DRL), in the management of network resources has been a groundbreaking method in handling the complexity of modern wireless networks. DRL-based approaches have helped address industrial IoT applications with a focus on real-time freshness requirements for data. Li et al. [17] proposed AoI-aware resource scheduling for Industrial IoT using deep reinforcement learning with the consideration of Age of Information (AoI) as a critical metric for data freshness in real-time applications. Their algorithm enhanced efficient utilization of resources while meeting strict timing constraints required by industrial processes, solving both average AoI optimization and AoI violation rate minimization to ensure system stability.

Akbari et al. [18] employed AoI to model the freshness of information in Virtual Network Function (VNF) scheduling for delay-sensitive industrial internet of things (IIoT) applications. They used single agent low-complex compound action actor-critic RL that allowed both discrete and continuous actions and jointly optimized VNF cost and AoI in regards to network resources under end-to-end QoS conditions. To alleviate single agent capacity limitations, they extended their solution to a multi-agent DRL setting, where agents work together.

2.3 Q-Learning Based Scheduling in LTE Networks

The application of reinforcement learning, or Q-learning, in scheduling wireless networks has received considerable attention. Feki and Zarai [19] proposed an algorithm to enhance performance throughout cellular networks by employing reinforcement learning in an LTE-advanced network environment. Their proposed scheduling policy, utilizing dynamic neural Q-learning, was able to achieve a multidimensional tradeoff between fairness and throughput with a desired level of channel quality indicator (CQI) based solutions to each UE class. The Q-learning algorithm took into account implementing different scheduling rule policies in every Transmission Time Interval (TTI), while the neural networks determined appropriate scheduling rules based on untested states.

Furthering the goal of the original Q-learning proposed, Feki et al. [20] Proposed a Q-learning-based scheduling methodology aimed at the more specific issues of LTE and LTE-advanced networks, specifically addressing Fairness, and total system throughput. While much of the past research has focused on optimizing both of these parameters concurrently, studies have not specifically highlighted making this trade-off in LTE technology involving transmission systems. The results of the simulation showed that the proposed algorithms performed better than the prior class of schedulers; however, the lack of delay was not considered, which would make them less useful for real-time service scenarios.

The evolution from simple Q-learning methods to enhanced methods is undeniable. Chen et al. [21] Developed a new downlink scheduling algorithm based on Q-learning that specifically targeted video traffic in LTE systems. The approach was able to demonstrate that, in terms of packet loss ratio, throughput, and latency, the performance for real-time video streams was significantly better than traditional scheduling algorithms such as EDF, EXP-PF, and MLWDF. The study concluded that it is important to include delay consideration in modern scheduling algorithms for real-time applications.

2.4 Deep Q-Networks and Neural Network Integration

The shift toward more complex neural network architectures is also evident in more recent works. In particular, Tang et al. [22] investigated deep reinforcement learning-based (TDD) uplink and downlink resource allocation approaches based on network properties such as intelligent, adaptive, and high-mobility network variability. They demonstrated the capabilities of deep learning to address the complexities of modern wireless networks.

Recent advances in deep learning for task scheduling in Internet of Things (IoT) edge computing are also noteworthy. Sheng et al. [23] Demonstrated that DRL-based approaches solved time scheduling and the allocation of resources simultaneously, considering task diversity and resource heterogeneity.

2.5 5G Network Slicing and Service Coexistence

With the advancement of 5G networks, new possibilities and challenges arose for intelligent scheduling. Alsenwi et al. [24] introduced a scheduling scheme for eMBB and URLLC traffic in 5G network slices using resource optimization for eMBB. They included a PGACL algorithm, while addressing URLLC traffic so that all types of data resources would be utilized. This study also showcased the complexity of scheduling multiple types with opposing objectives.

The innovation of 5G network slicing opened up the ability to provide multiple types of services in conjunction with each other. Malta et al. [25] worked on using a Deep Reinforcement Learning agent implementing dynamic resource allocation with 5G wireless network slicing based on traffic requirements spanning the 3GPP's 5G use cases including eMBB, URLLC, and mMTC. Their DRL agent evaluated several different decoding methods (OMA, NOMA, RSMA) and selected the most suitable dynamic decoding method according to prevailing network conditions.

There are challenges in jointly scheduling different services, which have been addressed with a variety of DRL methods. Research has shown that applying deep reinforcement learning to joint schedule eMBB and URLLC can skillfully manage multiple competing service requirements [26]. However, any punctured methods of URLLC scheduling may create significant rate loss to eMBB UEs.

2.6 Quality of Service and Real-Time Applications

Quality of Service (QoS) provisioning and real-time applications have been the subject of growing attention in recent scheduling research. Dong et al. [27] combined two different types of neural networks, Fully Connected Neural Networks (FNN) to allocate resources, and Cascade Neural Networks to enhance approximation quality with guaranteed QoS. This showed that hybrid neural network architectures were promising in more complex scheduling scenarios.

Husain et al. [28] proposed a very efficient packet scheduling for downlink data transmission in URLLC services. Their scheduling scheme was benchmarked against traditional scheduling schemes including PF and EXP-PF and all configurations demonstrated significant improvements over all the scenarios. For a small number of UEs, the new scheduling algorithm was very close to the performance of EXP-PF; however, as the UE density increased, the performance was consistently better than that of EXP-PF.

3 Research Gap Identification

Through analysis of both the academic literature and the current practices in the industry, this dissertation has unveiled a total of four critical gaps in 5G multi-service resource allocation:

- Static Parameters Updating in Resource Scheduling: The current scheduling algorithms use parameters which are static and do not adapt to the changing conditions of the network, nor the variations in traffic. Effectively these scheduling algorithms have fixed or static decision parameters and cannot modify those decisions on an ongoing basis resulting in either inefficient allocation or inefficient resource usage with no formal strategy in place. The model does not take the best achievable performance available under different conditions into account. This is important to emphasize particularly in regards to the aspect of heterogeneity in terms of service that will be shown from the service attributes within the 5G era, particularly noting the radical differences of traffic characteristics during different times of the day [29].

- Bias of Single-Objective Optimization in Multi-Metric Contexts: Resource allocation mechanisms adopt a biased quantitative performance metric over the other metrics, which results in unbalanced efficiencies from potential trade-offs between objectives. Conventional resource allocations do not simultaneously maximize throughput, minimize delay, maximize fairness, or minimize packet-loss. The severity of the issue is compounded with 5G where new services with heterogeneous rates of services emerge as inequality in terms of Quality-of-Service expectations [30].
- Lack of Intelligence in Service-Aware Resource Allocation Priority: Scheduling algorithms do not integrate sophisticated methods for weighting resource allocation criteria, according to service and network conditions. They do not have the capability to uniformly weigh the importance of channel quality, queue occupancy, and delay requirement with respect to the reliability of the network, and the specific requirements of the services. Consequently, their ineffective allocation of resources does not reflect the heterogeneous nature of modern applications in 5G networks [31].
- Scalability and Flexibility Limitations for Real-Time Deployment: The mainstream algorithms struggle with computational complexity and can never have the flexibility required for large-scale implementation through substantial deployments of 5G networks. They do not possess characteristics that enable pattern learning from historical behavior of the network nor do they change their approach based on past performance, therefore limiting their effectiveness within dynamic, high-density network environments that demand rapid decision-making [29]. This research pushes through the base limits above by proposing an intelligent, adaptive resource allocation strategy that learns to schedule in an optimal manner using deep reinforcement learning, dynamically weighs the importance of various metrics, and offers service-aware resource allocation priority, which is ultimately usable in real time for 5G networks.

4 Methodology

4.1 Deep Q-Network Algorithm Framework

The implementation of Deep Q-Networks (DQN) adheres to the conventional paradigm of deep reinforcement learning, wherein an agent acquires optimal policies for resource allocation by interacting with its environment. This agent functions within the context of a Markov Decision Process (MDP). Based on the original design [32], the Deep Q-Network (DQN) structure has two hidden layers each with 256 units and ReLU activations. Using the Adam optimizer, the DQN was trained with twelve output nodes that represented the permissible scheduling actions (action space) and four input features that described the state space. The ε-greedy exploration strategy and target network were used, which is in line with the original DQN framework. Figure 1 illustrates the DQN-based scheduler learning process. The agent uses MATLAB to interact with the 5G simulation environment, and the learning process is parameterized as follows:

- The policy network samples an action A, receives the current state S as input, and returns the reward R.
- The experience transition tuple (s, a, r, s) is saved in replay memory at each interaction, and mini-batches are sampled from it later.
- To encourage stability during training, a target network is implemented concurrently with the policy network, and weights are periodically copied to the target network.
- Mini-batches sampled from replay memory are used in the optimization process, which aims to minimize the loss between target and predicted Q-values in the policy network. Over several episodes, this framework allows the resource allocation policy to be improved.

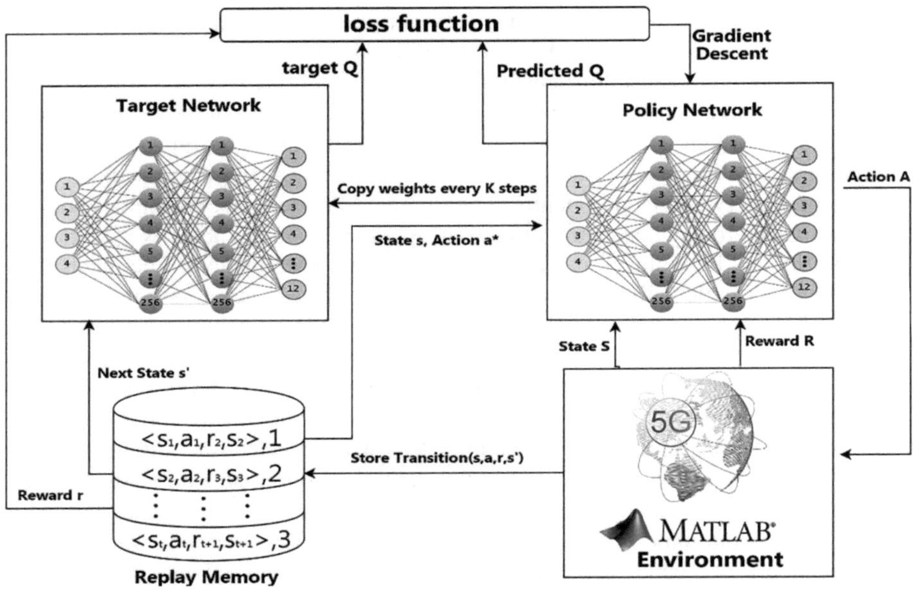

Fig. 1. DQN architecture.

The state space is a four-dimensional normalized vector that captures important descriptors of network performance [33]:

$$s(t) = \left[NorSysTh(t), DHoL(t), PLR(t), Fair(t)\right]^T \tag{1}$$

Where *NorSysTh* denotes the normalized system throughput, D_{HoL} is the average head-of-line delay, *PLR* is the packet loss ratio, and *Fairness* is the Jain-based fairness index.

Every element represents normalized system throughput, head-of-line packet delay, packet loss rate, and fairness index. This compact state representation embodies comprehensive network status information without making the computational complexity prohibitive to neural network approximation.

The action space consists of twelve discrete actions for different combinations of scheduling parameters:

$$a \in \{0, 1, 2, \ldots, 11\} \tag{2}$$

The discrete action encoding procedure converts every action to scheduling priority parameters by the mapping function:

$$a = 4 \times \theta_d + 2 \times \theta_q + \theta_c \tag{3}$$

This coding produces a delay importance $\theta_d \in 0, 1, 2$, queue importance $\theta_q \in 0, 1$, and channel importance $\theta_c \in 0, 1$, with 12 various parameter combinations for adaptive scheduling strategy selection.

The scheduling problem is approached as a multi-objective optimization problem which maximizes throughput while jointly minimizing delay, packet loss, and unfairness among UEs. Each of these competing objectives is represented with a utility function Eq. (4) that is based on normalized performance metrics to show a trade-off between competing objectives by implementing the metrics into scores from 0 to 1, so no one objective can dominate the optimization. The important parameters learned are used by the central resource allocation algorithm to compute the user scheduling priorities:

$$Score_i = (channelScore_i)^{\theta_c} \cdot (queueScore_i)^{\theta_q} \cdot (delayScore_i)^{\theta_d} \tag{4}$$

Each term is defined in Eqs. (5), (6), and (7).

Channel Score:

$$channelScore_i = min\left(1, \frac{\overline{G_i}}{\overline{G_{sys}}}\right) \tag{5}$$

Where $\overline{G_i}$ is the average channel gain for user i and, $\overline{G_{sys}}$ is the system average channel gain.

Queue Score:

$$queueScore_i = min\left(1, \frac{Q_i}{\overline{Q}}\right) \tag{6}$$

Where Q_i is the queue length of the user i and $\overline{Q}$ is the average queue length across all UEs.

Delay Score:

$$delayScore_i = \frac{D_i}{D_{max}^{service(i)}} \tag{7}$$

Where D_i is the current delay for the user i and, $D_{max}^{service(i)}$ is the maximum delay threshold for the service type of user i.

In contrast to traditional scheduling techniques that use fixed priority weights, the proposed framework allows the reinforcement learning agent to dynamically adjust the exponents $\theta_d, \theta_q, \theta_c$. The adjustable weights allow the scheduler to prioritize objectives differently at various network conditions, improving overall system performance. For example, a user who is currently experiencing poor channel conditions, a long queue, or has a large delay will be given a higher score, making it more likely that they will receive additional resource blocks. This formulation will improve throughput and fairness, but also indirectly help mitigate packet loss and reduce delay.

The reward function is formulated to incorporate the four important performance metrics: throughput, delay, fairness, and packet loss. To prevent preference from being inherent in any one goal each performance goal is normalized to [0, 1], and represented in a reward function as [33]:

$$R(t) = NorSysTh(t) + Fair(t) - DHoL(t) - PLR(t) \tag{8}$$

Where $NorSysTh(t)$, $Fair(t)$, $DHoL(t)$, and $PLR(t)$ denote the normalized system throughput, fairness index, head-of-line packet delay, and packet loss ratio respectively, all of which are computed using mathematical formulations that will be detailed in the subsequent Performance Measurement Metrics subsection. This structure allows the agent to maximize throughput and fairness while minimizing delay and packet loss, thereby mitigating the respective trade-offs for multi-service resource scheduling.

4.2 Traditional Scheduling Algorithms

The PF scheduling metric of the user i is expressed as [34]:

$$PF_i = \frac{r_i(t)}{\overline{R_i(t)}} \tag{9}$$

Where $r_i(t)$ is the instantaneous achievable rate and $\overline{R_i(t)}$ is the exponentially Weighted.

The M-LWDF metric incorporates delay sensitivity for real-time services and for non-real-time services, uses the PF metric. Equation (10) shows the metric used to model the MLWDF schedule [35]:

$$MLWDF_i = \begin{cases} \alpha_i \cdot W_i(t) \cdot \frac{r_i(t)}{\overline{R_i(t)}}, & if\ i \in RT. \\ \frac{r_i(t)}{\overline{R_i(t)}}, & if\ i \in NRT. \end{cases} \tag{10}$$

Where W_i is the head-of-line delay and α_i is given as:

$$\alpha_i = -\frac{\ln(\delta_i)}{\tau_i} \tag{11}$$

with target packet loss probability δ_i and τ_i being the maximum delay threshold for the user i service type.

Exponential Proportional Fair Algorithm

The EXP-PF measure combines exponential delay weighting with proportional fairness [36]:

$$EXPPF_i = \begin{cases} \exp\left(\frac{\alpha_i W_i(t) - \overline{W}}{1+\sqrt{\overline{W}}}\right) \cdot \frac{r_i(t)}{\overline{R_i(t)}}, & if\ i \in RT. \\ \frac{r_i(t)}{\overline{R_i(t)}}, & if\ i \in NRT. \end{cases} \tag{12}$$

Where $\overline{W}$ is the average weighted delay for all active UEs:

$$\overline{W} = \frac{1}{N}\sum\nolimits_{j=1}^{N} \alpha_j W_j(t) \tag{13}$$

The parameters in the above equation are defined similarly to those in Eq. (10), where N represents the number of active downlink RT traffic.

4.3 Performance Measurement Metrics

Normalized system throughput is expressed as [33]:

$$NorSysTh = \frac{\sum_{i=1}^{N} R_i(t)}{R_{max}} \tag{14}$$

Where $R_i(t)$ is the present throughput of the user i and R_{max} is the theoretical maximum system capacity.

The weighted delay metric is given by:

$$DHoL = \frac{\sum_{i=1}^{N} w_i^{service} \cdot \frac{d_i(t)}{D_{max}^{service(i)}}}{\sum_{i=1}^{N} w_i^{service}} \tag{15}$$

Where per-service weights are applied as $w^{VoIP}, w^{Video}, and\ w^{FTP}$ to reflect relative delay sensitivity. The standard D_{HoL} definition as in [33] was expanded by normalizing by the maximum tolerable delay for each service type and adding service-dependent weights. This formulation allows delays from heterogeneous services to be represented in a comparable manner while highlighting latency-sensitive traffic.

The weighted packet loss rate is computed as:

$$PLR = \frac{\sum_{i=1}^{N} w_i^{service} \cdot PLR_i}{\sum_{i=1}^{N} w_i^{service}} \tag{16}$$

Where $PLR_i = L_i/A_i$ represents the proportion of lost packets L_i and arrived packets A_i for user i. The packet loss ratio as in [33] has been modified by applying service-specific weights ω_i to the instantaneous loss values during each packet loss calculation. This weighted formulation penalizes losses in critical services so reliability is more representative of heterogeneous QoS needs.

Jain's fairness index was employed to quantify normalized throughput ratios [37]:

$$\mathrm{Fair} = \frac{\left(\sum_{i=1}^{N_{active}} x_i\right)^2}{N_{active} \cdot \sum_{i=1}^{N_{active}} x_i^2} \tag{17}$$

Where $x_i = R_i(t)/R_{req}^i$ is the normalized throughput ratio relative to minimum service requirements, and N_{active} is the number of active UEs.

A total of thirty independent simulation runs were conducted to assess the performance of each algorithm in this study, ensuring statistical validity. For every run, the mean of the performance metrics was first calculated throughout 150 Transmission Time Intervals (TTIs), and the overall mean was obtained as the result of a single episode.

The mean of the 30 episodes was calculated to derive a representative mean for each metric. The relative improvement of the proposed DQN-based scheduler over the baseline algorithms was assessed using the following standard formulation:

$$Improvement(\%) = \frac{X_{\text{DQN}} - X_{\text{Baseline}}}{X_{\text{Baseline}}} \times 100 \tag{18}$$

where $X_{\text{DQN}} and X_{\text{Baseline}}$ represent the evaluated metrics values attained by the DQN scheduler and the respective baseline algorithm.

5 Experimental Configuration and Simulation Setup

The simulation assessment included full performance analysis for four resource allocation algorithms: Deep Q-Network (DQN), Proportional Fair (PF), Modified Largest Weighted Delay First (M-LWDF), and Exponential Proportional Fair (EXP-PF). The performance assessment framework recorded performance information over 150 Transmission Time Intervals (TTIs) to provide detailed temporal analysis, complemented by per-episode aggregated measures for statistical analysis. The simulation employs a single-cell 5G network scenario as defined below:

1) System Specifications: Number of UEs (N) 10, Number of Resource Blocks (M) 25, Episode Duration (T) 150, and TTI Duration 1 ms.
2) Service Type Distribution: The number of UEs has been distributed across three service categories describing realistic heterogeneous conditions: VoIP Users 30% (Users 1, 4, 7), Video Users 40% (Users 2, 5, 8, 10), Ftp/browsing 30% (Users 3, 6, 9). This service distribution mimics typical cellular network traffic distribution where multimedia services account for a significant head of traffic volume and real-time applications are more sensitive to network latency.
3) Channel Model: The behavior of the channel is represented in terms of a normalized Channel Quality Indicator (CQI), which ranges between [0.25–0.83]. During each episode, the CQI is modified by adding random noise to simulate the abrupt changes typically experienced in channels. The modulation scheme switches between four discrete levels of modulation data signal for QPSK, 16QAM, 64QAM, and 256QAM, chosen adaptively based on the instantaneous CQI.
4) Traffic Model: Traffic arrivals are modeled as a Poisson process with natural variation in arrivals from the random arrival process for each episode. VoIP is modeled as ON-OFF bursting traffic. Video is modeled as sustained higher-rate flows generating periodic fluctuations and bursts. FTP/Browsing is modeled as variable-load traffic that occasionally includes heavy-tailed spikes. The packet sizes vary and relate to service type. The Packet drops are applied dynamically at a random rate based on a Random Early Detection (RED) packet dropping method.

The simulation conditions listed in Table 1 set the multi-service 5G network setup, including user distribution, traffic types, and Quality of Service requirements for heterogeneous service classes.

Table 1. Simulation environment parameters

Parameter	Value
Number of Users (UEs)	10
Number of Resource Blocks	25
Service Distribution	3 VoIP, 4 Video, 3 FTP/Browsing
Simulation Duration	150 TTI
Number of Episodes	30
VoIP Arrival Rate	150–180 packets/s
Video Arrival Rate	450–550 packets/s
FTP Arrival Rate	70–90 packets/s
VoIP Packet Size	100–150 bytes
Video Packet Size	1200–1800 bytes
FTP Packet Size	600–800 bytes
VoIP Channel Gain Range	0.45–0.56
Video Channel Gain Range	0.70–0.83
FTP Channel Gain Range	0.25–0.36
Bandwidth	10 MHz
Base Throughput per RB	1 Mbps
RED Parameters	
VoIP Min/Max Threshold	5K/20K bytes
Video Min/Max Threshold	20K/50K bytes
FTP Min/Max Threshold	30K/80K bytes
Max Drop Probability	0.1–0.2

Table 2 lists the training configuration parameters for DQN, such as the neural network model and the reinforcement learning hyperparameters tuned for the resource scheduling problem.

Table 3 presents a detailed performance comparison for the case of a high network load, providing a general performance snapshot for each performance index achieved by every algorithm.

The performance comparisons of the scheduling algorithms according to multiple key metrics are listed in Table 3. It is observed that the DQN-based scheduler achieves superior performance on most metrics. In throughput, the DQN obtains the highest rating with 0.7361, which translates into a 22.7% improvement over M-LWDF, the best traditional baseline (0.6000). For delay, the DQN obtained the best performance with 0.3473 s, which is a 31.5% improvement compared to the best traditional result for this performance metric found with M-LWDF (0.5069 s). Fairness also saw DQN improvements, with a 0.5596 score, which was 10.5% better than the best traditional algorithm for fairness (PF) (0.5065). For packet loss. PF has the most favorable result at

Table 2. DQN Training Configuration Parameters

Parameter	Value
Learning Rate (α)	0.005
Discount Factor (γ)	0.95
Batch Size	256
Experience Buffer Length	5×10^4
Use Double Q-Learning	True
Input Dimension	4
Hidden Layers	2
Hidden Layer Size	256
Output Dimension	12
Activation Function	ReLU
Optimizer	Adam
Max Episodes	5000
Episode Length	150

Table 3. Performance Results

Algorithm	Throughput	Delay	Fairness	Packet Loss	Reward
DQN	0.7361	0.3473	0.5596	0.0013	0.9471
PF	0.5092	0.5632	0.5065	0.0010	0.4515
M-LWDF	0.6000	0.5069	0.1685	0.0083	0.2533
EXP-PF	0.5608	0.5152	0.2192	0.0058	0.2591

0.0010, while DQN at 0.0013 is in a close second place. While DQN is slightly worse than PF, its performance is still much better than all other conventional algorithms.

Overall, DQN has superior performance in terms of every response metric, except packet loss. It is clear from the results that DQN consistently dominates in throughput, delay, fairness, and reward.

The performance of the proposed DQN-based scheduler was compared to three benchmark algorithms, PF, M-LWDF, and EXP-PF under four major performance metrics, including system throughput, packet delay, packet loss rate, and fairness index (Fig. 2). During each episode of the simulation, several dynamic parameters were either stored or changed in a manner that guaranteed that each episode was separate from the others. In the way, the parameters reflected the variability or stochasticity that occurs in real-world network conditions.

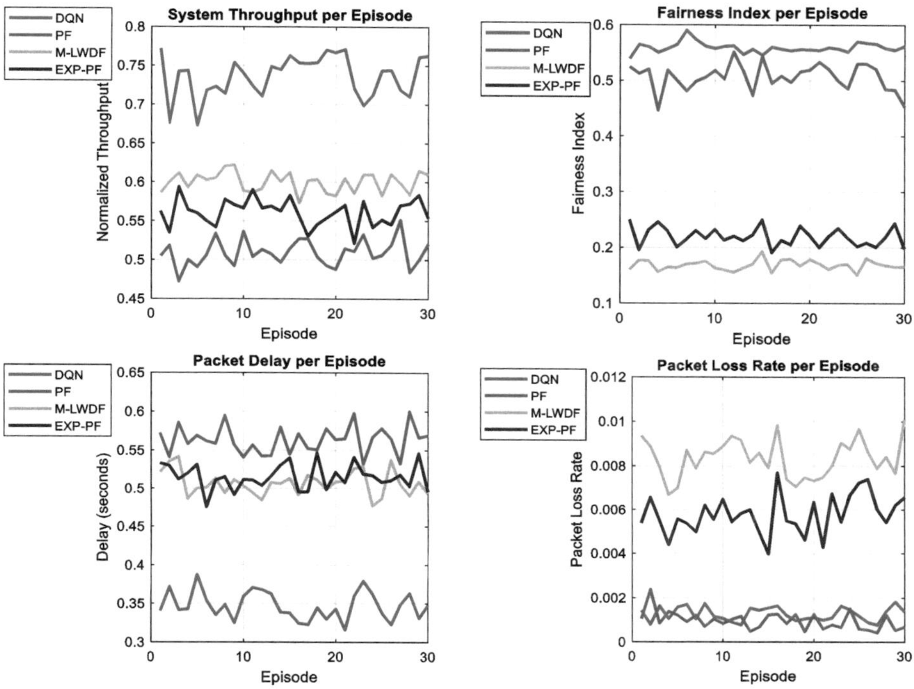

Fig. 2. Comparative Performance Analysis of Scheduling Algorithms Across Multiple Episodes

In terms of system throughput, the DQN algorithm outperformed all benchmarks consistently, reflecting normalized throughput values in the 0.65–0.75 range throughout the simulation episodes. This is consistent with our expectations of deep reinforcement learning being capable of effectively adjusting to changing demand and conditions, resulting in increased spectrum utilization. By comparison, PF had the lowest throughput performance, stabilizing at 0.5. M-LWDF and EXP-PF also returned lower throughput values, achieving throughput near 0.60 and 0.55, respectively. In terms of packet delay, the DQN scheduler achieved the lowest average delay, remaining in the 0.33–0.38 s range throughout the episodes. This significant improvement in the DQN delay performance is the result of the adaptability afforded to the proposed learning-based framework to allocate resources effectively, resulting in lower queuing times. Packet delays of the benchmark and conventional algorithms returned likewise higher average values, indicating similar frameworks with PF delivering the worst results, reaching up to 0.60 s. The M-LWDF and EXP-PF returned moderate values of roughly 0.48–0.55 s.

For packet loss rate (PLR), the trends differ from the previous metrics. PF and DQN had the lowest loss rates, which were approximately between 0.001 and 0.002, showing good transmission performance. M-LWDF and EXP-PF exhibited much larger PLRs, in the range of 0.006 to greater than 0.010, which showed that these schemes did not have the robustness needed to deliver reliable packets under changing load conditions. Finally, in terms of fairness, DQN again had the best performance keeping close to a fairness index of 0.58 per episode. PF also had a roughly equitable distribution of resources, stabilizing at around 0.52, but still a little below DQN. M-LWDF and EXP-PF had far lower fairness values, at around 0.15–0.20, which shows that they favor certain flows heavily over others.

Figure 3 provides temporal patterns of different metrics over the full period of transmission time intervals (TTI) in a single simulation run (150 TTI in total). Unlike average results that provide only summary values (averaged), these traces for each TTI exhibit the instantaneous behavior of each algorithm over the entire run and its ability, or inability, to adjust to different and continuously changing network conditions. Each Transmission Time Interval (TTI) represents a simulation iteration. Every TTI, the DQN picks an action based on the policies learned during its training, based on the learned policies, and transfers this action into resource allocations to UEs based on considerations of the user's delay, queue length, and channel quality.

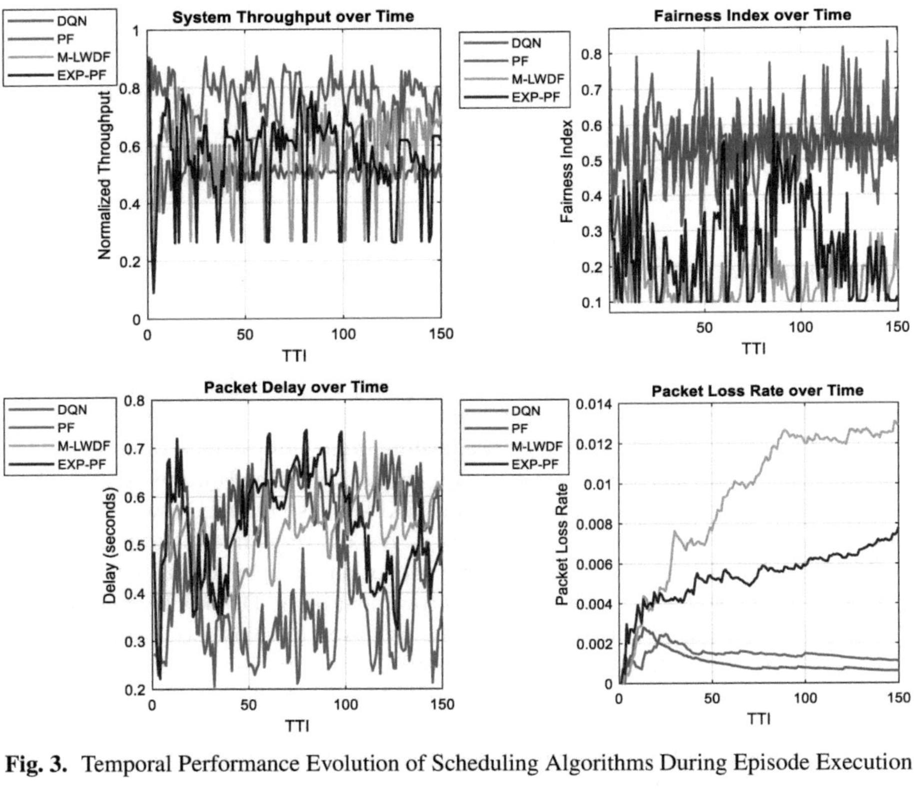

Fig. 3. Temporal Performance Evolution of Scheduling Algorithms During Episode Execution

Figure 3 plots the behavior of individual TTIs' performance metrics at Episode 1 and thus provides an inside look at algorithmic adaptation to evolving network conditions. Fine-grained timeline inspection demonstrates the adaptive character of DQN scheduling choices, with the fluctuations of the performance metrics around the optimal values being regulated. Yet, conventional algorithms are less consistent in their performance, reflecting their inadequacy in conforming to evolving network conditions and traffic profiles. The adaptive schedule by DQN allows continuous refinement of optimization, resulting in optimal long-term consistency in performance required for realistic deployment conditions. Multi-objective optimization analysis demonstrated DQN's ability to optimize multiple competing objectives simultaneously, in contrast to traditional algorithms that excel at one aspect and compromise system performance as a whole. DQN employs a learning-based approach to determine optimal operating regimes for peak aggregate system utility, a contribution to resource scheduling methodology for their heterogeneous network environment.

Table 4 illustrates that as the number of users increased from 10 to 15(5 VoIP, 6 Video, 4 FTP/Browsing), the overall system performance of all algorithms suffered from the higher traffic load and resulting resource contention. With respect to throughput, fairness, and delay, DQN continues to outperform the traditional algorithms in this simulated unseen environment, maintaining the highest aggregate throughput and the highest aggregate fairness, while keeping delay minimal. While packet loss does increase in comparison to the 10-user case, packet loss is still relatively low compared to other options, and DQN still achieves the best performance and overall reward. This demonstrates that the learning-based approach's functioning and reliability were both robust, generalizing well to previously unencountered situations, with higher densities of users.

Table 4. Performance Results.

Algorithm	Throughput	Delay	Fairness	Packet Loss	Reward
DQN	0.7148	0.4437	0.5203	0.0032	0.7882
PF	0.5057	0.6211	0.4653	0.0022	0.3477
M-LWDF	0.6228	0.5227	0.1473	0.0092	0.2382
EXP-PF	0.5848	0.5493	0.2030	0.0072	0.2314

5.1 Complexity Analysis

All simulations were run on a laptop with an Intel® Core™ i5-10300H CPU @ 2.50 GHz, 12 GB RAM (2667 MT/s), and NVIDIA GTX 1650 graphics card with 4 GB VRAM. The operating system was Windows and it had MATLAB R2024b software installed. The DQN was pre-trained for 5000 episodes with approximately 7 h of training time using GPU to facilitate the learning process. All execution time measurements represented inference performance utilizing the pre-trained model. All algorithms were run on CPU cores to enable a fair computational comparison.

The computational complexity of the proposed DQN-based scheduler was assessed against traditional scheduling algorithms utilizing MATLAB simulations. In order to analyze the computational overhead of the deep learning algorithm, ten simulation runs were performed collectively that comprised 150 TTIs. The execution time performance comparison for algorithms that were tested is shown in Table 5.

There are three primary areas that contribute to the increased execution time using DQN. First, DQN requires the computation of Q-values for all possible scheduling actions (12 actions) as it performs matrix multiplications, activation functions, and other operations in a multi-layered neural network. Traditional schedulers, on the other hand, perform using simple closed-form calculations. Second, the DQN algorithm must handle the 4-dimensional state vector with fairness index, DHOL, PLR, and throughput values, and must also perform normalization and other feature extracting operations at every TTI. The utility function generates additional computing time from the assessment of the channel score, delay score, and queue score for each user in the system. This requires iterated evaluations across all users to yield appropriate scheduling decisions, which adds a significant mathematical operation.

Table 5. Computational Performance of Scheduling Algorithms

Algorithm	Time per Run (s)	Time per TTI (ms)	Relative Performance
PF	0.980	6.54	1.00 (baseline)
MLWDF	1.028	6.86	1.05
EXP-PF	1.172	7.81	1.19
DQN	1.244	8.29	1.27

A notable finding was that the DQN scheduler exhibited a 26.8% computational overhead compared to PF (the fastest traditional algorithm) and 6.1% overhead compared to EXP-PF (the slowest traditional algorithm). This represents a moderate computational cost for enhanced scheduling intelligence. The relative overhead refers to the processing costs required to potentially defend increased intelligence when employing multi-dimensional state processing and probabilistic neural network inference. On the other hand, it holds to the same computational framework and evaluates to what extent scheduling performance is impacted across the operating conditions of all the algorithms in our comparison.

The focus of the execution time analysis was on the relative computational complexities rather than absolute timing constraints. The measured execution times were based on system and MATLAB simulation environment resource utilization, which makes direct comparison to theoretical timing requirements unreasonable.

Analysis of computational complexity indicated advantageous scalability properties for the proposed DQN-based scheduler. Most of the state metrics (throughput, packet loss rate, and any buffer-related metrics to accommodate HOL delay) required for the DQN scheduler were collected by the gNB as part of normal performance monitoring processes specified by 3GPP [38]. With the data required for observations coming from the gNB, the scalability aspects of a DQN scheduler regarding various network sizes were primarily concerned with the inference workload of the neural network.

The neural network inference workload was constant for all network sizes, given that both the input and output to the neural network consisted of a 4 with 12-action outputs. The only performance overhead incurred by larger networks was requiring additional evaluations of the utility function per user, as the number of action outputs and the neural network inference performance were unchanged. This architecture led to a suggestion that the DQN approach to scheduling in a dense 5G deployment can be scaled efficiently because it can leverage existing network performance monitoring infrastructure, and that the network evaluation process remains focused on optimizing the batch processing of evaluations of the utility function rather than re-processing the fundamental algorithm of the DQN.

5.2 Hyperparameter Sensitivity

The proposed DQN-based scheduling framework was evaluated for its sensitivity to important hyperparameters such as learning rate, discount factor, replay buffer size, and exploration rate to test the robustness of deployment. As shown in Table 5, the performance of DQN is influenced by the choice of hyperparameters. The maximum throughput value (0.7573) was achieved with a higher learning rate (0.01); however, the fairness was also relatively lower (0.5462) and the reward was less (0.9273) when the learning rate was higher than smaller values. The intermediate sizes were more stable in terms of fairness and reward: the learning rate of 0.005 achieved the highest reward (0.9390) alongside a low delay (0.3505) and the lowest fairness (0.5602), while 0.001 was only slightly lower in terms of reward (0.9370) with the highest fairness (0.5642) and the lowest packet loss (0.0011). These measures imply that learning rates in the range of 0.001–0.005 represent a reasonable trade-off in terms of balance and stability in performance, whereas larger learning rates represent a reasonable trade-off for fairness and reward.

Table 6. Sensitivity analysis of DQN performance under different hyperparameter settings.

Setting	Throughput	Delay	Fairness	Packet Loss	Reward
LR = 0.01	0.7573	0.3748	0.5462	0.0014	0.9273
LR = 0.001	0.7279	0.3539	0.5642	0.0011	0.9370
LR = 0.005	0.7304	0.3505	0.5602	0.0012	0.9390
RB = 10,000	0.7185	0.3608	0.4984	0.0012	0.8549
RB = 50,000	0.7459	0.3784	0.5455	0.0015	0.9116
RB = 100,000	0.7438	0.3804	0.5479	0.0014	0.9100
Decay = 0.01	0.7331	0.3486	0.5583	0.0013	0.9415
Initial $\varepsilon = 0.99$	0.7367	0.3485	0.5542	0.0013	0.9411

A small buffer size (10,000) for the replay buffer performed poorly across almost every metric, particularly fairness (0.4984) and reward (0.8549), due to having limited sample diversity. Medium buffer sizes (50,000 and 100,000) performed more than satisfactorily, with both achieving just about the same reward (0.9116 and 0.9100, respectively), and 50,000 was slightly higher on throughput (0.7459) and had lower delay

(0.3784), and marginally higher packet loss (0.0015). Additional results indicated a reasonable trade-off in the range of 50k-100k for the replay buffer, in the way of efficiency versus stability. Greater exploration amounting to a longer decay rate (0.01) and high exploration probability ($\varepsilon = 0.99$) yielded the highest rewards (0.9415 and 0.9411) and the lowest delays (0.3485 and 0.3486). This underscores the importance and need for further exploration to find high-quality scheduling strategies to help maximize long-term performance.

In general, a moderate learning rate ($\approx$0.005), memory between 50k–100k, and exploration that enables longer periods of exploration to perform on specification to have steady and improved reward and delays while still being fair.

The convergence performance of the DQN agent in the 5G environment was shown across 5000 training episodes. The results showed that the DQN agent can converge to a steady-state performance within a reasonable timeframe, around 200–300 training episodes, and this can be seen in the average reward value stable around ~18, as shown in Fig. 4.

The convergence analysis showed that the DQN agent exhibited robust, learned performance, and while the rewards of individual episodes exhibited natural variation (60–160 range), the moving average of the rewards remained stable (142–149). The DQN agent's average performance did not deteriorate, nor exhibit signs of catastrophic forgetting through the entirety of the training episodes. The convergence analysis confirmed that the DQN agent achieved stable, replicable performance within the multi-service environment effectively and reached its steady-state performance in less than 300 episodes.

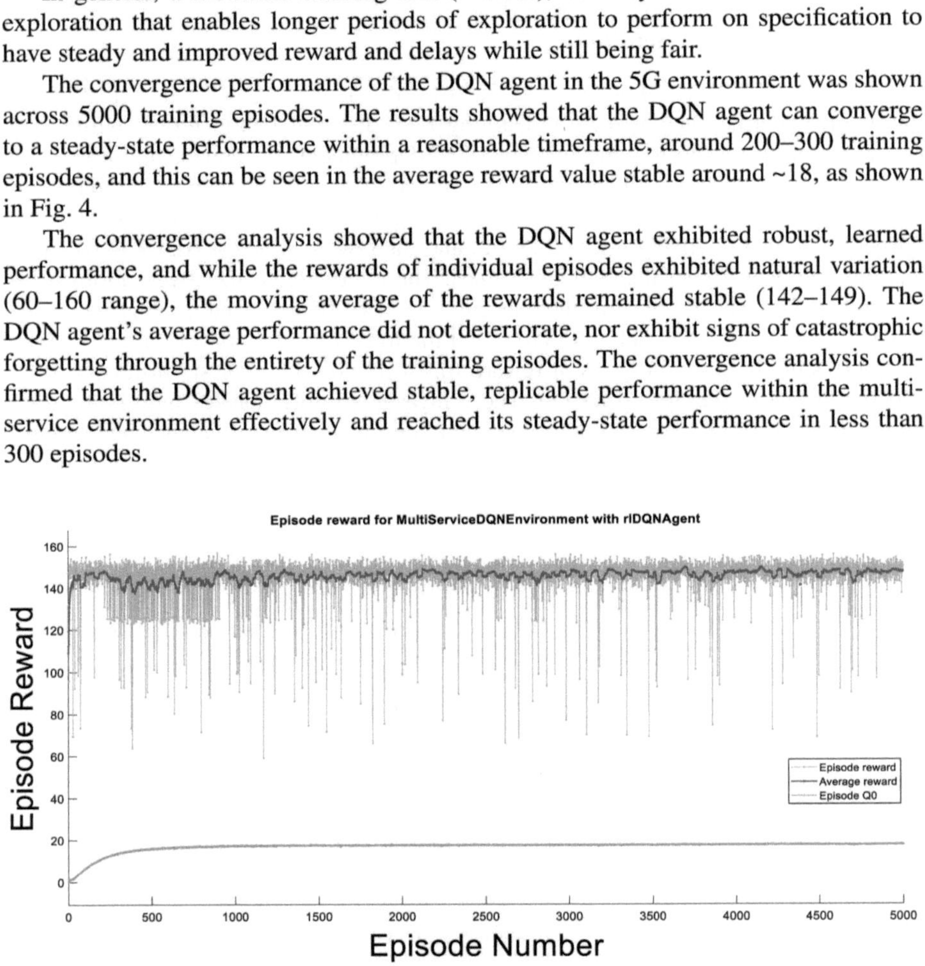

Fig. 4. Training with 5000 episodes in MATLAB.

6 Ablation Study

The ablation study investigates six different configurations where individual components were removed:

1. Throughput from state and reward.
2. DHoL (Downlink Head of Line delay) from state and reward.
3. Fairness from the state and reward.
4. Delay score from the utility function.
5. Channel score from the utility function.
6. Queue score from the utility function.

Each configuration was evaluated in the same network environment with the same hyperparameters as the full model for consistency in the comparison. Table 6 lists detailed results of the ablation study, comparing each reduced configuration to the full model baseline. The full model achieved the maximum reward of 0.9471, indicating that all components can work together and optimize system performance. Overall performance also signified the importance of each component when ordering comparatives. Channel score was most significant, and removing channel score from the utility function (presented in Eq. (4)) had the biggest impact on performance, lowering throughput by 21.1% and overall reward by 16.0%. This indicated that channel state information was fundamental from a resource allocation decision-making perspective.

Fairness was the second most relevant component; removing fairness from the state and reward formulation (presented in Eqs. (1) and (8)) resulted in a considerable drop of 24.8% overall reward with a similar throughput metric. This suggests that while fairness constraints may not be as relevant to instantaneous throughput, they are clearly essential for long-term optimization of a system as a whole, and maintaining user satisfaction over time.

The throughput component had moderate yet consistent impacts on overall performance. While removing throughput metrics from the state and reward formulation (presented in Eqs. (1) and (8)) caused a 9.7% drop in throughput, it also led to a 9.8% drop in reward. As seen with the DHoL and delay score components, they both played a substantive part in system performance, as both caused approximately 8% degradation on selected metrics when removed from the state and reward formulation. Interestingly, the queue score component (presented in Eq. (6)) had the least impact on performance when removed (6.5% drop in reward) while still benefiting overall performance. This component contributed positively to the overall score and supported that queue state was beneficial, though the state could be partially supplanted by the other components that have a higher impact (Table 7).

Table 7. DQN Ablation Study.

Configuration	Throughput	Delay	Fairness	Packet Loss	Reward
Full Model (Baseline)	0.7361	0.3473	0.5596	0.0013	0.9471
Without Throughput in State/Reward	0.6649	0.4397	0.6293	0.0006	0.8540
Without DHoL in State/Reward	0.6761	0.5045	0.6928	0.0002	0.8643

(continued)

Table 7. *(continued)*

Configuration	Throughput	Delay	Fairness	Packet Loss	Reward
Without Fairness in State/Reward	0.7296	0.4022	0.3877	0.0033	0.7118
Without Delay in Utility Function	0.6762	0.5054	0.6993	0.0002	0.8699
Without Channel in Utility Function	0.5804	0.4803	0.6953	0.0001	0.7954
Without Queue in Utility Function	0.6746	0.4727	0.6836	0.0002	0.8853

7 Conclusion and Future Work

The DQN-based scheduler was unequivocally superior to all other algorithms with respect to the total throughput, delay, and fairness metrics. Specifically, DQN reached a maximum throughput value of 0.7361, which is 22.7% larger than the M-LWDF throughput value of 0.6000. For delay, DQN attained the minimum delay value of 0.3473, which was 31.5% less than the M-LWDF delay value of 0.5069. Finally, DQN reached the highest fairness value of 0.5596, which was 10.5% greater than the PF fairness of 0.5065. These simulation results showed that not only did the DQN scheduler increase throughput, it also decreased delay and increased fairness. These demonstrate the validity of using DQN for intelligent resource scheduling for multi-service 5G networks.

Future works may involve expanding the proposed DQN framework to multi-cell environments, using 3GPP TR 38.901 channel models for quantification of inter-cell interference. The proposed DQN framework can be developed with security considerations, including adversarial training and cross-validation for examination of spoofed/tampered metrics. The framework can be also evaluated for scalability with 50–100 user equipment devices obtainable on a base station using higher network loads. The development of the DQN framework in O-RAN architectures will produce cloud-based mirrored training capabilities and near-real-time deployment of RIC. The future studies may also evaluate optimization of energy efficiency through model compression that minimizes computational burden. Approach and method need to be validated through progressive implementations of experimental testbeds. In addition, the practical viability of the DQN framework in commercial 5G environments needs to be assessed.

References

1. Dangi, R., Lalwani, P., Choudhary, G., You, I., Pau, G.: Study and investigation on 5G technology: a systematic review. Sensors **22**(1), 26 (2021). https://doi.org/10.3390/S22010026
2. Siddiqi, M.A., Yu, H., Joung, J.: 5G ultra-reliable low-latency communication implementation challenges and operational issues with IoT devices. Electronics **8**(9), 981 (2019). https://doi.org/10.3390/ELECTRONICS8090981

3. Kamal, M.A., Raza, H.W., Alam, M.M., Su'ud, M.M., Sajak, A.B.A.B.: Resource allocation schemes for 5G network: a systematic review. Sensors **21**(19), 6588 (2021). https://doi.org/10.3390/S21196588
4. Han, X., Xiao, K., Liu, R., Liu, X., Alexandropoulos, G.C., Jin, S.: Dynamic resource allocation schemes for eMBB and URLLC services in 5G wireless networks. Intell. Converg. Netw. **3**(2), 145–160 (2022). https://doi.org/10.23919/ICN.2022.0011
5. Jian, Y.-C., Chung, M.-S., Susanto, H., Leu, F.Y.: 5G base station scheduling. In: Barolli, L. (ed.) IMIS 2022. LNNS, vol. 496, pp. 315–324. Springer, Cham (2022). https://doi.org/10.1007/978-3-031-08819-3_33
6. Boutiba, K., Bagaa, M., Ksentini, A.: Optimal radio resource management in 5G NR featuring network slicing. Comput. Netw. **234**, 109937 (2023). https://doi.org/10.1016/j.comnet.2023.109937
7. 5G NR Resource Block Definition and RBs Calculation - Techplayon. https://www.techplayon.com/nr-resource-block-definition-and-rbs-calculation/. Accessed 02 June 2025
8. Saha, R.K., Cioffi, J.M.: Dynamic spectrum sharing for 5G NR and 4G LTE coexistence - a comprehensive review. IEEE Open J. Commun. Soc. **5**, 795–835 (2024). https://doi.org/10.1109/OJCOMS.2024.3351528
9. 5G NR Resource block - GaussianWaves. https://www.gaussianwaves.com/2022/02/5g-nr-resource-block/. Accessed 01 June 2025
10. Scheduling. https://www.3gpp.org/technologies/scheduling. Accessed 01 June 2025
11. NR-SR (NR Scheduling Request). https://www.telecomtrainer.com/nr-sr-nr-scheduling-request/. Accessed 01 June 2025
12. Vora, A., Kang, K.-D.: Effective 5G wireless downlink scheduling and resource allocation in cyber-physical systems. Technologies **6**(4), 105 (2018). https://doi.org/10.3390/technologies6040105
13. Aijaz, A., Dohler, M., Aghvami, A.H., Friderikos, V., Frodigh, M.: Realizing the tactile internet: haptic communications over next generation 5G cellular networks. IEEE Wirel. Commun. **24**(2), 82–89 (2017). https://doi.org/10.1109/MWC.2016.1500157RP
14. Maghsoudnia, A., Vlad, E., Gong, A., Dumitriu, D.M., Hassanieh, H.: Ultra-reliable low-latency in 5G: a close reality or a distant goal? In: Proceedings of the 23rd ACM Workshop on Hot Topics in Networks, New York, NY, USA, pp. 111–120. ACM, November 2024. https://doi.org/10.1145/3696348.3696862
15. Kwan, R., Leung, C., Zhang, J.: Proportional fair multiuser scheduling in LTE. IEEE Signal Process. Lett. **16**(6), 461–464 (2009). https://doi.org/10.1109/LSP.2009.2016449
16. Mamane, A., Fattah, M., El Ghazi, M., El Bekkali, M.: 5G enhanced mobile broadband multi-criteria scheduler for dense urban scenario. Telecommun. Syst. **80**(1), 33–43 (2022). https://doi.org/10.1007/s11235-022-00885-3
17. Li, H., Tang, L., Chen, S., Zheng, L., Zhong, S.: AoI-aware resource scheduling for industrial IoT with deep reinforcement learning. Electronics **13**(6), 1104 (2024). https://doi.org/10.3390/electronics13061104
18. Akbari, M., Abedi, M.R., Joda, R., Pourghasemian, M., Mokari, N., Erol-Kantarci, M.: Age of information aware VNF scheduling in industrial IoT using deep reinforcement learning. IEEE J. Sel. Areas Commun. **39**(8), 2487–2500 (2021). https://doi.org/10.1109/JSAC.2021.3087264
19. Feki, S., Zarai, F.: Cell performance-optimization scheduling algorithm using reinforcement learning for LTE-advanced network. In: 2017 IEEE/ACS 14th International Conference on Computer Systems and Applications (AICCSA), pp. 1075–1081. IEEE, October 2017. https://doi.org/10.1109/AICCSA.2017.114
20. Feki, S., Zarai, F., Belghith, A.: A Q-learning-based scheduler technique for LTE and LTE-advanced network. In: Proceedings of the 14th International Joint Conference on e-Business

and Telecommunications, SCITEPRESS - Science and Technology Publications, pp. 27–35 (2017). https://doi.org/10.5220/0006425200270035
21. Chen, X., Liu, Y., Wang, Y.: A novel downlink scheduler based on Q-learning for video traffic in LTE networks. In: 2018 International Conference on Network Infrastructure and Digital Content (IC-NIDC), pp. 115–119. IEEE, August 2018. https://doi.org/10.1109/ICNIDC.2018.8525617
22. Tang, F., Zhou, Y., Kato, N.: Deep reinforcement learning for dynamic uplink/downlink resource allocation in high mobility 5G HetNet. IEEE J. Sel. Areas Commun. **38**(12), 2773–2782 (2020). https://doi.org/10.1109/JSAC.2020.3005495
23. Sheng, S., Chen, P., Chen, Z., Wu, L., Yao, Y.: Deep reinforcement learning-based task scheduling in IoT edge computing. Sensors **21**(5), 1666 (2021). https://doi.org/10.3390/s21051666
24. Alsenwi, M., Tran, N.H., Bennis, M., Pandey, S.R., Bairagi, A.K., Hong, C.S.: Intelligent resource slicing for eMBB and URLLC coexistence in 5G and beyond: a deep reinforcement learning based approach, March 2020. http://arxiv.org/abs/2003.07651. Accessed 01 June 2025
25. Malta, S., Pinto, P., Fernández-Veiga, M.: Optimizing 5G network slicing with DRL: balancing eMBB, URLLC, and mMTC with OMA, NOMA, and RSMA. J. Netw. Comput. Appl. **234**, 104068 (2025). https://doi.org/10.1016/j.jnca.2024.104068
26. Li, J., Zhang, X.: Deep reinforcement learning-based joint scheduling of eMBB and URLLC in 5G networks. IEEE Wirel. Commun. Lett. **9**(9), 1543–1546 (2020). https://doi.org/10.1109/LWC.2020.2997036
27. Dong, R., She, C., Hardjawana, W., Li, Y., Vucetic, B.: Deep learning for radio resource allocation with diverse quality-of-service requirements in 5G, March 2020. http://arxiv.org/abs/2004.00507. Accessed 01 June 2025
28. Husain, Md.I., Haque, Md.E., Tariq, F.: An efficient packet scheduling algorithm for URLLC systems. In: 2020 International Conference on UK-China Emerging Technologies (UCET), pp. 1–4. IEEE, August 2020. https://doi.org/10.1109/UCET51115.2020.9205417
29. Bikkasani, D., Yerabolu, M.: AI-driven 5G network optimization: a comprehensive review of resource allocation, traffic management, and dynamic network slicing. Am. J. Artif. Intell. **8**(2), 55–62 (2024). https://doi.org/10.11648/j.ajai.20240802.14
30. Zhu, R., Aiyyappan, A., Varatharaj, J.R., Jeya Sheela John, J.: A standard network selection and resource allocation mechanism in 5G heterogeneous networks using hybrid heuristic algorithm with multi-objective constraints. EURASIP J. Wirel. Commun. Netw. **1**, 18 (2025). https://doi.org/10.1186/s13638-025-02441-4
31. Kim, B.-S.: A priority-aware dynamic scheduling algorithm for ensuring data freshness in 5G networks. Future Gener. Comput. Syst. **163**, 107542 (2025). https://doi.org/10.1016/j.future.2024.107542
32. Mnih, V., et al.: Human-level control through deep reinforcement learning. Nature **518**(7540), 529–533 (2015). https://doi.org/10.1038/nature14236
33. Eddine Benmadani, H., Azni, M., Essa Alharbi, T., Alzaidi, M.S., Tounsi, M.: Deep reinforcement learning-based dynamic scheduling for real-time applications in LTE and RAN slicing for eMBB in 5G. IEEE Access **13**, 33555–33570 (2025). https://doi.org/10.1109/ACCESS.2025.3541531
34. Kelly, F.P., Maulloo, A.K., Tan, D.K.H.: Rate control for communication networks: shadow prices, proportional fairness and stability. J. Oper. Res. Soc. **49**(3), 237–252 (1998). https://doi.org/10.1057/palgrave.jors.2600523
35. Afroz, F., Sandrasegaran, K., Ghosal, P.: Performance analysis of PF, M-LWDF and EXP/PF packet scheduling algorithms in 3GPP LTE downlink. In: 2014 Australasian Telecommunication Networks and Applications Conference, ATNAC 2014, pp. 87–92, January 2015. https://doi.org/10.1109/ATNAC.2014.7020879

36. Rhee, J.-H., Holtzman, J.M., Kim, D.-K.: Scheduling of real/non-real time services: adaptive EXP/PF algorithm. In: The 57th IEEE Semiannual Vehicular Technology Conference, 2003. VTC 2003-Spring, pp. 462–466. IEEE (2003). https://doi.org/10.1109/VETECS.2003.1207583
37. Jain, R., Chiu, D., Hawe, W.: A quantitative measure of fairness and discrimination for resource allocation in shared computer systems. academia.edu (1998). https://www.academia.edu/download/49798765/fairness.pdf. Accessed 23 May 2025
38. TSGC: 5G; Management and orchestration; 5G performance measurements (3GPP TS 28.552 version 16.9.0 Release 16) (2021). https://portal.etsi.org/TB/ETSIDeliverableStatus.aspx

Efficient Power Allocation in NOMA Networks Using Grey Wolf Optimizer and Genetic Algorithm

Hussein Ali Mohammed[1], Firas Abedi[1(✉)], Zubaidah Saleem Hasan[2], and Ahmed Hussain[3]

[1] Al-Furat Al-Awsat Technical University, Kufa, Iraq
{hussein.ali.inj,firasabedi}@atu.edu.iq
[2] AL-Zahraa University for Woman, Karballa, Iraq
zubaida.salim@alzahraa.edu.iq
[3] The Islamic University, Najaf, Iraq

Abstract. The rapid growth of wireless services demands schemes that can simultaneously support high capacity, low latency, and massive connectivity. Non-Orthogonal Multiple Access (NOMA) has emerged as a key enabler for next-generation networks, however its practical performance depends critically on efficient power and subchannel allocation. Two population-based metaheuristics the Genetic Algorithm (GA) and the Grey Wolf Optimizer (GWO) to solve the joint allocation problem in a realistic downlink NOMA setting with explicit multi-cell interference. Candidate solutions encoded user subchannel assignments and power splits, and their fitness was evaluated by a penalized objective that incorporates system throughput, fairness, and power constraints. Simulation experiments under different user densities and interference conditions compared GA and GWO against Orthogonal Multiple Access (OMA). The results showed that GWO consistently outperformed GA, and improved sum throughput by up to 13% over GA and more than 150% over OMA in interference-limited scenarios. GWO also converged nearly twice as fast (28 vs. 50 iterations on average), reduced per-iteration runtime by about 40%, and delivered higher fairness (JFI = 0.89 vs. 0.84) and energy efficiency (87.1 vs. 79.5 Mbps/W). These findings highlight the novelty of our study: a comprehensive comparative evaluation of GA and GWO under an interference-aware, multi-cell NOMA framework. The results confirmed that GWO provides a practical and computationally efficient solution for dense NOMA deployments, while also highlighted directions for future work in mobility-aware and MIMO-enabled networks.

Keywords: OMA · NOMA · Metaheuristic

1 Introduction

With the rapid evolution of wireless communication technologies, the expectations for future mobile networks have expanded to include ultralow latency,

W. A. Mahmoud et al. (Eds.): ACDN 2025, CCIS 2798, pp. 136–156, 2026.
https://doi.org/10.1007/978-3-032-15448-4_9

massive device connectivity, and high spectral efficiency. These demands, driven by trends such as Industry 4.0 [1], real-time augmented reality [2], and Software define networks [3], are beyond the capacity of conventional cellular systems. According to the International Telecommunication Union (ITU), future wireless networks (e.g., 5G Advanced and 6G) must support data rates of up to 10 Gbps, latency under 1 ms, and connection densities exceeding one million devices per square kilometer [4].

Traditional multiple access schemes, such as Time Division Multiple Access (TDMA), Frequency Division Multiple Access (FDMA), and Orthogonal Frequency Division Multiple Access (OFDMA), allocate orthogonal time or frequency resources to individual users to eliminate interference. While effective in earlier generations, these schemes limit the number of concurrent transmissions and do not scale efficiently with user density or bandwidth demand [5,6]. Consequently, researchers have proposed Non-Orthogonal Multiple Access (NOMA) as a solution to enhance spectrum reuse and user fairness in next-generation wireless networks.

NOMA enables simultaneous transmission to multiple users over the same frequency-time resources by leveraging differences in power levels and employing Successive Interference Cancellation (SIC) at the receiver side [7]. A key element in NOMA is user pairing, where strong and weak users are multiplexed on the same channel to maximize spectral efficiency and fairness. Such pairing is particularly important in dense macrocell environments with inter-cell interference, which better reflect practical deployment scenarios compared to isolated singlecell models. Despite these advantages, the resource allocation problem in NOMA covering power assignment, subchannel allocation, and user pairing— remains highly non-linear and non-convex [8,9]. Convex optimization methods often fail to scale, especially when channel state information is imperfect or user mobility is high. For this reason, the research community has turned to metaheuristic algorithms.

Among these, the Genetic Algorithm (GA) [10] and the Grey Wolf Optimizer (GWO) [11] stand out for complementary reasons. GA, one of the earliest evolutionary approaches applied to NOMA, is effective for combinatorial problem; however, it often suffers from slow convergence and entrapment in local optima under high-dimensional search spaces [12,13]. Particle Swarm Optimization (PSO) [14] and Differential Evolution (DE) [15] have also been studied; however, PSO is sensitive to parameter tuning and can stagnate in dynamic interference conditions, while DE may converge prematurely in large-scale problems [16]. In contrast, GWO provides a more adaptive balance between exploration and exploitation, requiring fewer control parameters and demonstrating strong performance in interference-limited wireless networks [10]. Recent hybrid variants, such as GWO-PSO [17], offer further improvements at the expense of added complexity and slower convergence [18,19]. This balance of simplicity, adaptability, and robustness motivates our choice of GA and GWO as the focus of this study.

Based on this context, the problem addressed in this paper was the joint allocation of power and subchannels in downlink NOMA systems under both interference-free and interference-limited conditions. The goal was to maximize system throughput while ensuring fairness constraints. The novelty of this work lies in its comprehensive comparative evaluation of GA and GWO under a realistic multi-cell NOMA framework with explicit inter-cell interference modeling and varying user densities. Unlike earlier works that focus on isolated single-cell or interference-free environments, this study systematically benchmarks convergence, complexity, and throughput, providing new insights into the applicability of metaheuristics for practical downlink NOMA systems. The main contributions of this study are as follows:

1. Formulating the resource allocation problem in a multi-cell downlink NOMA network, incorporating realistic co-channel interference.
2. Applying and comparing GA and GWO as population-based optimizers, highlighting their strengths and weaknesses under different user densities.
3. Providing a critical performance evaluation against an OMA baseline, with quantitative evidence showing throughput improvements of up to 13% over GA and more than 150% over OMA.
4. Discussing the practical implications of these findings and identifying future extensions toward MIMO configurations and hybrid algorithms.

2 Related Works

The body of research on NOMA has expanded rapidly over the last decade, driven by its inclusion as a key enabling technology for 5G and beyond. Early studies established the theoretical foundations of NOMA, demonstrating how superposition coding and SIC could achieve a higher spectral efficiency and improved fairness compared to OMA [20]in single-cell or two-user setups [7,21]. These works proved the principle but relied on simplified conditions ignoring realistic interference.

As NOMA moved toward practical deployment, researchers investigated resource allocation strategies such as user pairing, power control [22], and subchannel assignment [23]. Convex optimization and matching theory were among the first tools applied [24,25]. While these methods provide elegant formulations, they assume perfect CSI and static environments, which makes them less effective in dense networks or under mobility.

To overcome these limitations, metaheuristic algorithms have been explored. GA [26] was one of the earliest applied, owing to its suitability for non-linear and combinatorial optimization [27,28]. GA balances throughput and fairness suffers slow convergence and local optima traps in large search spaces. Later, swarm intelligence methods such as PSO [29] and DE were adopted [15]. PSO is relatively simple, still highly sensitive to parameter tuning and can stagnate in interference-limited scenarios, On the other hand DE offers fast convergence, while often loses diversity in large user networks.

More recently, GWO has attracted attention due to its balance between exploration and exploitation and its fewer control parameters [30]. Studies have shown that GWO outperforms GA, PSO, and DE in optimizing throughput under interference and high user density. However, GWO may converge prematurely if diversity is lost, and its performance in extremely dynamic networks remains underexplored. To improve this, hybrid methods such as GWO-PSO [17] and GWO-TLBO [19] have been proposed. These hybrids enhance accuracy; however increase complexity and may suffer from higher runtime overhead.

In summary, prior works highlight three key issues: (1) traditional convex methods' lack scalability in practical scenarios, (2) GA, PSO, and DE provide partial improvements; however, limited by convergence or sensitivity problems, and (3) GWO and hybrids show promising yet remain undertested in realistic multi-cell, interference-limited settings. This study addresses these gaps by comparing GA and GWO under the same system model with explicit interference modeling, offering new insights into their strengths and weaknesses in practical downlink NOMA scenarios.

3 System Model and Problem Formulation

3.1 Network Scenario

A downlink NOMA communication system consisting of a central base station (BS) and multiple user equipment (UE) devices randomly distributed within its coverage area was taken into account. The central BS represents the serving cell of interest, while six surrounding BSs form the first tier of interfering cells. Each BS and UE is equipped with a single antenna. The total system bandwidth B_{total} is divided into K orthogonal subchannels, each with a bandwidth of $B_k = B_{\text{total}}/K$ (Hz).

Let $n \in \mathcal{N}$ denote the set of users and $k \in \mathcal{K}$ the set of subchannels. The distance between user n and the central BS is d_n. The small-scale fading coefficient on subchannel k is denoted as $g_{k,n}$ and follows a Rayleigh distribution, while the large-scale path loss is modeled by $PL(d_n)$. Thus, the overall channel gain is expressed as

$$h_{k,n} = g_{k,n} \cdot PL(d_n), \tag{1}$$

consistent with standard channel modeling in cellular systems [31,32].

3.2 Signal and Interference Model

On each subchannel k, the BS transmits a superimposed signal consisting of all users multiplexed on that subchannel:

$$x_k = \sum_{n \in \mathcal{M}_k} \sqrt{p_{k,n}}\, s_{k,n}, \tag{2}$$

where $\mathcal{M}_k$ is the set of users sharing subchannel k, $p_{k,n}$ is the transmit power allocated to user n, and $s_{k,n}$ is the modulated symbol with unit power normalization, i.e., $\mathbb{E}[|s_{k,n}|^2] = 1$.

The received signal at user n is

$$y_{k,n} = h_{k,n} x_k + I_{k,n}^{\text{int}} + z_{k,n}, \tag{3}$$

where $z_{k,n} \sim \mathcal{N}(0, \sigma^2)$ is additive white Gaussian noise (AWGN) and $I_{k,n}^{\text{int}}$ represents inter-cell interference from neighboring BSs. Specifically,

$$I_{k,n}^{\text{int}} = \sum_{b \in \mathcal{B}} \sum_{m \in \mathcal{M}_b} p_{k,m}^{(b)} |h_{k,n}^{(b)}|^2, \tag{4}$$

where $\mathcal{B}$ is the set of interfering BSs, $\mathcal{M}_b$ is the set of users served by BS b, and $h_{k,n}^{(b)}$ is the channel gain from interfering BS b to user n.

In NOMA, stronger users perform successive interference cancellation (SIC) to decode weaker users' signals, while weaker users treat stronger signals as interference.

3.3 Optimization Objective

The system objective is to maximize the total throughput across all users and subchannels:

$$\max_{\{x_{k,n}, p_{k,n}\}} \sum_{k \in \mathcal{K}} \sum_{n \in \mathcal{N}} B_k \cdot \log_2 \left(1 + \frac{x_{k,n} p_{k,n} |h_{k,n}|^2}{I_{k,n}^{\text{int}} + I_{k,n}^{\text{intra}} + \sigma^2} \right), \tag{5}$$

where $x_{k,n} \in \{0, 1\}$ indicates whether user n is allocated to subchannel k, $I_{k,n}^{\text{intra}}$ denotes intra-cell interference from other NOMA users on the same subchannel, and B_k is the subchannel bandwidth (Hz). The log-based formulation follows Shannon's capacity expression [7].

3.4 Constraints

The optimization is subject to the following constraints:

$$\text{(Subchannel power budget)} \quad \sum_{n \in \mathcal{N}} x_{k,n} p_{k,n} \le P_k, \quad \forall k \tag{6}$$

$$\text{(Total transmission power)} \quad \sum_{k \in \mathcal{K}} \sum_{n \in \mathcal{N}} x_{k,n} p_{k,n} \le P_{\text{total}} \tag{7}$$

$$\text{(User multiplexing per subchannel)} \quad M_{\min} \le \sum_{n \in \mathcal{N}} x_{k,n} \le M_{\max}, \quad \forall k \tag{8}$$

$$\text{(Minimum user rate requirement)} \quad R_n \ge R_{n,\min}, \quad \forall n \tag{9}$$

$$\text{(Binary allocation)} \quad x_{k,n} \in \{0, 1\}, \quad \forall k, n. \tag{10}$$

This formulation yields a mixed-integer nonlinear programming (MINLP) problem, which is non-convex and NP-hard due to discrete allocation variables and interference-coupled rates. The objective is therefore to obtain high-quality, near-optimal solutions using metaheuristic algorithms (GA and GWO), as described in Sect. 4.

4 Optimization Techniques

This section solves the problem in Sect. 3 by mapping the mixed-integer nonlinear program (MINLP) into search variables and a single penalized objective function. We then detail GA and GWO based solvers that operate on this mapping.

4.1 Algorithm Mapping

Let $\mathbf{x} = \{x_{k,n}\} \in \{0,1\}^{K\times N}$ denote subchannel assignments and $\mathbf{p} = \{p_{k,n}\} \in \mathbb{R}_+^{K\times N}$ power allocations. Define the vectorized decision variable $\mathbf{z} = [\mathrm{vec}(\mathbf{x})^\top,\ \mathrm{vec}(\mathbf{p})^\top]^\top$. The feasible objective in (11) is

$$F(\mathbf{z}) \triangleq \sum_{k\in\mathcal{K}} \sum_{n\in\mathcal{N}} B_k \log_2\Big(1 + \tfrac{x_{k,n}p_{k,n}|h_{k,n}|^2}{I_{k,n}^{\mathrm{int}} + I_{k,n}^{\mathrm{intra}} + \sigma^2}\Big). \tag{11}$$

To apply metaheuristics on both feasible and infeasible candidates, we use a penalized fitness:

$$\begin{aligned}\varPhi(\mathbf{z}) = F(\mathbf{z}) &- \lambda_1 \underbrace{\sum_k \big[\sum_n x_{k,n}p_{k,n} - P_k\big]}_{\text{subchannel power violation}} - \lambda_2 \underbrace{\big[\sum_{k,n} x_{k,n}p_{k,n} - P_{\text{total}}\big]}_{\text{total power}} \\ &- \lambda_3 \underbrace{\sum_k \big(\big[\sum_n x_{k,n} - M_{\max}\big] + \big[M_{\min} - \sum_n x_{k,n}\big]\big)}_{\text{users per subchannel}} \\ &- \lambda_4 \underbrace{\sum_n [R_{n,\min} - R_n]}_{\text{minimum rate}}\end{aligned} \tag{12}$$

where $[u]_+ = \max\{u, 0\}$ and $\lambda_i > 0$ are penalty weights (we use $\lambda_1 = \lambda_2 = \lambda_3 = 10^3$, $\lambda_4 = 10^4$ unless otherwise stated). Maximizing $\varPhi$ is equivalent to maximizing the feasible F when penalties are large enough. Empirically, the chosen λ_i sufficed to eliminate constraint violations.

Representation and Decoding. A candidate solution encodes: (i) a pairing/assignment matrix $\mathbf{x}$ with at most $M_{\max}$ ones per row, and (ii) power entries $\mathbf{p}$ in $[0, P_k]$. After decoding, (i) a *repair* step is enforced to respect the user-per-subchannel bounds by greedily keeping the largest contributions to F, and (ii) per-subchannel powers are normalized to meet $\sum_n x_{k,n}p_{k,n} \le P_k$ and $\sum_{k,n} x_{k,n}p_{k,n} \le P_{\text{total}}$ by proportional scaling. SIC order on subchannel k follows descending $|h_{k,n}|$; accordingly, $I_{k,n}^{\mathrm{intra}}$ is computed as the residual from yet-to-be-canceled stronger users.

4.2 Genetic Algorithm (GA) for NOMA Allocation

GA is a population–based search method that explores many candidate solutions at once and evolves them over a sequence of generations [10]. Each candidate

Algorithm 1. GA for joint subchannel/power allocation

1: Initialize population $\{\mathbf{z}_0^{(i)}\}_{i=1}^{N_p}$; evaluate Φ.
2: **for** $t = 0$ To $T_{\max} - 1$ **do**
3: Select parents by roulette-wheel on Φ.
4: Apply crossover (binary + SBX) and mutation (bit-flip + Gaussian).
5: Repair and normalize each offspring; evaluate Φ via (12).
6: Elitism: keep best e solutions into next generation.
7: **end for**
8: Return $\arg\max_i \Phi(\mathbf{z}_{T_{\max}}^{(i)})$.

(an individual) encodes a complete resource–allocation decision (e.g., which users share a resource block and how transmit power is split among them). In every generation, GA evaluates the quality of each individual (its fitness), selects the better ones as parents (e.g., roulette–wheel or tournament selection), recombines parents to create new candidates (crossover), and applies small random mutations to maintain diversity. A few top individuals are copied unchanged (elitism) so improvements are not lost. With real–valued encodings and real coded crossover the simulated binary crossover (SBX) operator GA is well suited to continuous decision variables like power fractions, and simple "repair". In addition, penalty rules can keep solutions feasible under practical constraints (e.g., SIC and total–power limits). This combination makes GA a strong fit for NOMA resource allocation, which mixes discrete choices (pairing) with continuous ones (powers) and is typically nonconvex: GA can keep multiple promising pairings in the population, search globally over power splits, and steadily refine solutions without derivatives or convexity assumptions.
Chromosome. Two parts were concatenated: (a) a length-$K \times N$ binary string for $\mathbf{x}$, (b) a length-$K \times N$ real vector for $\mathbf{p}$. The following operators were applied:

- *Selection:* roulette-wheel on Φ.
- *Crossover:* two-point crossover on the binary part (assignments), and simulated binary crossover (SBX) on the real part (powers).
- *Mutation:* (i) bit-flip with prob. $p_{\text{mut}} = 0.05$ on $\mathbf{x}$, (ii) Gaussian perturbation on $\mathbf{p}$ (std. $0.05P_k$), then clip to $[0, P_k]$.
- *Repair & normalization:* as described above; recompute R_n and Φ.

The above GA procedure was summarized with Algorithm 1.

4.3 Grey Wolf Optimizer (GWO) for NOMA Allocation

GWO is a lightweight population–based search method inspired by the hunting and social hierarchy of grey wolves. A population of candidate solutions is organized into four roles: the best solution is the alpha, the next two are beta and delta, and the remainder are omega. At each iteration, the pack "encircles" the prey by updating every candidate with respect to the guidance of the alpha, beta, and delta—so the three best solutions jointly steer the rest of the

Algorithm 2. GWO for joint subchannel/power allocation

1: Initialize wolves $\{\tilde{\mathbf{z}}_0^{(i)}\}_{i=1}^{N_p}$; map, repair, evaluate Φ.
2: **for** $t = 0$ To $T_{\max} - 1$ **do**
3: Identify α, β, δ by Φ.
4: Update each wolf using (13); map, repair, evaluate Φ.
5: Decrease $a \leftarrow 2 - 2\frac{t+1}{T_{\max}}$.
6: **end for**
7: Return best mapped solution by Φ.

population. Early in the run, the algorithm emphasizes broad exploration of the search space; as iterations proceed, its control parameter gradually tightens the movement so candidates converge (exploitation) around the leaders. The procedure has only a few knobs, works directly with real-valued decision variables, and naturally admits simple feasibility handling (e.g., projecting power vectors to sum of one, repairing SIC violations, or adding penalties), which makes it attractive for mixed, nonconvex resource-allocation problems. In our NOMA setting, a candidate encodes a complete allocation (power split, and—if desired—pairing); GWO's leader-guided motion quickly concentrates search around high-quality splits that exploit power-domain multiplexing while avoiding wasteful high-power operation.

Position Vector. Each wolf stores a continuous vector $\tilde{\mathbf{z}} \in \mathbb{R}^{2KN}$ which is mapped to $\mathbf{x}$ and $\mathbf{p}$ by: (i) for each (k, n), set $x_{k,n} = 1$ among the top M_k largest logits on row k (*soft-to-hard* pairing), else 0; (ii) map the remaining entries by sigmoid then scale to $[0, P_k]$ for powers; finally apply repair/normalization and compute Φ.

GWO Update. Let α, β, δ be the top-3 wolves by Φ. Each wolf updates

$$\mathbf{D}_\alpha = |\mathbf{C}_1 \odot \tilde{\mathbf{z}}_\alpha - \tilde{\mathbf{z}}|, \quad \mathbf{D}_\beta = |\mathbf{C}_2 \odot \tilde{\mathbf{z}}_\beta - \tilde{\mathbf{z}}|, \quad \mathbf{D}_\delta = |\mathbf{C}_3 \odot \tilde{\mathbf{z}}_\delta - \tilde{\mathbf{z}}|,$$

$$\mathbf{X}_1 = \tilde{\mathbf{z}}_\alpha - \mathbf{A}_1 \odot \mathbf{D}_\alpha, \quad \mathbf{X}_2 = \tilde{\mathbf{z}}_\beta - \mathbf{A}_2 \odot \mathbf{D}_\beta, \quad \mathbf{X}_3 = \tilde{\mathbf{z}}_\delta - \mathbf{A}_3 \odot \mathbf{D}_\delta,$$

$$\tilde{\mathbf{z}}^{(t+1)} = \frac{\mathbf{X}_1 + \mathbf{X}_2 + \mathbf{X}_3}{3}, \tag{13}$$

with $\mathbf{A}_i = 2a\mathbf{r}_{1,i} - a$, $\mathbf{C}_i = 2\mathbf{r}_{2,i}$, $\mathbf{r}_{1,i}, \mathbf{r}_{2,i} \sim \mathcal{U}[0, 1]$, and a decreasing linearly from 2 to 0 (thus $|\mathbf{A}_i| > 1$ encourages exploration early, <1 exploitation later). After each update we map $\tilde{\mathbf{z}}$ to $(\mathbf{x}, \mathbf{p})$, repair/normalize, and evaluate Φ. The above GWO procedure is summarized by Algorithm 2.

4.4 Optimality of Penalization

When $\lambda_i \to \infty$ in (12), any infeasible $\mathbf{z}$ yields $\Phi(\mathbf{z}) < \Phi(\mathbf{z}^\star)$ for any feasible $\mathbf{z}^\star$ with $F(\mathbf{z}^\star)$ maximal, hence maximizing Φ recovers the constrained optimum. In practice, the chosen finite λ_i (Sect. 5.1) were sufficient to produce feasible solutions after repair/normalization in all runs. Therefore, Sect. 4 implements direct numerical solvers for the exact problem posed in Sect. 3, rather than introducing a new problem.

Table 1. System parameters

Parameter	Value
Cell radius	200 m
Total system bandwidth	5 MHz
Total transmit power	1 W
Noise power spectral density	−173 dBm/Hz
Channel model	Rayleigh fading
Number of users	4, 8, 12, 16
Number of sub-channels	2 to 10

5 Simulation Results and Discussion

To evaluate the effectiveness of the proposed optimization techniques, a series of simulations were conducted under controlled conditions. The focus was on measuring the overall system throughput in various configurations, particularly under the presence and absence of external interference. The performance of the GA and GWO methods was compared against a baseline OMA scheme.

5.1 Simulation Setup

The simulation environment models a downlink cellular system with a single central base station (BS) surrounded by six adjacent interfering cells. Users are randomly distributed within the central cell's coverage area, and each communication link is subject to Rayleigh fading and distance-dependent path loss. The main parameters used in the simulations are outlined in Table 1.

Each scenario was tested twice: once with co-channel interference from adjacent cells and once without them. The performance metric of interest is the sum rate, calculated as the aggregate throughput of all users. In this study, users were assumed to be randomly but statically distributed within the cell coverage area, and each communication link was modeled using Rayleigh small-scale fading combined with distance-dependent path loss. Dynamic mobility patterns and time-varying fading processes were not included, in order to isolate the impact of resource allocation strategies under controlled conditions. This simplification is consistent with several prior studies [33,34]; however, it also highlights the need for future work on mobility-aware resource allocation in NOMA systems. For interference-limited experiments, the central cell was surrounded by six first-tier interfering cells, each transmitting at the same power budget as the main cell. This setup creates a realistic co-channel interference environment consistent with standard cellular layouts [31].

In addition to throughput, three additional performance metrics were considered:

- **Fairness:** Measured using Jain's Fairness Index (JFI) [35], defined as

$$\text{JFI} = \frac{\left(\sum_{n=1}^{N} R_n\right)^2}{N \cdot \sum_{n=1}^{N} R_n^2}, \tag{14}$$

  where R_n is the rate achieved by user n and N is the number of users. Values close to 1 indicate high fairness.
- **Convergence time:** The average number of iterations and runtime required for each algorithm to reach 95% of its maximum throughput.
- **Energy efficiency:** Defined as the ratio of total throughput to the total transmission power (bits/s/Hz/W), providing insight into the cost-effectiveness of spectrum utilization.

To ensure reproducibility, the operating parameters of GA and GWO are summarized in Table 2. Both algorithms were run with a population size of 30 and a maximum of 100 iterations. For GA, crossover probability was set to 0.8 and mutation probability to 0.05, following common practice [33]. For GWO, the control parameter a was initialized at 2.0 and decreased linearly to 0 across iterations, as recommended in [11]. Each simulation scenario was repeated 100 times with independent channel realizations to ensure statistical significance.

Table 2. Simulation parameters for GA and GWO algorithms

Parameter	GA	GWO
Population size	30	30
Maximum iterations	100	100
Crossover probability	0.8	–
Mutation probability	0.05	–
Selection method	Roulette wheel	–
Control parameter a (initial value)	–	2.0 (linearly decreases to 0)
Number of independent runs	100	100
Termination criterion	Max iterations or convergence	Max iterations or convergence

5.2 Results with External Interference

Introducing co-channel interference from neighboring base stations creates a clear performance ordering. Across all user densities, NOMA with GWO attained the highest sum rate, NOMA with GA comes next, and OMA trails by a large margin. For example:

1. With 4 users, GWO reaches 63.9 Mbps, ahead of GA (56.0 Mbps) and OMA (46.7 Mbps).

2. With 16 users, GWO achieves 110.5 Mbps versus 106.2 Mbps (GA) and 40.3 Mbps (OMA).
3. These trends show that GWO's search dynamics are well matched to interference-limited settings, especially as user density grows.

Figure 1 reports the 4-user case. OMA tops out near 46.77 Mbps at three sub-channels and then saturates due to restricted user resource pairing. NOMA-GA improves the peak to about 56.03 Mbps at eight sub-channels through evolutionary tuning of power and channel assignments. NOMA-GWO goes further, reaching 63.95 Mbps at the same sub-channel count. Even at low load, GWO allocates resources more effectively under interference, confirming its stronger adaptability relative to both OMA and GA-based NOMA.

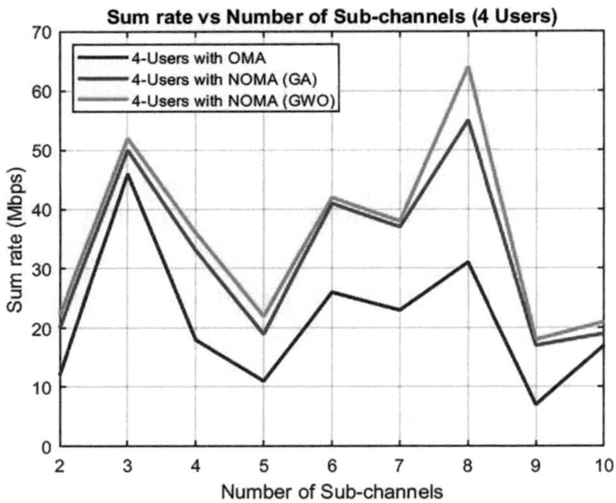

Fig. 1. Scenario 1: 4 users with external interference.

Figure 2 shows that with eight users the gap widens. OMA peaks at ≈32.84 Mbps with two sub-channels and gains little thereafter due to orthogonality constraints. NOMA-GA reaches 52.13 Mbps at nine sub-channels, while NOMA-GWO attains 62.60 Mbps at the same point. The nearly 2× jump from OMA to GWO reflects better convergence and more efficient use of shared spectrum under interference.

In the 12-user setting (Fig. 3), the orthogonal baseline peaks at 39.16 Mbps with five sub-channels, limited by the one user per-channel rule. NOMA-GA leverages power-domain multiplexing to reach 79.46 Mbps, and NOMA-GWO further improves to 87.13 Mbps at the same sub-channel count. As load and interference intensify, GWO's balance of exploration and exploitation yields more consistent high-quality allocations.

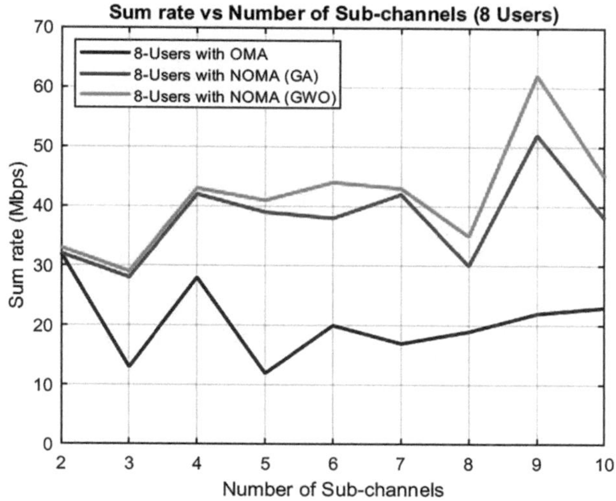

Fig. 2. Scenario 2: 8 users with external interference.

With sixteen users (Fig. 4), OMA peaks at 40.28 Mbps with seven sub-channels. NOMA-GA climbs to 106.23 Mbps, and NOMA-GWO edges higher to 110.51 Mbps at the same setting. The modest but consistent gain over GA underscores GWO's efficient convergence and resilience under heavy loading.

Table 3 summarizes the 12 user, 10 sub-channel case. GWO delivers ∼9.6% higher throughput than GA, converges in roughly half the iterations, and cuts per iteration runtime by ∼40%. Variance across 100 runs is also smaller (∼4% vs. ∼9%), indicating greater stability in the presence of interference. These differences matter in practice: faster, steadier convergence translates to lower decision latency and fewer re-optimizations in dynamic networks.

Table 3. Comparative performance of GA and GWO under 12-user, 10-subchannel scenario with external interference

Criterion	GA	GWO	Observation
Throughput (Mbps)	79.46	87.13	GWO improves sum rate by ∼9.6%
Convergence speed	∼50 iterations	∼28 iterations	Nearly 2× faster convergence
Runtime per iteration	0.21 s	0.12 s	∼40% lower runtime
Stability (variance across 100 runs)	∼9% fluctuation	∼4% fluctuation	More stable under interference

Additional metrics in Table 4 confirm that GWO's gains extend beyond throughput: fairness improves (JFI = 0.89 vs. 0.84 for GA), convergence accelerates, and energy efficiency increases. These properties make GWO a strong fit for dense NOMA deployments where equity and power budgets are tight.

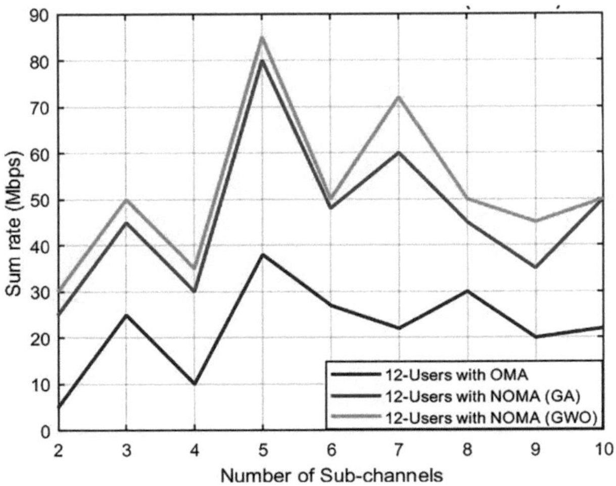

Fig. 3. Scenario 3: 12 users with external interference.

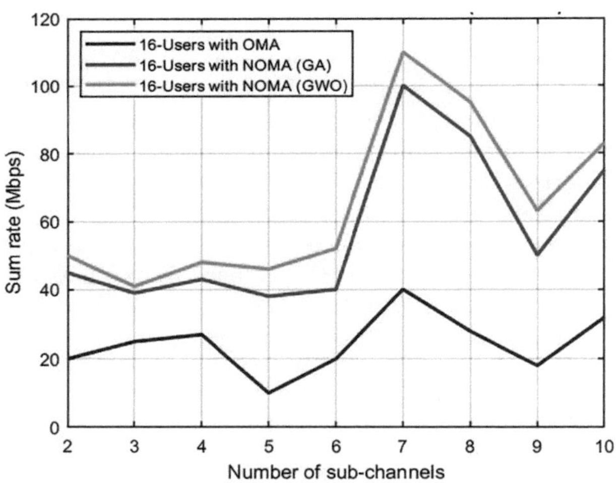

Fig. 4. Scenario 4: 16 users with external interference.

Table 4. Additional performance metrics under 12-user, 10-subchannel interference-limited scenario

Metric	OMA	GA	GWO
Fairness (JFI)	0.72	0.84	0.89
Convergence time (iterations)	–	∼50	∼28
Average runtime (s/iteration)	0.09	0.21	0.12
Energy efficiency (Mbps/W)	39.2	79.5	87.1

5.3 Results Without External Interference

Removing external interference lifts the achievable rates for all methods, but the relative ranking persists: GWO remains best, GA is a close second, and OMA is consistently lowest. For instance:

1. With 8 users, GWO attains 234.6 Mbps vs. 217.5 Mbps (GA) and 201.0 Mbps (OMA).
2. With 16 users, GWO reaches 215.4 Mbps, GA 186.6 Mbps, and OMA 118.4 Mbps.

In the 4-user interference-free case (Fig. 5), all schemes improve markedly. OMA reaches 240.89 Mbps at eight sub-channels, NOMA-GA rises to 254.81 Mbps, and NOMA-GWO leads with 258.01 Mbps. Although the margins narrow without interference, GWO maintains a consistent edge, indicating robust fine-tuning of power splits even in cleaner channels. For eight users (Fig. 6), OMA peaks at ≈201.05 Mbps with nine sub-channels, then saturates. NOMA-GA improves to 217.54 Mbps at nine sub-channels, while NOMA-GWO achieves 234.56 Mbps at ten sub-channels. GWO's exploration exploitation balance continues to yield better power and frequency allocations as complexity rises. With twelve users (Fig. 7), OMA reaches 191.76 Mbps at ten sub-channels. NOMA-GA attains 198.58 Mbps at the same point, while NOMA-GWO delivers 214.11 Mbps using only seven sub-channels. In other words, GWO achieves higher spectral efficiency with fewer resources a desirable property when bandwidth is constrained.

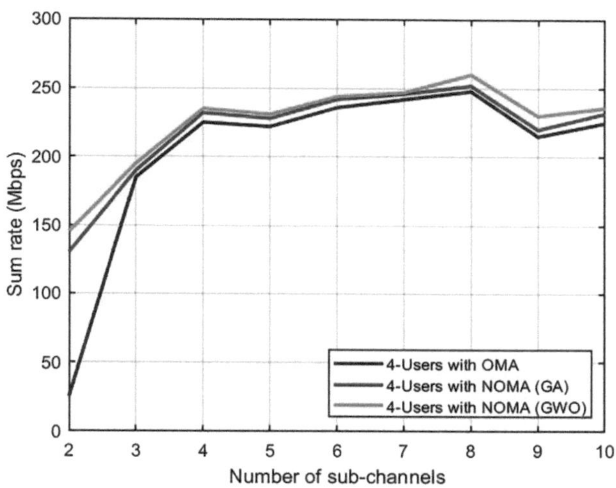

Fig. 5. Scenario 1: 4 users without external interference.

Finally, with sixteen users (Fig. 8), OMA peaks at 118.43 Mbps with ten sub-channels. NOMA-GA reaches 186.63 Mbps at seven sub-channels, and NOMA-GWO leads at 215.41 Mbps with eight sub-channels. The advantage at scale confirms that GWO better balances user demands and available spectrum.

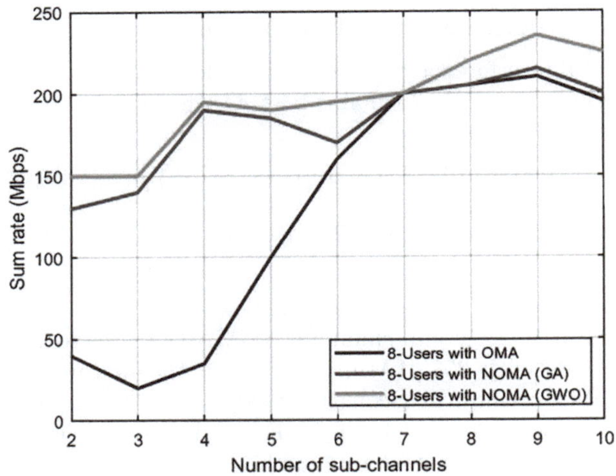

Fig. 6. Scenario 2: 8 users without external interference.

Table 5 highlights the consistent advantage of GWO over GA in a dense, interference-free scenario. While both methods deliver high throughput, GWO achieves a noticeable gain with faster convergence and lower runtime. It also produces more stable outcomes across repeated runs, indicating stronger reliability. These results confirm that even without external interference, GWO provides a more efficient and robust allocation strategy, reinforcing its suitability for large-scale NOMA deployments.

Table 5. Comparative performance of GA and GWO under 16-user, 8-subchannel scenario without external interference

Criterion	GA	GWO	Observation
Throughput (Mbps)	186.63	215.41	~15.4% higher sum rate
Convergence speed	~47 iterations	~26 iterations	Nearly 2× faster convergence
Runtime per iteration	0.25 s	0.14 s	~44% lower runtime
Stability (variance across 100 runs)	~8% fluctuation	~3% fluctuation	More stable in clean channels

Overall, pairing NOMA with metaheuristic optimization substantially outperforms OMA. GA delivers notable gains but can stagnate near local optima as load increases. GWO's hierarchical guidance and parameter light design enable quicker, steadier convergence to higher-quality allocations. Modeling inter-cell interference makes these trends directly relevant to practical deployments.

To establish statistical significance, each experiment was repeated 100 times with independent channel realizations. Table 6 lists mean and standard deviation for the 12 user, 10 sub-channels, and interference-limited case. Paired t-tests (GA

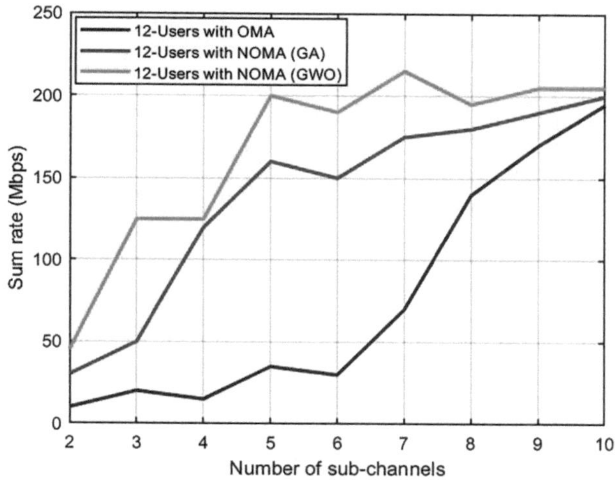

Fig. 7. Scenario 3: 12 users without external interference.

vs. GWO; OMA vs. NOMA) indicate that differences are significant at the 95% level ($p < 0.01$ in all comparisons), ruling out random variation as the cause of the observed gaps.

Table 6. Statistical analysis of throughput (Mbps) under 12-user, 10-subchannel scenario with interference

Method	Mean Throughput (Mbps)	Std. Dev. (Mbps)
OMA	39.16	2.8
GA	79.46	4.5
GWO	87.13	3.9

5.4 Comparisons of Sum-Rate and Energy-Efficiency Results to Other Methods

The proposed metaheuristics was compared to NOMA-DR [9], PD-NOMA [12], OMA [20], FTPA [23], and OFDMA [22], chosen to cover both optimized and rule-based baselines for rate and energy comparisons.

The sum rate in Fig. 9 grows monotonically with SNR for all schemes. NOMA-GA attains the highest rates, with NOMA-GWO closely tracking; above $\approx$10 dB their curves are nearly indistinguishable. This confirms that adaptive, search-based power allocation fully exploits power domain multiplexing and

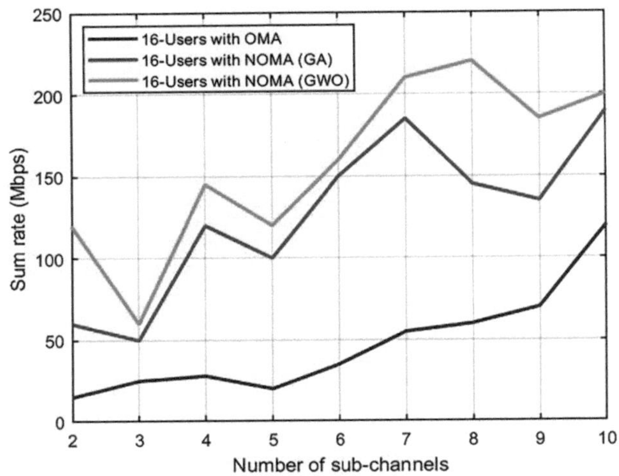

Fig. 8. Scenario 4: 16 users without external interference.

SIC. NOMA-DR lags at low SNR but steepens beyond ≈15 dB and eventually overtakes OMA, reflecting the increasing leverage of SIC as power disparities become more useful. PD-NOMA and FTPA remain lower because fractional/deterministic splits do not optimize the sum-rate objective. OFDMA is the lowest, as orthogonalization forfeits power-domain gains. The overall ordering of NOMA-GA $\gtrsim$ NOMA-GWO > NOMA-DR > OMA > PD-NOMA/FTPA > OFDMA aligns with theory and prior surveys.

Figure 10 reports energy efficiency (EE), defined as EE $= R_{\text{sum}}/(P_{\text{tx}} + P_{\text{c}})$ with P_{c} modeling circuit power. Because R_{sum} grows sublinearly while the denominator increases roughly linearly, EE rises early and then plateaus or declines. NOMA-GWO achieves the best EE across the entire power range, peaking near (4.4×10^7) bits/J at moderate powers (∼2–6 W), with NOMA-GA a close second. NOMA-DR and PD-NOMA approach the top tier at medium powers but fade as $P_{\max}$ increases. OMA peaks early and then degrades, while FTPA and OFDMA decline beyond ≈2 W, indicative of operation beyond the EE-optimal region. These patterns are consistent with fractional-programming results that predict a unique EE-optimal transmit power and the advantage of NOMA with optimized power allocation.

For EE-centric operation, the target was the onset of the EE plateau (here ∼2–6 W) and prefer adaptive NOMA allocators (GWO/GA). For throughput centric regimes (high SNR), GWO/GA clearly dominated OMA/OFDMA; fixed rules such as PD-NOMA/FTPA were also lightweighted. Reporting both sum rate and EE provides a fuller view of the power performance trade-off and helps avoid configurations that add watts without adding useful bits.

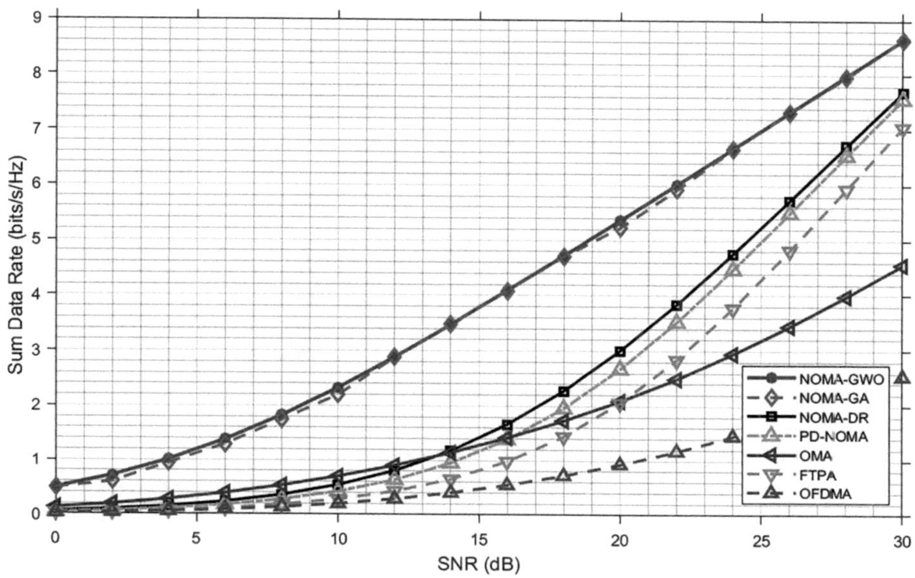

Fig. 9. Sum rate versus SNR with 16 users.

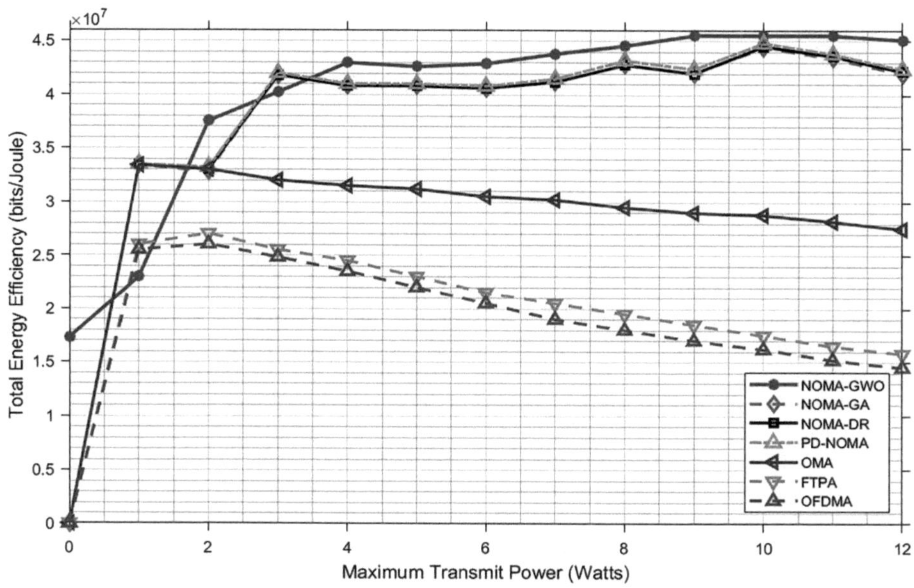

Fig. 10. Energy efficiency versus maximum transmit power with 16 users.

6 Conclusion

Resource allocation for downlink NOMA was evaluated using GA and GWO. Across a range of user loads and interference conditions, NOMA consistently outperformed OMA, with the gap widening as the number of users grew. Among the optimizers, GWO delivered the highest sum rates in nearly all scenarios, showing strong adaptability in both interference-limited and cleaner environments. GA also improved performance; however, it was occasionally hindered by slower convergence and weaker local exploitation. A statistical analysis confirmed that the observed gains were significant at the 95% confidence level, underscoring the robustness of GWO's advantage over GA and OMA. These results point to nature-inspired optimizers particularly GWO as practical tools for real-time resource management in next-generation wireless systems. The main limitation of the study is the assumption of static user distributions and quasi-static channels; while common for tractability, this may limit direct transfer to highly dynamic deployments. Future work should incorporate mobility and time-varying fading, extend the analysis to MIMO configurations, and evaluate performance under latency and energy efficiency constraints. Hybrid approaches that combine multiple optimization strategies (or blend learning-based and heuristic methods) are also promising for increasingly complex network settings.

References

1. Artetxe, E., Barambones, O., Calvo, I., Fernández-Bustamante, P., Martin, I., Uralde, J.: Wireless technologies for industry 4.0 applications. Energies **16**(3), 1349 (2023)
2. Morín, D.G., Pérez, P., Armada, A.G.: Toward the distributed implementation of immersive augmented reality architectures on 5G networks. IEEE Commun. Mag. **60**(2), 46–52 (2022)
3. Preveze, B., Alkhayyat, A., Abedi, F., Jawad, A.M., Abosinnee, A.S.: SDN-driven internet of health things: a novel adaptive switching technique for hospital healthcare monitoring system. Wirel. Commun. Mob. Comput. **2022**(1), 3150756 (2022)
4. Zhang, Z., et al.: 6G wireless networks: vision, requirements, architecture, and key technologies. IEEE Veh. Technol. Mag. **14**(3), 28–41 (2019)
5. Agiwal, M., Roy, A., Saxena, N.: Next generation 5G wireless networks: a comprehensive survey. IEEE Commun. Surv. Tut. **18**(3), 1617–1655 (2016)
6. Kareem, Z.H., Malik, R.Q., Jawad, S., Abedi, F.: Reinforcement learning-driven task offloading and resource allocation in wireless IoT networks. IEEE Access (2025)
7. Ding, Z., Lei, X., Karagiannidis, G.K., Schober, R., Yuan, J., Bhargava, V.K.: A survey on non-orthogonal multiple access for 5G networks: research challenges and future trends. IEEE J. Sel. Areas Commun. **35**(10), 2181–2195 (2017)
8. Khan, M.J., Singh, I.: Cooperative power-domain non-orthogonal multiple access (NOMA) in 5G systems: potentials and challenges. In: 5G and Beyond Wireless Networks, pp. 13–36 (2024)
9. Abuajwa, O., Mitani, S.: Dynamic resource allocation for energy-efficient downlink NOMA systems in 5G networks. Heliyon **10**(9) (2024)

10. Mirjalili, S.: Genetic algorithm. In: Evolutionary Algorithms and Neural Networks: Theory and Applications, vol. 780, pp. 43–55. Springer, Cham (2018). https://doi.org/10.1007/978-3-319-93025-1_4
11. Mirjalili, S., Mirjalili, S.M., Lewis, A.: Grey wolf optimizer. Adv. Eng. Softw. **69** 46–61 (2014)
12. Kirtay, S., Bocekci, V.G., Yildiz, K.: Genetic algorithm based approach for optimization of fair power allocation in Pd-NOMA systems. Tehnički vjesnik **32**(3), 948–957 (2025)
13. Odida, M.O.: The evolution of mobile communication: a comprehensive survey on 5G technology. J. Sen. Net. Data Comm. **4**(1), 01–11 (2024)
14. Masaracchia, A., Da Costa, D.B., Duong, T.Q., Nguyen, M.N., Nguyen, M.T.: A PSO - based approach for user-pairing schemes in NOMA systems: theory and applications. IEEE Access **7**, 90550–90564 (2019)
15. Dong, Z., Shang, T., Li, Q., Tang, T.: Differential evolution-based optimal power allocation scheme for NOMA-VLC systems. Opt. Exp. **28**(15), 21627–21640 (2020)
16. Ahsan, W., Yi, W., Qin, Z., Liu, Y., Nallanathan, A.: Resource allocation in uplink NOMA-IoT networks: a reinforcement-learning approach. IEEE Trans. Wirel. Commun. **20**(8), 5083–5098 (2021)
17. Şenel, F.A., Gökçe, F., Yüksel, A.S., Yiğit, T.: A novel hybrid PSO–GWO algorithm for optimization problems. Eng. Comput. **35**(4), 1359–1373 (2019)
18. Rehman, B., et al.: Joint user grouping and power control using whale optimization algorithm for NOMA uplink systems. PeerJ Comput. Sci. **8**(4), e882 (2022)
19. Azarshab, M., Fathian, M., Amiri, B.: An enhanced teaching-learning-based optimization (TLBO) with grey wolf optimizer (GWO) for text feature selection and clustering. arXiv preprint arXiv:2402.11839 (2024)
20. Wang, C.L., Chen, J.Y., Chen, Y.J.: Power allocation for a downlink non-orthogonal multiple access system. IEEE Wirel. Commun. Lett. **5**(5), 532–535 (2016)
21. kamal, S., Nazar, B., Hathal, H.: Non-orthogonal multiple access schemes survey: an overview of non-orthogonal multiple access techniques. J. Eng. Sustain. Dev. (2023)
22. Chang, Z., et al.: Energy-efficient and secure resource allocation for multiple-antenna NOMA with wireless power transfer. IEEE Trans. Green Commun. Netw. **2**(4), 1059–1071 (2018)
23. Saito, Y., Benjebbour, A., Kishiyama, Y., Nakamura, T.: System-level performance of downlink non-orthogonal multiple access (NOMA) under various environments. In: 2015 IEEE 81st Vehicular Technology Conference, VTC Spring, pp. 1–5. IEEE (2015)
24. Di, B., Bayat, S., Song, L., Li, Y.: Radio resource allocation for downlink non-orthogonal multiple access (NOMA) networks using matching theory. In: 2015 IEEE Global Communications Conference (GLOBECOM), pp. 1–6 (2014)
25. Chandra, R., Borugadda, S.: Multi agent deep reinforcement learning with deep Q-network based energy efficiency and resource allocation in NOMA wireless systems. In: 2023 Second International Conference on Electrical, Electronics, Information and Communication Technologies (ICEEICT), pp. 1–8 (2023)
26. Chebbi, S., Habachi, O., Sabir, E., Cances, J. P., Meghdadi, V.: GWO-based user clustering and power allocation for downlink MIMO-NOMA systems. 2024 International Conference on Software, Telecommunications and Computer Networks (SoftCOM), pp. 1–6 (2024)

27. Moltafet, M., Azmi, P., Mokari, N., Javan, M.R., Mokdad, A.A.: Optimal and fair energy efficient resource allocation for energy harvesting-enabled-PD-NOMA-based HetNets. IEEE Trans. Wirel. Commun. **17**, 2054–2067 (2018)
28. Bai, X., Wang, S., Ma, J., Xu, J.: Research on UAV-NOMA communication system based on improved grey wolf optimization algorithm. In: Proceedings of the 2024 2nd International Conference on Communication Networks and Machine Learning (2024)
29. Souto, V.D.P., Souza, R.D., Filho, B.F.: PSO-based optimization of STAR-RIS aided NOMA wireless communication networks. In: 2024 19th International Symposium on Wireless Communication Systems (ISWCS), pp. 1–6 (2024)
30. Águila-León, J., Vargas-Salgado, C., Díaz-Bello, D., Montalvá, C.M.: Optimizing photovoltaic systems: a meta-optimization approach with GWO-enhanced PSO algorithm for improving MPPT controllers. Renew. Energy (2024)
31. Tse, D., Viswanath, P.: Fundamentals of Wireless Communication. Cambridge University Press, New York (2005)
32. Goldsmith, A.: Wireless Communications. Cambridge University Press, Cambridge (2005)
33. Kara, F.: Deep learning based channel estimation for MIMO systems in 5G and beyond. Phys. Commun. **40**, 101097 (2020)
34. Sharma, S.K.: Multifunctional Antennas and Arrays for Wireless Communication Systems. IEEE-Press/Wiley-Interscience (2021)
35. Jain, R., Chiu, D.M., Hawe, W.R.: A quantitative measure of fairness and discrimination for resource allocation in shared computer systems. Technical report, TR-301, Digital Equipment Corporation (1984)

Author Index

W. A. Mahmoud et al. (Eds.): ACDN 2025, CCIS 2798, p. 157, 2026.
https://doi.org/10.1007/978-3-032-15448-4

MIX
Papier aus verantwortungsvollen Quellen
Paper from responsible sources
FSC® C105338

If you have any concerns about our products,
you can contact us on
ProductSafety@springernature.com

In case Publisher is established outside the EU,
the EU authorized representative is:
Springer Nature Customer Service Center GmbH
Europaplatz 3, 69115 Heidelberg, Germany

Printed by Libri Plureos GmbH
in Hamburg, Germany